WILLIAM SHAKESPEARE

Twelfth Night · Othello

Shakespeare Plays in Rinehart Editions

Henry IV (Part I) • *Much Ado About Nothing* • *Hamlet*

King Lear • *The Tempest*

As You Like It • *Julius Caesar* • *Macbeth*

Twelfth Night • *Othello*

WILLIAM SHAKESPEARE

Twelfth Night · Othello

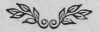

Edited with an introduction and notes by Alan S. Downer

HOLT, RINEHART AND WINSTON
NEW YORK · CHICAGO · SAN FRANCISCO
TORONTO · LONDON

21917-0318

Sixth Printing, January, 1967

Introduction and notes © 1958 by Alan S. Downer
Typography Design by Stefan Salter
All Rights Reserved
Printed in the United States of America
Library of Congress Catalog Card Number 58–7244

SHAKESPEARE

AND THE ELIZABETHAN IDEA OF THEATER

1. The Microcosm

For the fullest appreciation of Shakespeare's work, it is necessary to remember that a play is both a visual and a literary art. It does not undervalue the magnificence of the poetry to remind ourselves that language is only one of the tools that the playwright employs in achieving his ends. The words he writes are intended to be conveyed to the audience by actors: by actors in costumes chosen or designed to signify character, status, attitude; by actors whose gestures and actions may be as memorable and effective as the words they speak; by actors moving in patterns or arranged in tableaux or groupings that may crystallize the play's meaning more clearly and more directly than a critic's commentary, an author's preface, or a tutor's outline. The Renaissance inherited and cherished the idea of drama as a *speaking picture;* and the spectator in an Elizabethan theater must have had something of the experience of seeing a series of paintings in the mode of Titian, or Veronese, taking shape and dissolving into one another before his eyes, speaking to him in color and color contrasts, in conventional gesture, in design and grouping, with the added instrument of spoken dialogue to clarify the meaning and enrich the texture of the action.

The Elizabethan playhouse, the only theater that Shakespeare knew and the architectural pattern of which he must have had in mind as he wrote, was perfectly designed as a vehicle for this concept of the *speaking picture*. Designed is perhaps too positive a word; the theater building might more accurately be said to have happened as a necessary response to the concept. Although the first public, commercial playhouse was not erected in London until 1576, less than ten years before Shakespeare came down from his native Stratford, the conditions for public performance had been established for several centuries. In the Biblical plays of the medieval craft cycles, in the folk plays of the village square or common, in the interludes in banquet halls, in the moralities and history plays of the traveling professionals playing in inn yards on their "pageant" wagons—the elements of the theater varied but little: an open, almost undecorated playing area, either a cleared space on the ground or a large elevated platform without scenery or curtains to distract from or shut off the actor; an audience encircling the acting area in intimate and unbroken contact with the players.

For the spectator of these plays, the dramatic experience was almost wholly conveyed by the actor and what he said and did. Physical devices, on which the modern playwright leans heavily for his effects, were undemanded. The afternoon sun might be beating down on the villain as he went about his business in the dark of the moon, Herod might hold his court in the street before the village butcher shop, St. George might be played by the cobbler's son, but the spectator saw only the darkness, the royal court, the mythical hero. The English audience was trained to look to the actor, who brought with him or built up in his speech whatever sense of time or place was necessary for an understanding of the action. For always action, and the actor, took the eye and the mind.

The playhouse that James Burbage erected in London in 1576 was devised for the method of presentation that had become conventional in the professional acting companies. He began with a circular shell, without a roof, the basic plan of those popular places of amusement, the bear-baiting pits (see *Twelfth Night,* III, 1, line 115). Against the inside wall of the circular shell, Burbage erected a large platform, entrance to which was through doors placed at either end. This was the main acting area, intended to support the actors and project the meaning of their action. With no scenery to attract the viewer's eye, or to signify time, place, or implication, the actor or actors stood alone, and—in interpreting the situation and the developing theme of the play—gestures and patterns of movement took on an importance not unlike that of the figures in a sculpture group.

There were other acting areas. From the pageant wagons with their three levels came the idea that the platform represented earth, the cellar beneath it (reached by way of a trap door in the stage), hell, and the roof over the stage, heaven. So the audience of *Othello* (III, 3, line 445) received a more direct understanding of the change that had come over the hero than is possible in a modern theater. The player on the stage between the heavenly roof and the infernal cellar reflected the still conventional Ptolemaic idea of the universe, with the earth in perilous balance between paradise and perdition.

At the back of the main platform, between the entrance doors, there may have been a curtained alcove or inner stage, used for scenes that seem to require a sense of isolation, like the cellar where Sir Toby Belch conducts his evening revels or the chamber where Othello sacrifices his wife. The existence of this inner stage has been much questioned by scholars, and its function may have been filled by a temporary structure erected on the main platform. It is quite possible that some playhouses had neither an inner stage nor a curtained structure, that only readers accustomed to the conventions of a realistic theater demand such visual support for their imaginations.

But there seems to be no question that there was, halfway between the main stage and the heavenly roof, a curtained room used originally as a musician's gallery but available when the dramatic situation involved simultaneous action, say, in the street and on a city wall, or on two floors of the same house. At the same level, above each entrance door, was a praticable window at which, for example, Brabantio stood to be goaded by the taunts of Iago in the "street" below.

The audience, a cross section of the citizens of London, stood in the open air around the stage or sat in the three tiers of galleries that lined the walls. But what the audience looked upon was not, as in the modern theater, a framed picture of a reproduction of a suburban living room, or an army barracks, or a public square; the audience looked upon a structure which was a skeletonic representation in miniature (microcosm) of the great universe (macrocosm) of which they themselves were a part.

2. The Macrocosm

While as individuals Elizabethan playgoers were as diverse as any group gathered in any popular, public theater, they had a greater homogeneity than might be found in the audience at, say, a contemporary urban movie. They were all Englishmen, intensely concerned with the political and patriotic affairs of a state that was

beginning to sense its own importance in the world. They were all
Christians, and the doctrines of the state church (taken over with
little alteration from the teachings of the Roman church which it
had replaced) were drummed into them from childhood.

They were told over and over again that man's life was a pilgrimage and that his ultimate goal was the City of God. They heard
repeatedly that man might lose sight of this goal, might focus his
concern on such things of this world as possessions, political power,
the love of woman, the pursuit of pleasure; that in so doing man
placed himself in the hands of Fortune who would inevitably desert
him and bring him to dust. They were taught that God had divinely
established a world order in which every creature, natural and super-
natural, human and animal, and every object and element had an
assigned place and function, which place and function might be
evaded or neglected with disastrous results not only for the individual but for society at large. They knew that the divinely fixed order
in the universe, in the state, in society, in the family, and within the
individual must be maintained at all costs; that the chief duty of
man was to hold to the strait and narrow path between an excess of
concern and an excess of unconcern for the world and his fellow
men and women. Finally, they felt deeply that God's grace hung
over all, awaiting any man who recognized his own identity, fulfilled
his assigned function, and understood that Christian doctrine had
replaced Mosaic law.

These principles of right action (and of evil action, in their
reverse) are the governing principles by which the audience would
evaluate what happened in a Shakespearean play. For the Elizabethans a drama was to be seen, not as a particular "case history,"
but as a mirror of life in the most general sense; the drama reflects,
as Hamlet suggests, not the image of Hamlet, Prince of Denmark,
but the image of (human) nature. Our heritage, from the philosophical and scientific attitudes of the nineteenth century, tends to en-
courage us to look upon man in life and literature as an individual;
the Elizabethan attitude is captured in the familiar words of John
Donne: "No man is an island, entire of itself; every man is a piece
of the continent, a part of the main . . . . any man's death dimin-
ishes me because I am involved in mankind; and therefore never
send to know for whom the bell tolls: it tolls for thee."

3. The Idea of a Theater

This idea of drama was one that the physical playhouse was de-signed to support. In 1566 appeared an English translation of a French treatise, *Theatrum Mundi* by Pierre Boaistuau. To the trans-lation, which was to have a long life in many editions, the printer affixed the title, *The Theater or Rule of the World*, explaining that he added *Rule* to interpret to the English who had never seen a play-house what *Theater* meant. The text itself is a conglomeration of histories, legends and fables; grim warnings of catastrophe; and ac-counts of misery, holocaust, collapse, mass murder, unexpected death and destruction, cataclysm, and every conceivable affliction that has visited man from lice to earthquakes, drunkenness to as-sassination, featuring both the image of Fortune and her wheel and the image of man's life as a pilgrimage to the Holy City. Everything that could happen in an Elizabethan play is recorded in *Theatrum Mundi*, bound up and controlled by the idea of a theater with which the original Dedication concludes:

I have addressed to [the general reader] this theater, in which he may contemplate & be advised of his infirmity and misery, & not withdrawn from himself, to this end that in making a view and review of all the parts of his life, he may thereby be moved to detect and abhor his vile nature; and if we will be equal judges in human actions: what else is this world but a theater? Whereas some play or use the state of artificers and men of base condition and calling, & others do represent the state of kings, dukes, earls, marquisses, barons, and others constituted in dignities. And nevertheless when all these have cast off their vizards and masking garments, and that death cometh and maketh an end of this bloody tragedy, then they acknowledge themselves all to be mortal men.

It was in the light of this widely accepted idea of a theater that James Burbage erected his first playhouse and called it simply, but with more significance than we today attach to the name, The Theater. Nearly a quarter of a century later it became necessary to move the acting company to another location. With a typically English combination of sentiment and economy, The Theater was dismantled and reassembled elsewhere and renamed—but in the same conceit—The Globe. And tradition reports that hanging over the entrance of the renovated playhouse was a picture of Atlas supporting the earth, with the motto which Shakespeare himself has made famous: "All the world's a stage."

The melancholy and philosophical Jaques, to whom Shakespeare assigns the statement in *As You Like It,* sums up the roles that man as actor in the great world is called upon to fill: the infant, the schoolboy, the lover, the soldier, the justice, the old man, and "second childishness." These had been, for centuries, the Seven Ages of Man, and for Jaques, as for Boaistuau and the Renaissance audience, the statement is both descriptive and metaphorical. If the place of every man in society—tinker, tailor, scholar, sailor, doctor, lawyer, merchant, chief—was fixed by immutable decree, so too were the functions and qualities, the duties and perquisites of each degree, estate, or occupation. Every man was, so to speak, assigned a stereotype, a role to play, and his success in filling the part was the measure of the value of his life. A king was good or bad measured by his success in maintaining just order in his kingdom; an army officer was saved or lost measured by his success in evaluating those under his command; the head of a household was to be praised or blamed for the degree of his perception in guiding the lives he was appointed to control. Thus the king, the commander, the father, the young man or woman in love, were social stereotypes that are translated into dramatic stereotypes to be evaluated according to their deviation from the ideal. This is not to suggest that the spectators were consciously loyal, obedient, faithful, reverent; it would be unfair to expect that the Elizabethans lived by the code to which they subscribed any more than we do. But the code existed, and was invoked in the theater (if not in life), and these stereotypes are fitted into actions that endlessly repeat themselves—the ruler who brings chaos into his state, the wife who breaks faith with a husband, the subordinate who betrays his leader, the man who devotes his energies to Fortune.

Identifiable stereotypes and conventional actions suggest to the spectator the enduring facts of existence, as he has been taught to think about those facts. The Shakespearean play presents essential and eternal truths rather than particular instances. Malvolio and Othello are not just individuals, but representatives of humanity at large, and this generalizing habit of character interpretation was encouraged by the playhouse itself. The Elizabethan stage, this little world, this microcosm, was the mirror of the greater world of general human experience and belief. The particular action on the stage was seen both in its literal or "realistic" context and in the larger symbolic or metaphorical connotations.

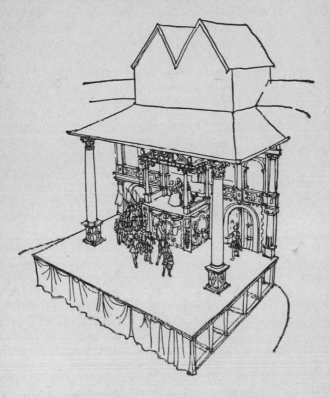

4. Playhouse and Playwright

This idea of theater affected the art of the playwright in many ways, three of which are of immediate concern to an understanding of Shakespeare: the symbolic treatment of place, time, and action.

The formal unchanging background of the Elizabethan stage

From *The Globe Restored,* by C. W. Hodges. New York: Coward-McCann, Inc., and London: Ernest Benn Ltd., 1953. By permission of the author and the publishers.

permitted the shifting of locale with the greatest freedom and rapidity. Geographical and architectural accuracy were never a problem; indeed a situation could be performed without any reference to place, if the dramatist pleased. Shakespeare places *Twelfth Night* in "Illyria," but without any attempt to reproduce the conditions of an outpost of the Roman Empire. Illyria has a romantic sound, it permits a pun on *Elysium,* and that is sufficient for a symbolic drama. More dramatically significant is the shifting of the action of *Othello* from Venice to Cyprus. The original story, which Shakespeare was adapting to the stage, made nothing of this; many critics have seen, in Shakespeare's use of a dual locale, merely the necessity of getting Othello and his wife away from a place of order and law to an isolated post where a catastrophe could occur. But to the more sensitive Elizabethan mind, Venice might suggest Venus in her socialized and acceptable form, and Cyprus (the birthplace of Venus) the goddess of love without the control of society—a kind of symbolic geography for the action of *Othello.*

The formal, unchanging background of the Elizabethan stage permitted the action to proceed without reference to a clock or a calendar. Time was a tool to be used as convenience or dramatic necessity dictated. In *Twelfth Night,* Shakespeare employs time with the precision of an itinerary compiled by a tourist agency.

In *Othello,* on the other hand, Shakespeare manipulates time with great freedom. The marriage ceremony of Othello and Desdemona is hardly completed when the general is ordered to Cyprus. He departs at once, Desdemona following on another ship. In Cyprus the consummation of the marriage is once again interrupted by a brawl engineered by Iago, as a result of which Lieutenant Cassio is cashiered. Next day—and the time scheme is insisted upon —Iago begins to plant suspicion of Cassio in Othello's mind, most effectively by a circumstantial tale of a night when he had shared a bed with the lieutenant and heard Cassio talking in his sleep, wooing Desdemona, and cursing the fate that had married her to the Moor. That Othello should swallow such a chronological impossibility has been taken as a sign of the carelessness of Shakespeare's untaught genius, or of his skill in suggesting that Othello is far gone in unreason. But such a question could hardly arise for the Elizabethan spectator. For him, dramatic action was not framed in time; time was at the mercy of the playwright and was controlled by the design of the dramatic action.

The formal, unchanging background of the Elizabethan stage permitted the *design* of a dramatic action to stand forth with great clarity. The attention of the audience, undistracted by illusionistic scenery, was necessarily focused upon the actors and the stage pictures created by their groupings. Optical science has long recognized the ability of the eye to retain images, even after the original picture has been changed; the Elizabethan habit of mind of recognizing analogies between apparently dissimilar orders of being made optical memory an effective tool of the dramatist.

For example, in *Twelfth Night,* Act I, scene 5, the spectators would see Olivia with Malvolio and her servants being cross-examined by Feste as he proves her a fool. In Act II, scene 4, they would see the Duke with Viola and his servants as Feste prepares to sing "the song we had last night." The two situations present the same picture: the fool in the center of the audience that he is to entertain. In each he exhibits one of his professional talents: the play of wit, the charm of song. In each he aims at something more than entertainment: the jesting demonstrates the folly of Olivia in loving the dead more than the living; the song (so different from the one requested by the Duke [lines 42-47]) mocks the passion of Orsino as sentimental rather than natural. Further, in the striking scene before Malvolio's prison (IV, 2), Feste has the stage to himself as he traps the benighted steward into repeated declarations of his own folly. Thus, in the various entanglements of a bustling comedy, Feste holds firmly the central position, paradoxically, he is the wise man who by proof and contrast demonstrates how "wise men, folly fall'n, quite taint their wit." Unlike Olivia, Orsino, and Malvolio, the Fool's uniform clothes only his body; he wears not motley in his brain.

Thus with Feste as agent the design of the play, the analogous relation between the parts of the action, is established for the audience. As is usual in Shakespeare, the unifying idea is most obvious in the lowest or broadest action: Malvolio, the ambitious steward, is so sick of self-love that he assumes a ridiculous costume and, aspiring to wed his lady, steps quite out of the place assigned to him in the order of things. Olivia and Orsino, whose loves are also shown to be folly, are disguised in a metaphorical sense. Like Viola, they are not what they appear to be; unlike Viola, and unlike Feste, they have been led to "disguise" themselves out of blindness to the nature of their own purposes. The action of the play, as guided by

Feste, leads first to the literal recognition scene, a dramatic convention, in which Viola and Sebastian are brought face to face and in an extended passage of fifty lines (V, 1, 217 ff.) identify themselves. The conventional dramatic action leads to a recognition on the part of the Duke and of Olivia which is both literal and metaphorical. The Duke penetrates both the external disguise of Viola and the deception he has practiced upon himself. Olivia, too, emerges from her "most extracting frenzy." If Malvolio stubbornly clings to his conviction that he has been notoriously abused, he provides comic emphasis to the central idea of the play: the confusions that arise from a foolish determination to go against nature can be resolved by a willing surrender to nature's ordering of things. And we may look to be well edified (and amused) when the Fool delivers the madmen.

Othello presents a similar dramatic pattern in a tragic action. Here the agent is Iago, not a professional fool but a professed villain; the subjects of his attention are Othello, a general, and Cassio, a lieutenant. As in *Twelfth Night,* the meaning of the action is stated more directly on the lower level, the level of the lieutenant. Cassio knows his weakness, that he has no head for liquor, but he allows himself to be worked on by Iago to whose character and motives he is utterly blind. The result for Cassio is drunkenness and the commission of an act of which he is immediately ashamed once he has returned to his senses. He berates himself: "Drunk? and speak parrot? and squabble? swagger? swear? . . . O God, that men should put an enemy in their mouths to steal away their brains! That we should with joy, pleasance, revel, and applause transform ourselves into beasts!" (II, 3, 265-277.)

This bitter speech is not simply an attack on alcohol. The language refers directly to the larger and familiar Elizabethan concept that man was to be distinguished from the lower animals by his reasoning power. In surrendering his reason, he surrendered also his rightful place in the hierarchy, became the slave of passion or will—a beast, not a man.

Cassio's story, simple to understand and evaluate, parallels and helps to clarify Othello's. Othello too is a good man and a soldier. His weakness is not strong drink, but strong passion, though it is a weakness he knows nothing about. Manipulated by Iago, he surrenders completely the rational powers that had made him a successful leader of men, and, enslaved by jealousy ("the green-ey'd monster"), becomes himself a beast. Like Cassio, he lives to repent his action and to achieve some measure of self-knowledge, but too late.

Recognition has always been one of the most attractive elements in drama. On the level of narrative, it is the basis of the fascination of the mystery play; on the metaphorical level, it permits the achievement of self-knowledge that is one of the distinctive characteristics of tragedy. But, as we have observed in *Twelfth Night,* recognition can be the central concern of comedy also. In fact the parallels between the structure of *Twelfth Night* and the structure of *Othello* are as striking as the differences in their total effects. In both plays a major figure who does not know his own nature (Othello, Orsino) is propelled by an agent (Iago, Feste) through a situation which results in his discovery of his own nature. In both the agent carries on parallel or analogous actions with secondary characters (Cassio, Roderigo; Olivia, Malvolio). If one play is tragic and the other comic, the difference lies not so much in the basic situation as in the purpose of the agent and the wilfulness of the characters he is acting upon. Feste's intent is gracious; Orsino, Olivia, and Malvolio are living in a dream of their own choosing. Iago's purpose is revenge; Othello and Roderigo (also Cassio, if not to the same degree) live wholly in the world of possession, reputation, and material values. Olivia and the Duke can be mocked into recognition before it is too late; Othello and Roderigo can be manipulated past the point of no return.

In both plays the central idea or organizing principle of the action is based upon the moral code conventionally accepted by the audience and the playwright. This is not to say that Shakespeare's purpose is to demonstrate the code, or to prove its inevitable operation. The theme of a Shakespearean play, like its familiar analogous structure, is significant chiefly as unifying device. It is not the point of the action, but the point of departure for a dramatic experience. Since both theme and analogous structure are based upon ideas and attitudes which the spectator is assumed to share, they provide the spectator with a perspective for evaluating the characters and their behavior. Theme and structure are thus largely responsible for the kinetic reactions of the spectators, so important a part of the dramatic experience.

For it must never be forgotten that, if the original purpose of the Renaissance artist was to delight and instruct, the essential purpose of any playwright is to create not merely a drama but a dramatic experience. Whether the scene be imaginary Illyria or identifiable Cyprus, whether the characters be fantastic dukes and stewards, or recognizable husbands and wives, whether the situation be unfamiliar (murder) or commonplace (puppy-love), the playwright must devise a structure which will permit the spectator to live through the action on the stage as if it were a part of his daily routine. A play in performance becomes a part of the life of the audience. It cannot be put aside, like a novel, to be resumed at convenience. It is a living experience, or it is nothing.

When Jaques in *As You Like It* muses that "all the world's a stage," he is echoing a hundred philosophical predecessors. But he is also stating very precisely Shakespeare's idea of theater. On the bare boards of The Globe was the world, and the actors were mankind. Entrance and exit were birth and death, and each man in his time played many parts from infant to "second childishness." During the two-hour traffic of the stage, the life reflected from the macrocosm was intensified, organized, clarified, enriched. The spectator who left The Globe was not quite the same man who entered it. Beyond delight and instruction, this dramatic experience was Shakespeare's great gift to his immediate audiences. Indeed it was the greatest legacy of his age to nations unknown and to three centuries of playgoers about whom he never thought.

ALAN S. DOWNER

Princeton, N. J.

TEXTUAL NOTE

The text of *Twelfth Night* is based on the Folio of 1623; that of *Othello* on the Quarto of 1622 and the Folio of 1623. Spelling and punctuation have been modernized.

SOME SUGGESTED READINGS

The best recent study of Shakespeare's life is *Shakespeare of London* by Marcette Chute, New York: Dutton, 1950. Useful general background material may be found in *A Shakespeare Primer* by Gerald Sanders, New York: Rinehart, 1950; *The Backgrounds of Shakespeare's Plays* by Karl J. Holzknecht, New York: American Book, 1950. An introduction to the study of the Elizabethan stage and dramatic art may be found in the present editor's *The British Drama: A Handbook and Brief Chronicle*, New York: Appleton, 1950. The advanced student should consult *Shakespeare's Stage* by A. M. Nagler, New Haven: Yale University Press, 1958; *A Companion to Shakespeare Studies*, edited by Harley Granville-Barker and G. B. Harrison, New York: Cambridge University Press, 1934. Samplings of Shakespeare criticism of three centuries are included in three convenient small anthologies: D. Nicol Smith, *Shakespeare Criticism* (to Carlyle), Oxford: Oxford University Press, 1916; Ann Bradby, *Shakespeare Criticism, 1919-1935*, Oxford: Oxford University Press, 1936; Leonard F. Dean, *Shakespeare: Modern Essays in Criticism*, Oxford: Oxford University Press, 1957.

CONTENTS

Twelfth Night

or

What You Will

Characters

ORSINO, *Duke of Illyria.*

SEBASTIAN, *brother to* VIOLA.

ANTONIO, *a sea-captain, friend to* SEBASTIAN.

SEA-CAPTAIN, *friend to* VIOLA.

VALENTINE,
CURIO, } *gentlemen attending on the Duke.*

SIR TOBY BELCH, *uncle to* OLIVIA.

SIR ANDREW AGUECHEEK.

MALVOLIO, *steward to* OLIVIA

FABIAN, *a gentleman,*
FESTE, *a clown,* } *servants to* OLIVIA.

OLIVIA, *a rich countess.*

VIOLA.

MARIA, OLIVIA'S *woman.*

LORDS, PRIESTS, SAILORS, OFFICERS, MUSICIANS,
and other ATTENDANTS

SCENE: *A city in Illyria, and the sea-coast near it.*

1

[ACT I · 1] *The Duke's palace.*

Enter ORSINO, *Duke of Illyria,* CURIO, *and other* LORDS,
MUSICIANS *attending.*

DUKE.   If music be the food of love, play on!
Give me excess of it, that, surfeiting,
The appetite may sicken, and so die.
That strain again! It had a dying fall.
O, it came o'er my ear like the sweet sound   5
That breathes upon a bank of violets,
Stealing and giving odor. Enough! no more!
'Tis not so sweet now as it was before.
O spirit of love, how quick and fresh art thou,
That, notwithstanding thy capacity   10
Receiveth as the sea, nought enters there,
Of what validity and pitch soe'er,
But falls into abatement and low price
Even in a minute! So full of shapes is fancy
That it alone is high fantastical.   15
    CURIO.   Will you go hunt, my lord?
    DUKE.   What, Curio?
    CURIO.   The hart.
    DUKE.   Why, so I do, the noblest that I have.
O, when mine eyes did see Olivia first,
Methought she purg'd the air of pestilence!   20
That instant was I turn'd into a hart;
And my desires, like fell and cruel hounds,
E'er since pursue me.

Enter VALENTINE

How now! what news from her?
    VALENTINE.   So please my lord, I might not be admitted,
But from her handmaid do return this answer: 25

[ACT I · 1] 2 surfeiting *being overful* / 4 fall *cadence* / 5 sound
i.e., of the wind / 9 quick *alive* / 10 capacity *receptive power* / 12
validity and pitch *high value* / 13 abatement *devaluation* / 14 fancy
love / 15 alone *above all others* / 17 hart *deer* (*with inevitable puns
on heart and deer*) / 21 turn'd into a hart *Diana, goddess of the hunt,
the moon, and chastity, while bathing was spied upon by Acteon. In
punishment she turned him into a stag, and he was torn to pieces by his
own hunting dogs* / 22 fell *fierce*

The element itself, till seven years' heat,
Shall not behold her face at ample view;
But like a cloistress she will veiled walk,
And water once a day her chamber round
With eye-offending brine: all this to season   30
A brother's dead love, which she would keep fresh
And lasting in her sad remembrance.
   DUKE. O, she that hath a heart of that fine frame
To pay this debt of love but to a brother,
How will she love when the rich golden shaft   35
Hath kill'd the flock of all affections else
That live in her; when liver, brain, and heart,
These sovereign thrones, are all supplied and fill'd,
Her sweet perfections, with one self king!
Away before me to sweet beds of flowers;   40
Love-thoughts lie rich when canopied with bowers.

                                Exeunt.

[ACT I · 2] *The sea-coast.*

Enter VIOLA, *a* CAPTAIN, *and* SAILORS.

   VIOLA. What country, friends, is this?
   CAPTAIN. This is Illyria, lady.
   VIOLA. And what should I do in Illyria?
My brother he is in Elysium.
Perchance he is not drown'd. What think you, sailors?   5
   CAPTAIN. It is perchance that you yourself were saved.
   VIOLA. O my poor brother! and so perchance may he be.
   CAPTAIN. True, madam; and, to comfort you with chance,
Assure yourself, after our ship did split,
When you and those poor number saved with you   10
Hung on our driving boat, I saw your brother,
Most provident in peril, bind himself,
Courage and hope both teaching him the practice,
To a strong mast that liv'd upon the sea;

---

26 element *heavens* / 28 cloistress *nun* / 30 season *preserve* / 35
shaft *Cupid's arrow* / 36 affections *thoughts and emotions* / 37 liver,
brain, and heart *the seat of love, thought, and emotion*
   [ACT I · 2] 4 Elysium *heaven* / 5 Perchance *by some chance* / 11
driving *storm-driven* / 14 liv'd *floated*

Where, like Arion on the dolphin's back,   15
I saw him hold acquaintance with the waves
So long as I could see.
   VIOLA.   For saying so, there's gold.
Mine own escape unfoldeth to my hope,
Whereto thy speech serves for authority,   20
The like of him. Know'st thou this country?
   CAPTAIN.   Ay, madam, well; for I was bred and born
Not three hours' travel from this very place.
   VIOLA.   Who governs here?
   CAPTAIN.   A noble duke, in nature as in name.   25
   VIOLA.   What is his name?
   CAPTAIN.   Orsino.
   VIOLA.   Orsino! I have heard my father name him.
He was a bachelor then.
   CAPTAIN.   And so is now, or was so very late;   30
For but a month ago I went from hence,
And then 'twas fresh in murmur—as, you know,
What great ones do the less will prattle of—
That he did seek the love of fair Olivia.
   VIOLA.   What's she?   35
   CAPTAIN.   A virtuous maid, the daughter of a count
That died some twelvemonth since, then leaving her
In the protection of his son, her brother,
Who shortly also died; for whose dear love,
They say, she hath abjur'd the company   40
And sight of men.
   VIOLA.   O that I serv'd that lady,
And might not be delivered to the world,
Till I had made mine own occasion mellow,
What my estate is!
   CAPTAIN.   That were hard to compass,
Because she will admit no kind of suit,   45
No, not the Duke's.
   VIOLA.   There is a fair behavior in thee, captain;
And though that nature with a beauteous wall

---

15 Arion *a legendary bard who, captured by pirates, lept into the sea
where a dolphin, charmed by his music, carried him to safety* / 16 hold
acquaintance *rise and fall* / 19 unfoldeth to *encourages* / 43 Till I . . .
mellow *till I was sure the time was ripe* / 44 estate *condition*

Doth oft close in pollution, yet of thee
I will believe thou hast a mind that suits   50
With this thy fair and outward character.
I prithee, and I'll pay thee bounteously,
Conceal me what I am, and be my aid
For such disguise as haply shall become
The form of my intent. I'll serve this duke.   55
Thou shalt present me as an eunuch to him.
It may be worth thy pains, for I can sing
And speak to him in many sorts of music
That will allow me very worth his service.
What else may hap, to time I will commit,   60
Only shape thou thy silence to my wit.
   CAPTAIN.   Be you his eunuch, and your mute I'll be.
When my tongue blabs, then let mine eyes not see.
   VIOLA.   I thank thee. Lead me on.   *Exeunt.*

[ACT I · 3] *Olivia's house.*

Enter SIR TOBY BELCH *and* MARIA.

   SIR TOBY.   What a plague means my niece, to take the
death of her brother thus? I am sure care's an enemy to life.
   MARIA.   By my troth, Sir Toby, you must come in earlier
o' nights. Your cousin, my lady, takes great exceptions to your
ill hours.   5
   SIR TOBY.   Why, let her except before excepted.
   MARIA.   Ay, but you must confine yourself within the
modest limits of order.
   SIR TOBY.   Confine? I'll confine myself no finer than I am.
These clothes are good enough to drink in, and so be these   10
boots too; an they be not, let them hang themselves in their
own straps.
   MARIA.   That quaffing and drinking will undo you. I heard
my lady talk of it yesterday, and of a foolish knight that you
brought in one night here to be her wooer.   15

---

51 character *appearance* / 56 eunuch *singing boy* / 59 allow me *cause
me to be accepted as* / 59 worth his service *worthy to serve him* / 62
mute *silent actor*
   [ACT I · 3] 4 cousin *also coz, loosely used of any kinship* / 6 before excepted *with all necessary exceptions* (*legal phrase*) / 9 Confine
clothe myself / 11 an *if*

SIR TOBY. Who? Sir Andrew Aguecheek?

MARIA. Ay, he.

SIR TOBY. He's as tall a man as any's in Illyria.

MARIA. What's that to the purpose?

SIR TOBY. Why, he has three thousand ducats a year.   20

MARIA. Ay, but he'll have but a year in all these ducats. He's a very fool and a prodigal.

SIR TOBY. Fie, that you'll say so! He plays o' the viol-de-gamboys, and speaks three or four languages word for word without book, and hath all the good gifts of nature.   25

MARIA. He hath indeed, almost natural; for besides that he's a fool, he's a great quarreller; and but that he hath the gift of a coward to allay the gust he hath in quarrelling, 'tis thought among the prudent he would quickly have the gift of a grave.   30

SIR TOBY. By this hand, they are scoundrels and substractors that say so of him. Who are they?

MARIA. They that add, moreover, he's drunk nightly in your company.

SIR TOBY. With drinking healths to my niece. I'll drink to   35 her as long as there is a passage in my throat and drink in Illyria. He's a coward and a coystrill that will not drink to my niece till his brains turn o' the toe like a parish-top. What, wench! *Castiliano vulgo!* for here comes Sir Andrew Agueface.   40

Enter SIR ANDREW.

SIR ANDREW. Sir Toby Belch! How now, Sir Toby Belch!

SIR TOBY. Sweet Sir Andrew!

SIR ANDREW. Bless you, fair shrew.

MARIA. And you too, sir.

SIR TOBY. Accost, Sir Andrew, accost.   45

SIR ANDREW. What's that?

SIR TOBY. My niece's chambermaid.

SIR ANDREW. Good Mistress Accost, I desire better acquaintance.

---

18 tall *valiant* / 20 ducat *Italian coin* / 23 viol-de-gamboys *base viol* / 26 almost natural *almost like an idiot* / 28 gust *appetite* / 31 substractors *slanderers* / 37 coystrill *stable boy* / 39 Castiliano vulgo *keep a straight face* [?] (*Sir Toby's exuberant diction often demands imaginative interpretation from the reader and spectator*)

MARIA. My name is Mary, sir.   50

SIR ANDREW. Good Mistress Mary Accost,—

SIR TOBY. You mistake, knight. "Accost" is front her, board her, woo her, assail her.

SIR ANDREW. By my troth, I would not undertake her in this company. Is that the meaning of "accost"?   55

MARIA. Fare you well, gentlemen.

SIR TOBY. An thou let part so, Sir Andrew, would thou mightst never draw sword again.

SIR ANDREW. An you part so, mistress, I would I might never draw sword again. Fair lady, do you think you have 60 fools in hand?

MARIA. Sir, I have not you by the hand.

SIR ANDREW. Marry, but you shall have; and here's my hand.

MARIA. Now, sir, "thought is free." I pray you, bring your 65 hand to the buttery-bar and let it drink.

SIR ANDREW. Wherefore, sweetheart? What's your metaphor?

MARIA. It's dry, sir.

SIR ANDREW. Why, I think so. I am not such an ass but 70 I can keep my hand dry. But what's your jest?

MARIA. A dry jest, sir.

SIR ANDREW. Are you full of them?

MARIA. Ay, sir, I have them at my fingers' ends. Marry, now I let go your hand, I am barren.   *Exit* 75

SIR TOBY. O knight, thou lack'st a cup of canary. When did I see thee so put down?

SIR ANDREW. Never in your life, I think, unless you see canary put me down. Methinks sometimes I have no more wit than a Christian or an ordinary man has; but I am a great 80 eater of beef and I believe that does harm to my wit.

SIR TOBY. No question.

SIR ANDREW. An I thought that, I'd forswear it. I'll ride home to-morrow, Sir Toby.

SIR TOBY. *Pourquoi*, my dear knight?   85

SIR ANDREW. What is *"pourquoi"*—do or not do? I would

---

63 Marry *a mild oath* / 66 buttery-bar *where drinks were served* / 71 dry *a dry hand was a sign of sexual debility* / 76 canary *sweet wine* / 85 Pourquoi *why*

I had bestowed that time in the tongues that I have in fencing, dancing, and bear-baiting. O, had I but followed the arts!

SIR TOBY.   Then hadst thou had an excellent head of hair.

SIR ANDREW.   Why, would that have mended my hair?   90

SIR TOBY.   Past question; for thou seest it will not curl by nature.

SIR ANDREW.   But it becomes me well enough, does 't not?

SIR TOBY.   Excellent; it hangs like flax on a distaff, and I hope to see a housewife take thee between her legs, and spin   95
it off.

SIR ANDREW.   Faith, I'll home to-morrow, Sir Toby. Your niece will not be seen, or if she be, it's four to one she'll none of me. The Count himself here hard by woos her.

SIR TOBY.   She'll none o' the Count. She'll not match above   100
her degree, neither in estate, years, nor wit; I have heard her swear 't. Tut, there's life in 't, man.

SIR ANDREW.   I'll stay a month longer. I am a fellow o' the strangest mind in the world; I delight in masques and revels sometimes altogether.   105

SIR TOBY.   Art thou good at these kickshawses, knight?

SIR ANDREW.   As any man in Illyria, whatsoever he be, under the degree of my betters; and yet I will not compare with an old man.

SIR TOBY.   What is thy excellence in a galliard, knight?   110

SIR ANDREW.   Faith, I can cut a caper.

SIR TOBY.   And I can cut the mutton to 't.

SIR ANDREW.   And I think I have the back trick simply as strong as any man in Illyria.

SIR TOBY.   Wherefore are these things hid? Wherefore have   115
these gifts a curtain before 'em? Are they like to take dust, like Mistress Mall's picture? Why dost thou not go to church in a galliard and come home in a coranto? My very walk should be a jig. I would not so much as make water but in a

---

95 housewife *pronounced hussy, with a pun on harlot* / 95 spin it off *with a pun: cause your hair to fall out as a result of venereal disease* / 101 degree *rank, status* / 102 life *"While there's life, there's hope"* / 106 kickshawses *trifles* / 109 old man *veteran* / 110 galliard *lively dance* / 111 cut a caper *do a high kick* / 112 mutton *often served with caper sauce* / 113 back-trick *a special "caper" in a galliard* / 117 Mistress Mall's *i.e., my lady's* / 118 coranto *quick-step*

sink-a-pace. What dost thou mean? Is it a world to hide virtues   120
in? I did think, by the excellent constitution of thy leg, it was
formed under the star of a galliard.

SIR ANDREW.   Ay, 'tis strong, and it does indifferent well
in a flame-colored stock. Shall we set about some revels?

SIR TOBY.   What shall we do else? Were we not born under   125
Taurus?

SIR ANDREW.   Taurus! That's sides and heart.

SIR TOBY.   No, sir, it is legs and thighs. Let me see thee
caper. Ha! Higher! Ha, ha! Excellent!   *Exeunt.*

[ACT I · 4] *The Duke's palace.*

Enter VALENTINE, *and* VIOLA *in man's attire.*

VALENTINE.   If the Duke continue these favors towards
you, Cesario, you are like to be much advanced. He hath
known you but three days, and already you are no stranger.

VIOLA.   You either fear his humor or my negligence, that
you call in question the continuance of his love. Is he incon-   5
stant, sir, in his favors?

VALENTINE.   No, believe me.

Enter DUKE, CURIO, *and* ATTENDANTS.

VIOLA.   I thank you. Here comes the Count.

DUKE.   Who saw Cesario, ho?

VIOLA.   On your attendance, my lord; here.   10

DUKE.   Stand you a while aloof. Cesario,
Thou know'st no less but all. I have unclasp'd
To thee the book even of my secret soul.
Therefore, good youth, address thy gait unto her.
Be not denied access, stand at her doors,   15
And tell them, there thy fixed foot shall grow
Till thou have audience.

VIOLA.   Sure, my noble lord,
If she be so abandon'd to her sorrow

---

120 sink-a-pace *cinq-pace, dance of five steps* / 124 stock *stocking* /
126 Taurus *the "Sign of the Bull" in the zodiac. The signs were supposed
to govern the parts of the body, and to determine the qualities and
abilities of men*
    [ACT I · 4] 4 humor *capriciousness* / 4 negligence *neglect of duty*

As it is spoke, she never will admit me.

   DUKE.   Be clamorous and leap all civil bounds   20
Rather than make unprofited return.

   VIOLA.   Say I do speak with her, my lord, what then?

   DUKE.   O, then unfold the passion of my love,
Surprise her with discourse of my dear faith.
It shall become thee well to act my woes.   25
She will attend it better in thy youth
Than in a nuncio's of more grave aspect.

   VIOLA.   I think not so, my lord.

   DUKE.   Dear lad, believe it;
For they shall yet belie thy happy years,
That say thou art a man. Diana's lip   30
Is not more smooth and rubious; thy small pipe
Is as the maiden's organ, shrill and sound;
And all is semblative a woman's part.
I know thy constellation is right apt
For this affair. Some four or five attend him,—   35
All, if you will; for I myself am best
When least in company. Prosper well in this,
And thou shalt live as freely as thy lord,
To call his fortunes thine.

   VIOLA   I'll do my best
To woo your lady,—[aside] yet, a barful strife!   40
Whoe'er I woo, myself would be his wife.   *Exeunt.*

[ACT I · 5] *Olivia's house.*

Enter MARIA *and* FESTE.

   MARIA.   Nay, either tell me where thou hast been, or I
will not open my lips so wide as a bristle may enter in way
of thy excuse. My lady will hang thee for thy absence.

   FESTE.   Let her hang me! He that is well hanged in this
world needs to fear no colors.   5

   MARIA.   Make that good.

---

24 surprise *overpower* / 27 nuncio *messenger* / 31 rubious *ruby-red*
/ 32 shrill and sound *high and clear* / 33 part *role* / 34 constellation
nature (*as determined by the stars at nativity*) / 40 barful *full of im-*
pediments

   [ACT I · 5] 5 colors *i.e., nothing* (*with a pun on collar, the hang-*
man's noose) / 6 Make that good *prove it*

FESTE.   He shall see none to fear.

MARIA.   A good lenten answer. I can tell thee where that saying was born, of "I fear no colors."

FESTE.   Where, good Mistress Mary?   10

MARIA.   In the wars; and that may you be bold to say in your foolery.

FESTE.   Well, God give them wisdom that have it; and those that are fools, let them use their talents.

MARIA.   Yet you will be hanged for being so long absent;   15 or, to be turned away, is not that as good as a hanging to you?

FESTE.   Many a good hanging prevents a bad marriage; and, for turning away, let summer bear it out.

MARIA.   You are resolute, then?

FESTE.   Not so, neither; but I am resolved on two points.   20

MARIA.   That if one break, the other will hold; or, if both break, your gaskins fall.

FESTE.   Apt, in good faith; very apt. Well, go thy way. If Sir Toby would leave drinking, thou wert as witty a piece of Eve's flesh as any in Illyria.   25

MARIA.   Peace, you rogue, no more o' that. Here comes my lady. Make your excuse wisely, you were best.

Exit.

Enter LADY OLIVIA *and retinue, with* MALVOLIO.

FESTE.   Wit, an 't be thy will, put me into good fooling! Those wits that think they have thee do very oft prove fools; and I that am sure I lack thee may pass for a wise man; for   30 what says Quinapalus? "Better a witty fool than a foolish wit." —God bless thee, lady!

OLIVIA.   Take the fool away.

FESTE.   Do you not hear, fellows? Take away the lady.

OLIVIA.   Go to, you're a dry fool. I'll no more of you; be-   35 sides, you grow dishonest.

FESTE.   Two faults, madonna, that drink and good counsel will amend; for give the dry fool drink, then is the fool not

---

8 good lenten *mighty thin* / 14 talents *with a pun on talons* / 18 bear it out *make it endurable* / 21 one *i.e., the lace that attaches the breeches* (*gaskins*) *to the jacket* / 24 witty . . . flesh *be as good a wife* / 31 Quinapalus *a philosopher invented by Feste for the occasion* / 35 dry *stupid* / 36 dishonest *unreliable*

dry. Bid the dishonest man mend himself; if he mend, he is
no longer dishonest; if he cannot, let the botcher mend him. 40
Any thing that's mended is but patched; virtue that trans-
gresses is but patched with sin, and sin that amends is but
patched with virtue. If that this simple syllogism will serve,
so; if it will not, what remedy? As there is no true cuckold but
calamity, so beauty's a flower. The lady bade take away the 45
fool; therefore, I say again, take her away.

OLIVIA. Sir, I bade them take away you.

FESTE. Misprision in the highest degree! Lady, *"cucullus
non facit monachum";* that's as much to say as I wear not
motley in my brain. Good madonna, give me leave to prove 50
you a fool.

OLIVIA. Can you do it?

FESTE. Dexteriously, good madonna.

OLIVIA. Make your proof.

FESTE. I must catechize you for it, madonna. Good my 55
mouse of virtue, answer me.

OLIVIA. Well, sir, for want of other idleness, I'll bide your
proof.

FESTE. Good madonna, why mourn'st thou?

OLIVIA. Good fool, for my brother's death.   60

FESTE. I think his soul is in hell, madonna.

OLIVIA. I know his soul is in heaven, fool.

FESTE. The more fool, madonna, to mourn for your
brother's soul being in heaven. Take away the fool, gentlemen.   65

OLIVIA. What think you of this fool, Malvolio? Doth he
not mend?

MALVOLIO. Yes, and shall do till the pangs of death shake
him. Infirmity, that decays the wise, doth ever make the better fool.   70

FESTE. God send you, sir, a speedy infirmity, for the better increasing your folly! Sir Toby will be sworn that I am no
fox, but he will not pass his word for twopence that you are
no fool.

---

39 mend *reform* / 40 botcher *tailor* / 43 syllogism *logical argument* / 45
calamity *i.e., adverse fortune* (*equivalent to the unfaithful wife that makes
a husband a cuckold*) / 48 Misprision *error* / 48 cucullus . . . monachum
the cowl does not make the monk / 50 motley *jester's costume*

OLIVIA.   How say you to that, Malvolio?   75

MALVOLIO.   I marvel your ladyship takes delight in such a barren rascal. I saw him put down the other day with an ordinary fool that has no more brain than a stone. Look you now, he's out of his guard already. Unless you laugh and minister occasion to him, he is gagged. I protest, I take these   80 wise men, that crow so at these set kind of fools, no better than the fools' zanies.

OLIVIA.   O, you are sick of self-love, Malvolio, and taste with a distempered appetite. To be generous, guiltless, and of free disposition, is to take those things for bird-bolts that you   85 deem cannon-bullets. There is no slander in an allowed fool, though he do nothing but rail; nor no railing in a known discreet man though he do nothing but reprove.

FESTE.   Now Mercury endue thee with leasing, for thou speak'st well of fools!   90

Re-enter MARIA.

MARIA.   Madam, there is at the gate a young gentleman much desires to speak with you.

OLIVIA.   From the Count Orsino, is it?

MARIA.   I know not, madam. 'Tis a fair young man, and well attended.   95

OLIVIA.   Who of my people hold him in delay?

MARIA.   Sir Toby, madam, your kinsman.

OLIVIA.   Fetch him off, I pray you. He speaks nothing but madman; fie on him! [*Exit* MARIA.] Go you, Malvolio; if it be a suit from the Count, I am sick, or not at home,—what you   100 will, to dismiss it. [*Exit* MALVOLIO.] Now you see, sir, how your fooling grows old, and people dislike it.

FESTE.   Thou hast spoke for us, madonna, as if thy eldest son should be a fool; whose skull Jove cram with brains! for —here he comes—

Enter SIR TOBY.

---

one of thy kin has most weak *pia mater*.   105

OLIVIA. By mine honor, half drunk. What is he at the
gate, cousin?

SIR TOBY. A gentleman.

OLIVIA. A gentleman! What gentleman?

SIR TOBEY. 'Tis a gentleman here—a plague o' these   110
pickle-herring! How now, sot!

FESTE. Good Sir Toby!

OLIVIA. Cousin, cousin, how have you come so early by
this lethargy?

SIR TOBY. Lechery! I defy lechery. There's one at the gate.   115

OLIVIA. Ay, marry, what is he?

SIR TOBY. Let him be the devil, an he will, I care not;
give me faith, say I. Well, it's all one.   *Exit.*

OLIVIA. What's a drunken man like, fool?

FESTE. Like a drowned man, a fool, and a madman. One   120
draught above heat makes him a fool, the second mads him,
and a third drowns him.

OLIVIA. Go thou and seek the crowner and let him sit o'
my coz, for he's in the third degree of drink, he's drowned.
Go, look after him.   125

FESTE. He is but mad yet, madonna; and the fool shall
look to the madman.   *Exit.*

Re-enter MALVOLIO.

MALVOLIO. Madam, yond young fellow swears he will
speak with you. I told him you were sick; he takes on him to
understand so much, and therefore comes to speak with you.   130
I told him you were asleep; he seems to have a fore-knowl-
edge of that too, and therefore comes to speak with you. What
is to be said to him, lady? He's fortified against any denial.

OLIVIA. Tell him he shall not speak with me.

MALVOLIO. Has been told so; and he says, he'll stand at   135
your door like a sheriff's post, and be the supporter to a bench,
but he'll speak with you.

OLIVIA. What kind o' man is he?

MALVOLIO. Why, of mankind.

---

105 pia mater *brain* / 121 above heat *i.e., above temperate drinking*
/ 123 crowner *coroner* / 123 sit o' *hold an inquest on* / 129 takes on
him *presumes* / 136 post *sign of office at sheriff's door*

OLIVIA.   What manner of man?   140

MALVOLIO.   Of very ill manner. He'll speak with you, will you or no.

OLIVIA.   Of what personage and years is he?

MALVOLIO.   Not yet old enough for a man, nor young enough for a boy; as a squash is before 'tis a peascod, or a   145
codling when 'tis almost an apple; 'tis with him in standing water, between boy and man. He is very well-favored and he speaks very shrewishly. One would think his mother's milk were scarce out of him.

OLIVIA.   Let him approach. Call in my gentlewoman.   150

MALVOLIO.   Gentlewoman, my lady calls.   *Exit.*

Re-enter MARIA.

OLIVIA.   Give me my veil. Come, throw it o'er my face. We'll once more hear Orsino's embassy.

Enter VIOLA.

VIOLA.   The honorable lady of the house, which is she?

OLIVIA.   Speak to me; I shall answer for her. Your will?   155

VIOLA.   Most radiant, exquisite, and unmatchable beauty, —I pray you, tell me if this be the lady of the house, for I never saw her. I would be loath to cast away my speech, for besides that it is excellently well penned, I have taken great pains to con it. Good beauties, let me sustain no scorn. I am   160
very comptible, even to the least sinister usage.

OLIVIA.   Whence came you, sir?

VIOLA.   I can say little more than I have studied, and that question's out of my part. Good gentle one, give me modest assurance if you be the lady of the house, that I may proceed   165
in my speech.

OLIVIA.   Are you a comedian?

VIOLA.   No, my profound heart; and yet, by the very fangs of malice I swear, I am not that I play. Are you the lady of the house?   170

OLIVIA.   If I do not usurp myself, I am.

---

145 squash *unripe peapod* / 146 codling *unripe apple* / 146 standing water *between ebb and flow* / 147 well-favored *handsome* / 160 con *learn* / 161 comptible *sensitive* / 167 comedian *i.e., player*

VIOLA.   Most certain, if you are she, you do usurp yourself; for what is yours to bestow is not yours to reserve. But
this is from my commission. I will on with my speech in your
praise, and then show you the heart of my message.   175

OLIVIA.   Come to what is important in 't. I forgive you
the praise.

VIOLA.   Alas, I took great pains to study it, and 'tis poeti-
cal.

OLIVIA.   It is the more like to be feigned. I pray you, keep   180
it in. I heard you were saucy at my gates, and allowed your
approach rather to wonder at you than to hear you. If you
be not mad, be gone; if you have reason, be brief. 'Tis not
that time of moon with me to make one in so skipping a
dialogue.   185

MARIA.   Will you hoist sail, sir? Here lies your way.

VIOLA.   No, good swabber, I am to hull here a little
longer. Some mollification for your giant, sweet lady. Tell me
your mind. I am a messenger.

OLIVIA.   Sure, you have some hideous matter to deliver,   190
when the courtesy of it is so fearful. Speak your offi e.

VIOLA.   It alone concerns your ear. I bring no overture of
war, no taxation of homage. I hold the olive in my hand;
my words are as full of peace as matter.

OLIVIA.   Yet you began rudely. What are you? What would   195
you?

VIOLA.   The rudeness that hath appeared in me have I
learned from my entertainment. What I am, and what I
would, are as secret as maidenhead; to your ears, divinity; to
any other's, profanation.   200

OLIVIA.   Give us the place alone; we will hear this divinity.
[Exit MARIA.] Now, sir, what is your text?

VIOLA.   Most sweet lady,—

OLIVIA.   A comfortable doctrine, and much may be said
of it. Where lies your text?   205

VIOLA.   In Orsino's bosom.

OLIVIA.   In his bosom! In what chapter of his bosom?

---

174 from my commission *not part of my instructions* / 176 forgive you
excuse you from repeating / 183 'Tis not . . . with me *I am not at
present so under the influence of the moon* (*so lunatic*) / 198 entertainment *reception* / 199 divinity *sacred discourse*

VIOLA.   To answer by the method, in the first of his heart.
OLIVIA.   O, I have read it; it is heresy. Have you no more
to say?   210
VIOLA.   Good madam, let me see your face.
OLIVIA.   Have you any commission from your lord to ne-
gotiate with my face? You are now out of your text, but we
will draw the curtain and show you the picture. Look you, sir,
such a one I was this present. Is't not well done?   215

                                                      Unveiling.

VIOLA.   Excellently done, if God did all.
OLIVIA.   'Tis in grain, sir; 't will endure wind and weather.
VIOLA.   'Tis beauty truly blent, whose red and white
Nature's own sweet and cunning hand laid on.
Lady, you are the cruell'st she alive,   220
If you will lead these graces to the grave
And leave the world no copy.
OLIVIA.   O, sir, I will not be so hard-hearted; I will give
out divers schedules of my beauty. It shall be inventoried, and
every particle and utensil labelled to my will: as, item, two   225
lips, indifferent red; item, two gray eyes, with lids to them;
item, one neck, one chin, and so forth. Were you sent hither
to praise me?
VIOLA.   I see you what you are, you are too proud;
But, if you were the devil, you are fair.   230
My lord and master loves you. O, such love
Could be but recompens'd, though you were crown'd
The nonpareil of beauty!
OLIVIA.   How does he love me?
VIOLA.   With adorations, with fertile tears,
With groans that thunder love, with sighs of fire.   235
OLIVIA.   Your lord does know my mind; I cannot love him.
Yet I suppose him virtuous, know him noble;
Of great estate, of fresh and stainless youth,
In voices well divulg'd, free, learn'd, and valiant,
And in dimension and the shape of nature   240
A gracious person; but yet I cannot love him.

---

208 method *in accordance with the style of a preacher* / 217 in grain
fast dyed / 224 schedules *catalogues* / 225 utensil *detail* / 225 will
testament / 233 nonpareil *without an equal* / 239 voices well divulg'd
well spoken of in public testimony

He might have took his answer long ago.

   VIOLA.   If I did love you in my master's flame,
With such a suff'ring, such a deadly life,
In your denial I would find no sense.   245
I would not understand it.

   OLIVIA.   Why, what would you?

   VIOLA.   Make me a willow cabin at your gate,
And call upon my soul within the house;
Write loyal cantons of contemned love
And sing them loud even in the dead of night;   250
Halloo your name to the reverberate hills
And make the babbling gossip of the air
Cry out "Olivia!" O, you should not rest
Between the elements of air and earth,
But you should pity me!

   OLIVIA   You might do much.   255
What is your parentage?

   VIOLA.   Above my fortunes, yet my state is well.
I am a gentleman.

   OLIVIA.   Get you to your lord.
I cannot love him. Let him send no more,—
Unless, perchance, you come to me again   260
To tell me how he takes it. Fare you well!
I thank you for your pains; spend this for me.

   VIOLA.   I am no fee'd post, lady. Keep your purse.
My master, not myself, lacks recompense.
Love make his heart of flint that you shall love;   265
And let your fervor, like my master's, be
Plac'd in contempt! Farewell, fair cruelty.   *Exit.*

   OLIVIA. "What is your parentage?"
"Above my fortunes, yet my state is well.
I am a gentleman." I'll be sworn thou art.   270
Thy tongue, thy face, thy limbs, actions, and spirit
Do give thee five-fold blazon. Not too fast! Soft, soft!
Unless the master were the man. How now!
Even so quickly may one catch the plague?
Methinks I feel this youth's perfections   275

---

249 cantons *songs* / 251 reverberate *echoing* / 263 fee'd post *hired messenger* / 272 blazon *gentleman's coat of arms* / 273 were *were as attractive as*

With an invisible and subtle stealth
To creep in at mine eyes. Well, let it be.
What ho, Malvolio!

Re-enter MALVOLIO.

MALVOLIO.   Here, madam, at your service.
OLIVIA.   Run after that same peevish messenger,
The County's man. He left this ring behind him,   280
Would I or not. Tell him I'll none of it.
Desire him not to flatter with his lord,
Nor hold him up with hopes. I'm not for him.
If that the youth will come this way to-morrow,
I'll give him reasons for 't. Hie thee, Malvolio.   285
MALVOLIO.   Madam, I will.   *Exit.*
OLIVIA.   I do I know not what, and fear to find
Mine eye too great a flatterer for my mind.
Fate, show thy force; ourselves we do not owe;
What is decreed must be, and be this so.   *Exit.*   290

[ACT II · 1] *The sea-coast.*

Enter ANTONIO *and* SEBASTIAN.

ANTONIO.   Will you stay no longer? Nor will you not that
I go with you?
SEBASTIAN.   By your patience, no. My stars shine darkly
over me. The malignancy of my fate might perhaps distemper
yours, therefore I shall crave of you your leave that I may   5
bear my evils alone. It were a bad recompense for your love,
to lay any of them on you.
ANTONIO.   Let me yet know of you whither you are bound.
SEBASTIAN.   No, sooth, sir; my determinate voyage is mere
extravagancy. But I perceive in you so excellent a touch of   10
modesty that you will not extort from me what I am willing to
keep in; therefore it charges me in manners the rather to express myself. You must know of me then, Antonio, my name

---

280 County *Count* (*i.e., Duke*) / 288 great . . . mind *more powerful
an influence over me than is my judgment* / 289 owe *own*
   [ACT II · 1] 4 malignancy *evil disposition* / 9 sooth *truly* / 9 mere
extravagancy *to wander without plan* / 12 it charges me . . . to *good
manners dictate that I*

is Sebastian, which I called Roderigo. My father was that Sebastian of Messaline, whom I know you have heard of. He   15
left behind him myself and a sister, both born in an hour. If
the heavens had been pleased, would we had so ended! But
you, sir, altered that; for some hour before you took me from
the breach of the sea was my sister drowned.

ANTONIO.   Alas the day!   20

SEBASTIAN.   A lady, sir, though it was said she much re-
sembled me, was yet of many accounted beautiful; but,
though I could not with such estimable wonder overfar believe that, yet thus far I will boldly publish her: she bore a
mind that envy could not but call fair. She is drowned already,   25
r, with salt water, though I seem to drown her remembrance
gain with more.

ANTONIO.   Pardon me, sir, your bad entertainment.

SEBASTIAN.   O good Antonio, forgive me your trouble.

ANTONIO.   If you will not murder me for my love, let me   30
our servant.

BASTIAN.   If you will not undo what you have done, that
him whom you have recovered, desire it not. Fare ye
nce. My bosom is full of kindness, and I am yet so
manners of my mother, that upon the least occasion   35
ne eyes will tell tales of me. I am bound to the Count
court. Farewell.   *Exit.*

NIO.   The gentleness of all the gods go with thee!
any enemies in Orsino's court,
uld I very shortly see thee there.   40
ne what may, I do adore thee so
nger shall seem sport, and I will go.   *Exit.*

[ACT II · 2] *A street.*

Enter VIOLA, *followed by* MALVOLIO.

LVOLIO.   Were you not e'en now with the Countess
?

LA.   Even now, sir. On a moderate pace I have since
d but hither.

---

reach *breakers* / 23 estimable wonder *an admirable estimate* / 33 re-
ered *rescued* / 35 manners *temperament* / 36 tell tales *i.e., by weeping*

MALVOLIO.   She returns this ring to you, sir; you might   5
have saved me my pains, to have taken it away yourself. She
adds, moreover, that you should put your lord into a desperate assurance she will none of him; and one thing more, that
you be never so hardy to come again in his affairs, unless it
be to report your lord's taking of this. Receive it so.   10

VIOLA.   She took the ring of me. I'll none of it.

MALVOLIO.   Come, sir, you peevishly threw it to her; and
her will is,·it should be so returned. If it be worth stopping
for, there it lies in your eye; if not, be it his that finds it.

Exit.

VIOLA.   I left no ring with her. What means this lady?   15
Fortune forbid my outside have not charm'd her!
She made good view of me; indeed so much,
That sure methought her eyes had lost her tongue,
For she did speak in starts distractedly.
She loves me, sure: the cunning of her passion
Invites me in this churlish messenger.
None of my lord's ring! Why, he sent her none.
I am the man. If it be so—as 'tis—
Poor lady, she were better love a dream.
Disguise, I see thou art a wickedness
Wherein the pregnant enemy does much.
How easy is it for the proper-false
In women's waxen hearts to set their forms!
Alas, our frailty is the cause, not we!
For such as we are made of, such we be.
How will this fadge? My master loves her dearly;
And I, poor monster, fond as much on him;
And she, mistaken, seems to dote on me.
What will become of this? As I am man,
My state is desperate for my master's love;
As I am woman,—now alas the day!—
What thriftless sighs shall poor Olivia breathe!
O time! thou must untangle this, not I.
It is too hard a knot for me t' untie!   *Exit.*

[ACT II · 2] 7 put . . . desperate assurance *convince the Duke*
his cause is hopeless / 18 lost *made her lose* / 26 pregnant *resour*
/ 27 proper-false *men who are handsome deceivers* / fadge
out / 35 desperate *without hope* / 37 thriftless *unprofitable*

[ACT II · 3] *Olivia's house.*

Enter SIR TOBY *and* SIR ANDREW.

SIR TOBY.   Approach, Sir Andrew. Not to be a-bed after midnight is to be up betimes; and *"diliculo surgere,"* thou know'st,—

SIR ANDREW.   Nay, by my troth, I know not; but I know, to be up late is to be up late.   5

SIR TOBY.   A false conclusion! I hate it as an unfilled can. To be up after midnight and to go to bed then, is early; so that to go to bed after midnight is to go to bed betimes. Does not our lives consist of the four elements?

SIR ANDREW.   Faith, so they say; but I think it rather con-   10 sists of eating and drinking.

SIR TOBY.   Thou'rt a scholar; let us therefore eat and drink. Marian, I say! a stoup of wine!

Enter FESTE.

SIR ANDREW.   Here comes the fool, i' faith.

FESTE.   How now, my hearts! Did you never see the pic-   15 ture of "We Three"?

SIR TOBY.   Welcome, ass. Now let's have a catch.

SIR ANDREW.   By my troth, the fool has an excellent breast. I had rather than forty shillings I had such a leg, and so sweet a breath to sing, as the fool has. In sooth, thou wast in very   20 gracious fooling last night, when thou spok'st of Pigrogromi-tus, of the Vapians passing the equinoctial of Queubus. 'Twas very good, i' faith. I sent thee sixpence for thy leman. Hadst it?

FESTE.   I did impeticos thy gratillity; for Malvolio's nose   25 is no whipstock. My lady has a white hand, and the Myrmi-dons are no bottle-ale houses.

SIR ANDREW.   Excellent! Why, this is the best fooling, when all is done. Now, a song.

[ACT II · 3] 2 betimes *early* / 2 diliculo surgere *early to rise* (*is good for the health*) / 6 can *drinking pot* / 9 four elements *i.e, fire, air, earth, and water* (*components of all matter*) / 13 stoup *large pot* / 16 "We Three" *a picture of two idiots, the spectator being the third* / 17 catch *round* / 18 breast *voice* / 21 Pigrogromitus . . . Queubus *nonsensical learning* / 23 leman *sweetheart* / 25 impeticos *pocket* / 25 gratillity *little tip* (*the rest of the speech is nonsense*)

SIR TOBY.   Come on; there is sixpence for you. Let's have   30
a song.

SIR ANDREW.   There's a testril of me too. If one knight
give a—

FESTE.   Would you have a love-song, or a song of good
life?   35

SIR TOBY.   A love-song, a love-song.

SIR ANDREW.   Ay, ay. I care not for good life.

FESTE.   [*Sings.*]

> O mistress mine, where are you roaming?
> O, stay and hear, your true love's coming,
>   That can sing both high and low.   40
> Trip no further, pretty sweeting;
> Journeys end in lovers meeting,
>   Every wise man's son doth know.

SIR ANDREW.   Excellent good, i' faith.

SIR TOBY.   Good, good.   45

FESTE.   [*Sings.*]

> What is love? 'Tis not hereafter.
> Present mirth hath present laughter;
>   What's to come is still unsure.
> In delay there lies no plenty;
> Then come kiss me, sweet and twenty,   50
>   Youth's a stuff will not endure.

SIR ANDREW.   A mellifluous voice, as I am true knight.

SIR TOBY.   A contagious breath.

SIR ANDREW.   Very sweet and contagious, i' faith.

SIR TOBY.   To hear by the nose, it is dulcet in contagion.   55
But shall we make the welkin dance indeed? Shall we rouse
the night-owl in a catch that will draw three souls out of one
weaver? Shall we do that?

SIR ANDREW.   An you love me, let's do 't. I am dog at a
catch.   60

FESTE.   By 'r lady, sir, and some dogs will catch well.

---

32 testril *sixpence* / 34 good life *morality* / 50 sweet and twenty *sweet
to the twentieth degree* / 53 contagious *catchy* (*and, malodorous*) / 56
welkin *the stars in the heavens* / 59 dog *skillful*

SIR ANDREW. Most certain. Let our catch be, "Thou knave."

FESTE. "Hold thy peace, thou knave," knight? I shall be constrained in 't to call thee knave, knight. 65

SIR ANDREW. 'Tis not the first time I have constrained one to call me knave. Begin, fool. It begins, "Hold thy peace."

FESTE. I shall never begin if I hold my peace.

SIR ANDREW. Good, i' faith. Come, begin.

Catch sung.

Enter MARIA.

MARIA. What a caterwauling do you keep here! If my lady 70 have not called up her steward Malvolio and bid him turn you out of doors, never trust me.

SIR TOBY. My lady's a Cataian, we are politicians, Malvolio's a Peg-a-Ramsey, and "Three merry men be we." Am not I consanguineous? Am I not of her blood? Tilly-vally, 75 Lady! [*Sings.*] "There dwelt a man in Babylon, lady, lady!"

FESTE. Beshrew me, the knight's in admirable fooling.

SIR ANDREW. Ay, he does well enough if he be disposed, and so do I too. He does it with a better grace, but I do it more natural. 80

SIR TOBY. [*Sings.*] "O, the twelfth day of December,"—

MARIA. For the love o' God, peace!

Enter MALVOLIO.

MALVOLIO. My masters, are you mad, or what are you? Have you no wit, manners, nor honesty, but to gabble like tinkers at this time of night? Do ye make an alehouse of my 85 lady's house, that ye squeak out your coziers' catches without any mitigation or remorse of voice? Is there no respect of place, persons, nor time in you?

SIR TOBY. We did keep time, sir, in our catches. Sneck up!

MALVOLIO. Sir Toby, I must be round with you. My lady 90 bade me tell you that, though she harbors you as her kinsman, she's nothing allied to your disorders. If you can separate

---

73 Cataian *Cathayan, slang for humbug* / 73 politicians *statesmen* / 74 Peg-a-Ramsey *of no account* / 75 Tilly-vally *hoity-toity* / 86 coziers' *cobblers'* / 87 respect of *consideration for* / 89 Sneck up *go to the devil* / 90 round *outspoken*

yourself and your misdemeanors, you are welcome to the
house; if not, an it would please you to take leave of her, she
is very willing to bid you farewell.   95

SIR TOBY.   "Farewell, dear heart, since I must needs be
gone."

MARIA.   Nay, good Sir Toby.

FESTE.   "His eyes do show his days are almost done."

MALVOLIO.   Is 't even so?   100

SIR TOBY.   "But I will never die."

FESTE.   Sir Toby, there you lie.

MALVOLIO.   This is much credit to you.

SIR TOBY.   "Shall I bid him go?"

FESTE.   "What an if you do?"   105

SIR TOBY.   "Shall I bid him go, and spare not?"

FESTE.   "O no, no, no, no, you dare not."

SIR TOBY.   Out o' tune, sir! Ye lie. Art any more than a
steward? Dost thou think, because thou art virtuous, there
shall be no more cakes and ale?   110

FESTE.   Yes, by Saint Anne, and ginger shall be hot i' the
mouth too.

SIR TOBY.   Thou'rt i' the right. Go, sir, rub your chain
with crumbs. A stoup of wine, Maria!

MALVOLIO.   Mistress Mary, if you prized my lady's favor   115
at anything more than contempt, you would not give means
for this uncivil rule. She shall know of it, by this hand.

                                                              Exit.

MARIA.   Go shake your ears.

SIR ANDREW: 'Twere as good a deed as to drink when a
man's a-hungry, to challenge him the field, and then to break   120
promise with him and make a fool of him.

SIR TOBY.   Do 't, knight. I'll write thee a challenge, or I'll
deliver thy indignation to him by word of mouth.

MARIA.   Sweet Sir Toby, be patient for to-night. Since the
youth of the Count's was to-day with my lady, she is much   125
out of quiet. For Monsieur Malvolio, let me alone with him.
If I do not gull him into a nayword, and make him a common
recreation, do not think I have wit enough to lie straight in
my bed. I know I can do it.

---

111 ginger *used in spicing ale* / 113 chain *of office, as steward* / 127
gull *trick* / 127 nayword *byword* / 128 recreation *laughing stock*

SIR TOBY. Possess us, possess us. Tell us something of 130
him.

MARIA. Marry, sir, sometimes he is a kind of puritan.

SIR ANDREW. O, if I thought that, I'd beat him like a dog!

SIR TOBY. What, for being a puritan? Thy exquisite reason, dear knight? 135

SIR ANDREW. I have no exquisite reason for 't, but I have
reason good enough.

MARIA. The devil a puritan that he is, or anything con-
stantly, but a time-pleaser; an affectioned ass, that cons state
without book and utters it by great swarths; the best per- 140
suaded of himself, so crammed, as he thinks, with excellen-
cies, that it is his grounds of faith that all that look on him
love him; and on that vice in him will my revenge find notable
cause to work

SIR TOBY. What wilt thou do? 145

MARIA. I will drop in his way some obscure epistles of
love; wherein, by the color of his beard, the shape of his leg,
the manner of his gait, the expressure of his eye, forehead,
and complexion, he shall find himself most feelingly per-
sonated. I can write very like my lady your niece. On a for- 150
gotten matter we can hardly make distinction of our hands.

SIR TOBY. Excellent! I smell a device.

SIR ANDREW. I have 't in my nose too

SIR TOBY. He shall think by the letters that thou wilt drop
that they come from my niece, and that she's in love with 155
him.

MARIA. My purpose is, indeed, a horse of that color.

SIR ANDREW. And your horse now would make him an
ass.

MARIA. Ass, I doubt not. 160

SIR ANDREW. O, 'twill be admirable!

MARIA. Sport royal, I warrant you. I know my physic
will work with him. I will plant you two, and let the fool
make a third, where he shall find the letter. Observe his con-

---

130 Possess us *tell us how* / 139 time-pleaser *sycophant* / 139 state
courtly behavior and speech / 140 swarths *quantities* / 140 best persuaded *with the best opinion* / 149 feelingly *exactly* / 160 Ass *with a
pun on as* / 164 construction *interpretation*

struction of it. For this night, to bed, and dream on the event.   165
Farewell.   *Exit.*

SIR TOBY.   Good night, Penthesilea.

SIR ANDREW.   Before me, she's a good wench.

SIR TOBY.   She's a beagle, true-bred, and one that adores
me. What o' that?   170

SIR ANDREW.   I was adored once too.

SIR TOBY.   Let's to bed, knight. Thou hadst need send for
more money.

SIR ANDREW.   If I cannot recover your niece, I am a foul
way out.   175

SIR TOBY.   Send for money, knight. If thou hast her not i'
th' end, call me Cut.

SIR ANDREW.   If I do not, never trust me, take it how you
will.

SIR TOBY.   Come, come, I'll go burn some sack; 'tis too   180
late to go to bed now. Come, knight; come, knight.

                                                            Exeunt.

[A C T   I I • 4] *The Duke's palace.*

Enter DUKE, VIOLA, CURIO, *and others.*

DUKE.   Give me some music. Now,—good morrow,
        friends,—
Now, good Cesario, but that piece of song,
That old and antique song we heard last night.
Methought it did relieve my passion much,
More than light airs and recollected terms   5
Of these most brisk and giddy-paced times.
Come, but one verse.

CURIO.   He is not here, so please your lordship, that should
sing it.

DUKE.   Who was it?   10

CURIO.   Feste, the jester, my lord; a fool that the lady
Olivia's father took much delight in. He is about the house.

---

167 Penthesilea *Queen of the Amazons* / 169 beagle *a small hunting
dog* / 174 recover *win* / 175 out *i.e., out of pocket* / 177 Cut *horse*
/ 180 burn some sack *heat some wine*
   [ACT II • 4] 5 recollected *artificial*

DUKE.   Seek him out, and play the tune the while.

Exit CURIO. *Music plays.*

Come hither, boy. If ever thou shalt love,
In the sweet pangs of it remember me;   15
For such as I am all true lovers are,
Unstaid and skittish in all motions else,
Save in the constant image of the creature
That is belov'd. How dost thou like this tune?

VIOLA.   It gives a very echo to the seat   20
Where Love is thron'd.

DUKE.   Thou dost speak masterly.
My life upon 't, young though thou art, thine eye
Hath stay'd upon some favor that it loves.
Hath it not, boy?

VIOLA.   A little, by your favor.

DUKE.   What kind of woman is 't?

VIOLA.   Of your complexion.   25

DUKE.   She is not worth thee, then. What years, i' faith?

VIOLA.   About your years, my lord.

DUKE.   Too old, by heaven. Let still the woman take
An elder than herself; so wears she to him,
So sways she level in her husband's heart.   30
For, boy, however we do praise ourselves,
Our fancies are more giddy and unfirm,
More longing, wavering, sooner lost and won,
Than women's are.

VIOLA.   I think it well, my lord.

DUKE.   Then let thy love be younger than thyself,   35
Or thy affection cannot hold the bent.
For women are as roses, whose fair flower
Being once display'd, doth fall that very hour.

VIOLA.   And so they are; alas, that they are so!
To die, even when they to perfection grow!   40

Re-enter CURIO *and* FESTE.

---

17 motions else *other thoughts and feelings* / 20 seat *heart* / 23 favor
face / 24 by your favor *both, if you please and, by your face* / 28 still
always / 29 wears she *adapts herself* / 30 sways she level *maintains
a balance* / 36 the bent *intensity* / 38 display'd *full blown*

DUKE.   O, fellow, come, the song we had last night.
Mark it, Cesario, it is old and plain.
The spinsters and the knitters in the sun
And the free maids that weave their thread with bones
Do use to chant it. It is silly sooth,   45
And dallies with the innocence of love,
Like the old age.

    FESTE.   Are you ready, sir?

    DUKE.   Ay; prithee, sing.   *Music.*

Song

    FESTE.

      Come away, come away, death,   50
        And in sad cypress let me be laid.
      Fly away, fly away, breath;
        I am slain by a fair cruel maid.
      My shroud of white, stuck all with yew,
        O, prepare it!   55
      My part of death, no one so true
        Did share it.

      Not a flower, not a flower sweet,
        On my black coffin let there be strown.
      Not a friend, not a friend greet   60
        My poor corpse, where my bones shall be thrown.
      A thousand thousand sighs to save,
        Lay me, O, where
      Sad true lover never find my grave,
        To weep there!   65

    DUKE.   There's for thy pains.

    FESTE.   No pains, sir; I take pleasure in singing, sir.

    DUKE.   I'll pay thy pleasure then.

    FESTE.   Truly, sir, and pleasure will be paid, one time or
another.   70

    DUKE.   Give me now leave to leave thee.

    FESTE.   Now, the melancholy god protect thee, and the
tailor make thy doublet of changeable taffeta, for thy mind

---

43 spinsters *spinners* / 44 weave . . . bones *make lace* / 45 silly sooth
simple truth / 46 dallies *plays* / 51 cypress *coffin* / 73 doublet *jacket*
73 changeable *iridescent, opalescent*

is a very opal. I would have men of such constancy put to sea,
that their business might be everything and their intent every-   75
where; for that's it that always makes a good voyage of
nothing. Farewell.   *Exit.*

  DUKE.   Let all the rest give place.

CURIO *and* ATTENDANTS *retire.*

                         Once more, Cesario,
Get thee to yond same sovereign cruelty.
Tell her, my love, more noble than the world,   80
Prizes not quantity of dirty lands.
The parts that Fortune hath bestow'd upon her,
Tell her, I hold as giddily as Fortune;
But 'tis that miracle and queen of gems
That Nature pranks her in attracts my soul.   85
  VIOLA.   But if she cannot love you, sir?
  DUKE.   I cannot be so answer'd.
  VIOLA.   Sooth, but you must.
Say that some lady, as perhaps there is,
Hath for your love as great a pang of heart
As you have for Olivia. You cannot love her;   90
You tell her so. Must she not then be answer'd?
  DUKE.   There is no woman's sides
Can bide the beating of so strong a passion
As love doth give my heart; no woman's heart
So big, to hold so much. They lack retention.   95
Alas, their love may be call'd appetite—
No motion of the liver, but the palate—
That suffer surfeit, cloyment, and revolt;
But mine is all as hungry as the sea,
And can digest as much. Make no compare   100
Between that love a woman can bear me
And that I owe Olivia.
  VIOLA.   Ay, but I know—
  DUKE.   What dost thou know?
  VIOLA.   Too well what love women to men may owe.
In faith, they are as true of heart as we.   105

---

75 intent *destination* / 85 pranks *adorns* / 93 bide *endure* / 97 motion of the liver *genuine passion*

My father had a daughter lov'd a man,
As it might be, perhaps, were I a woman,
I should your lordship.

    DUKE.   And what's her history?

    VIOLA.   A blank, my lord. She never told her love,
But let concealment, like a worm i' the bud,   110
Feed on her damask cheek. She pin'd in thought,
And with a green and yellow melancholy
She sat, like Patience on a monument,
Smiling at grief. Was not this love indeed?
We men may say more, swear more; but indeed   115
Our shows are more than will, for still we prove
Much in our vows, but little in our love.

    DUKE.   But died thy sister of her love, my boy?

    VIOLA.   I am all the daughters of my father's house,
And all the brothers too;—and yet I know not.   120
Sir, shall I to this lady?

    DUKE.   Ay, that's the theme.
To her in haste. Give her this jewel; say
My love can give no place, bide no denay.   *Exeunt.*

[ACT II · 5] *Olivia's garden.*

Enter SIR TOBY, SIR ANDREW, *and* FABIAN.

    SIR TOBY.   Come thy ways, Signor Fabian.

    FABIAN.   Nay, I'll come. If I lose a scruple of this sport,
let me boiled to death with melancholy.

    SIR TOBY.   Wouldst thou not be glad to have the niggardly
rascally sheep-biter come by some notable shame?   5

    FABIAN.   I would exult, man. You know, he brought me
out o' favor with my lady about a bear-baiting here.

    SIR TOBY.   To anger him we'll have the bear again, and we
will fool him black and blue. Shall we not, Sir Andrew?

    SIR ANDREW.   An we do not, it is pity of our lives.   10

Enter MARIA.

---

111 damask *mingled white and red* / 112 green and yellow *pale and
sallow* / 116 will *what we feel* / 123 denay *denial*

    [ACT II · 5] 2 scruple *least possible portion* / 5 sheep-biter *dog* /
7 bear-baiting *a popular and brutal sport* / 9 black and blue *within
an inch of his life*

SIR TOBY.   Here comes the little villain. How now, my metal of India!

MARIA.   Get ye all three into the box-tree; Malvolio's coming down this walk. He has been yonder i' the sun practising behavior to his own shadow this half hour. Observe him, for the love of mockery, for I know this letter will make a contemplative idiot of him. Close, in the name of jesting! Lie thou there [*throws down a letter*], for here comes the trout that must be caught with tickling.   *Exit.* 15

Enter MALVOLIO.

MALVOLIO.   'Tis but fortune. All is fortune. Maria once told me she did affect me; and I have heard herself come thus near, that, should she fancy, it should be one of my complexion. Besides, she uses me with a more exalted respect than any one else that follows her. What should I think on 't? 20

SIR TOBY.   Here's an overweening rogue!   25

FABIAN.   O, peace! Contemplation makes a rare turkey-cock of him. How he jets under his advanced plumes!

SIR ANDREW.   'Slight, I could so beat the rogue!

FABIAN.   Peace, I say.

MALVOLIO.   To be Count Malvolio!   30

SIR TOBY.   Ah, rogue!

SIR ANDREW.   Pistol him, pistol him.

FABIAN.   Peace, peace!

MALVOLIO.   There is example for 't. The lady of the Strachy married the yeoman of the wardrobe.   35

SIR ANDREW.   Fie on him, Jezebel!

FABIAN.   O, peace! now he's deeply in. Look how imagination blows him.

MALVOLIO.   Having been three months married to her, sitting in my state,—   40

SIR TOBY.   O, for a stone-bow, to hit him in the eye!

MALVOLIO.   Calling my officers about me, in my branched

---

12 metal of India *golden lass* / 13 box-tree *hedge* / 17 Close *hide* / 19 tickling *the bare hand* / 21 she *Olivia* / 27 jets *struts* / 27 under his . . . plumes *with his tail-feathers up* / 36 Jezebel *a proud Queen of Israel* / 38 blows him *puffs him up* / 40 state *chair of state* / 41 stone-bow *cross-bow that shoots stones* / 42 branched *embroidered*

velvet gown, having come from a day-bed, where I have left
Olivia sleeping,—

SIR TOBY.   Fire and brimstone!   45

FABIAN.   O, peace, peace!

MALVOLIO.   And then to have the humor of state; and
after a demure travel of regard, telling them I know my place
as I would they should do theirs, to ask for my kinsman
Toby,—   50

SIR TOBY.   Bolts and shackles!

FABIAN.   O peace, peace, peace! Now, now.

MALVOLIO.   Seven of my people, with an obedient start,
make out for him. I frown the while, and perchance wind up
my watch, or play with my—some rich jewel. Toby ap-   55
proaches, curtsies there to me,—

SIR TOBY.   Shall this fellow live?

FABIAN.   Though our silence be drawn from us with cars,
yet peace.

MALVOLIO.   I extend my hand to him thus, quenching my   60
familiar smile with an austere regard of control,—

SIR TOBY.   And does not Toby take you a blow o' the lips
then?

MALVOLIO.   Saying, "Cousin Toby, my fortunes, having
cast me on your niece, give me this prerogative of speech,"— 65

SIR TOBY.   What, what?

MALVOLIO.   "You must amend your drunkenness."

SIR TOBY.   Out, scab!

FABIAN.   Nay, patience, or we break the sinews of our plot.

MALVOLIO.   "Besides, you waste the treasure of your time   70
with a foolish knight,"—

SIR ANDREW.   That's me, I warrant you.

MALVOLIO.   "One Sir Andrew,"—

SIR ANDREW.   I knew 'twas I; for many do call me fool.

MALVOLIO.   What employment have we here?   75

                                    Taking up the letter.

FABIAN.   Now is the woodcock near the gin.

---

47 humor *demeanor* / 48 demure travel of regard *dignified glancing
about* / 55 my *Malvolio touches his steward's chain* / 61 control *authority* / 75 employment *business* / 76 woodcock *proverbially a stupid
bird* / 76 gin *trap*

SIR TOBY.   O, peace, and the spirit of humors intimate reading aloud to him!

MALVOLIO.   By my life, this is my lady's hand. These be her very C's, her U's, and her T's; and thus makes she her   80 great P's. It is, in contempt of question, her hand.

SIR ANDREW.   Her C's, her U's, and her T's: why that?

MALVOLIO.   [Reads.] "To the unknown beloved, this, and my good wishes":—her very phrases! By your leave, wax. Soft! And the impressure her Lucrece, with which she uses to   85 seal: 'tis my lady. To whom should this be?

FABIAN.   This wins him, liver and all.

MALVOLIO.   [Reads.]

> "Jove knows I love;
>   But who?
> Lips, do not move;   90
> No man must know."

"No man must know." What follows? The numbers altered! "No man must know!" If this should be thee, Malvolio?

SIR TOBY.   Marry, hang thee, brock!

MALVOLIO.   [Reads.]

> "I may command where I adore;   95
>   But silence, like a Lucrece knife,
> With bloodless stroke my heart doth gore.
>   M, O, A, I, doth sway my life."

FABIAN.   A fustian riddle!

SIR TOBY.   Excellent wench, say I.   100

MALVOLIO.   "M, O, A, I, doth sway my life." Nay, but first, let me see, let me see, let me see.

FABIAN.   What dish o' poison has she dressed him!

SIR TOBY.   And with what wing the staniel checks at it!

MALVOLIO.   "I may command where I adore." Why, she   105 may command me. I serve her; she is my lady. Why, this is evident to any formal capacity, there is no obstruction in this. And the end,—what should that alphabetical position por-

---

81 in contempt of *without* / 85 Lucrece *the emblem on Olivia's seal ring* / 92 numbers *meter* / 94 brock *badger* / 96 knife *Lucrece committed suicide* / 99 fustian *nonsensical* / 104 staniel *hawk* / 104 checks at it *is led astray by it* / 107 formal *normal*

tend? If I could make that resemble something in me!—
Softly! M, O, A, I,—   110

SIR TOBY.   O, ay, make up that. He is now at a cold scent.

FABIAN.   Sowter will cry upon 't for all this, though it be
as rank as a fox.

MALVOLIO.   M,—Malvolio; M,—why, that begins my
name.   115

FABIAN.   Did not I say he would work it out? The cur is
excellent at faults.

MALVOLIO.   M,—but then there is no consonancy in the
sequel. That suffers under probation; A should follow, but
O does.   120

FABIAN.   And O shall end, I hope.

SIR TOBY.   Ay, or I'll cudgel him, and make him cry O!

MALVOLIO.   And then I comes behind.

FABIAN.   Ay, an you had any eye behind you, you might
see more detraction at your heels than fortunes before you.   125

MALVOLIO.   M, O, A, I; this simulation is not as the
former; and yet, to crush this a little, it would bow to me, for
every one of these letters are in my name. Soft! here follows
prose.

[Reads.] "If this fall into thy hand, revolve. In my stars I am   130
above thee, but be not afraid of greatness: some are born great,
some achieve greatness, and some have greatness thrust upon 'em.
Thy Fates open their hands, let thy blood and spirit embrace them;
and, to inure thyself to what thou art like to be, cast thy humble
slough and appear fresh. Be opposite with a kinsman, surly with   135
servants; let thy tongue tang arguments of state; put thyself into
the trick of singularity. She thus advises thee that sighs for thee.
Remember who commended thy yellow stockings, and wished to
see thee ever cross-gartered. I say, remember. Go to, thou art
made, if thou desir'st to be so; if not, let me see thee a steward 140
still, the fellow of servants, and not worthy to touch Fortune's
fingers. Farewell. She that would alter services with thee,
                          THE FORTUNATE–UNHAPPY."

Daylight and champain discovers not more; this is open. I

---

112 Sowter *a clumsy hound* / 118 consonancy *consistency* / 119 probation *examination* / 126 simulation *veiled meaning* / 130 revolve *consider* / 134 inure *accustom* / 134 humble slough *lowly garb* / 137
singularity *unusual behavior* / 139 cross-gartered *garters crossing above
and below the knee* / 144 champain *open country*

will be proud, I will read politic authors, I will baffle Sir Toby, 145
I will wash off gross acquaintance, I will be point-device the
very man. I do not now fool myself to let imagination jade
me; for every reason excites to this, that my lady loves me.
She did commend my yellow stockings of late, she did praise
my leg being cross-gartered; and in this she manifests herself 150
to my love, and with a kind of injunction drives me to these
habits of her liking. I thank my stars I am happy. I will be
strange, stout, in yellow stockings, and cross-gartered, even
with the swiftness of putting on. Jove and my stars be praised!
Here is yet a postcript.   155

[*Reads.*] "Thou canst not choose but know who I am. If thou
entertain'st my love, let it appear in thy smiling. Thy smiles become thee well; therefore in my presence still smile, dear my
sweet, I prithee."

Jove, I thank thee. I will smile; I will do everything that 160
thou wilt have me.   *Exit.*

FABIAN.   I will not give my part of this sport for a pension
of thousands to be paid from the Sophy.

SIR TOBY.   I could marry this wench for this device—

SIR ANDREW.   So could I too,   165

SIR TOBY.   And ask no other dowry with her but such another jest.

Re-enter MARIA.

SIR ANDREW.   Nor I neither.

FABIAN.   Here comes my noble gull-catcher.

SIR TOBY.   Wilt thou set thy foot o' my neck?   170

SIR ANDREW.   Or o' mine either?

SIR TOBY.   Shall I play my freedom at tray-trip, and become thy bond-slave?

SIR ANDREW.   I' faith, or I either?

SIR TOBY.   Why, thou hast put him in such a dream, that 175
when the image of it leaves him he must run mad.

MARIA.   Nay, but say true: does it work upon him?

SIR TOBY.   Like aqua-vitae with a midwife.

---

145 politic authors *writers on statecraft* / 146 point-device *exactly* / 147
jade *trick* / 153 strange, stout *distant, haughty* / 163 Sophy *Shah of
Persia* / 172 play *wager* / 172 tray-trip *gambling game* / 178 aqua-
vitae *brandy*

MARIA.   If you will then see the fruits of the sport, mark
his first approach before my lady. He will come to her in yel-   180
low stockings, and 'tis a color she abhors, and cross-gartered,
a fashion she detests; and he will smile upon her, which will
now be so unsuitable to her disposition, being addicted to a
melancholy as she is, that it cannot but turn him into a notable contempt. If you will see it, follow me.   185

SIR TOBY.   To the gates of Tartar, thou most excellent devil
of wit!

SIR ANDREW.   I'll make one too.   *Exeunt.*

[ACT III · 1] *Olivia's garden.*

Enter VIOLA *and* FESTE *with a tabor.*

VIOLA.   Save thee, friend, and thy music! Dost thou live
by thy tabor?

FESTE.   No, sir, I live by the church.

VIOLA.   Art thou a churchman?

FESTE.   No such matter, sir: I do live by the church; for I   5
do live at my house, and my house doth stand by the church.

VIOLA.   So thou mayst say, the king lies by a beggar, if
a beggar dwells near him; or, the church stands by thy tabor,
if thy tabor stand by the church.

FESTE.   You have said, sir. To see this age! A sentence is   10
but a cheveril glove to a good wit. How quickly the wrong
side may be turned outward!

VIOLA.   Nay, that's certain. They that dally nicely with
words may quickly make them wanton.

FESTE.   I would, therefore, my sister had had no name,   15
sir.

VIOLA.   Why, man?

FESTE.   Why, sir, her name's a word, and to dally with
that word might make my sister wanton. But, indeed, words
are very rascals since bonds disgraced them.   20

VIOLA.   Thy reason, man?

---

186 Tartar *hell*
     [ACT III · 1] 2 tabor *a small drum* / 11 cheveril *kidskin* / 14 wan-
ton *ambiguous and unchaste* / 20 rascals *helpless, inferior* / 20 disgraced *i.e., since a man's word is no longer to be trusted without a
bond, or added assurance*

FESTE.   Troth, sir, I can yield you none without words; and words are grown so false, I am loath to prove reason with them.

VIOLA.   I warrant thou art a merry fellow and car'st for   25
nothing.

FESTE.   Not so, sir, I do care for something; but in my conscience, sir, I do not care for you: if that be to care for nothing, sir, I would it would make you invisible.

VIOLA.   Art not thou the Lady Olivia's fool?   30

FESTE   No, indeed, sir; the Lady Olivia has no folly She will keep no fool, sir, till she be married; and fools are as like husbands as pilchards are to herrings, the husband's the bigger. I am indeed not her fool, but her corrupter of words.

VIOLA.   I saw thee late at the Count Orsino's.   35

FESTE.   Foolery, sir, does walk about the orb like the sun, it shines everywhere. I would be sorry, sir, but the fool should be as oft with your master as with my mistress. I think I saw your wisdom there.

VIOLA.   Nay, an thou pass upon me, I'll no more with   40
thee. Hold, there's expenses for thee.

FESTE.   Now Jove, in his next commodity of hair, send thee a beard!

VIOLA.   By my troth, I'll tell thee, I am almost sick for one,—[aside] though I would not have it grow on my chin.   45
Is thy lady within?

FESTE.   Would not a pair of these have bred, sir?

VIOLA.   Yes, being kept together and put to use.

FESTE.   I would play Lord Pandarus of Phrygia, sir, to bring a Cressida to this Troilus.   50

VIOLA.   I understand you, sir; 'tis well begged.

FESTE.   The matter, I hope, is not great, sir, begging but a beggar. Cressida was a beggar. My lady is within, sir. I will conster to them whence you come: who you are and what you would are out of my welkin—I might say "element," but the   55
word is overworn.   *Exit.*

VIOLA.   This fellow is wise enough to play the fool,
And to do that well craves a kind of wit.

---

33 pilchard *small fish* / 39 your wisdom *you* / 40 pass upon *thrust at* / 48 to use *out at interest* / 54 conster *interpret* / 55 welkin *sky* / 55 element *sky*

He must observe their mood on whom he jests,
The quality of persons, and the time,   60
Not, like the haggard, check at every feather
That comes before his eye. This is a practice
As full of labor as a wise man's art;
For folly that he wisely shows is fit;
But wise men, folly-fall'n, quite taint their wit.   65

Enter SIR TOBY *and* SIR ANDREW.

SIR TOBY.   Save you, gentleman.

VIOLA.   And you, sir.

SIR ANDREW.   *Dieu vous garde, monsieur.*

VIOLA.   *Et vous aussi; votre serviteur.*

SIR ANDREW.   I hope, sir, you are; and I am yours.   70

SIR TOBY.   Will you encounter the house? My niece is de-
sirous you should enter, if your trade be to her.

VIOLA.   I am bound to your niece, sir; I mean, she is the
list of my voyage.

SIR TOBY.   Taste your legs, sir; put them to motion.   75

VIOLA.   My legs do better understand me, sir, than I understand what you mean by bidding me taste my legs.

SIR TOBY.   I mean, to go, sir, to enter.

VIOLA.   I will answer you with gait and entrance. But we
are prevented.   80

Enter OLIVIA *and* MARIA *her Gentlewoman.*

Most excellent accomplished lady, the heavens rain odors on
you!

SIR ANDREW.   That youth's a rare courtier. "Rain odors;"
well.

VIOLA.   My matter hath no voice, lady, but to your own   85
most pregnant and vouchsafed ear.

SIR ANDREW.   "Odors," "pregnant," and "vouchsafed"; I'll
get 'em all three all ready.

OLIVIA.   Let the garden door be shut, and leave me to my
hearing. [*Exeunt all but* OLIVIA *and* VIOLA.] Give me your   90
hand, sir.

VIOLA.   My duty, madam, and most humble service.

---

61 haggard *untrained hawk* / 61 check *go after* / 74 list *destination* /
76 understand *i.e., stand under* / 86 pregnant *ready*

OLIVIA.   What is your name?

VIOLA.   Cesario is your servant's name, fair princess.

OLIVIA.   My servant, sir! 'Twas never merry world   95
Since lowly feigning was call'd compliment.
You're servant to the Count Orsino, youth.

VIOLA.   And he is yours, and his must needs be yours.
Your servant's servant is your servant, madam.

OLIVIA.   For him, I think not on him. For his thoughts,   100
Would they were blanks, rather than fill'd with me!

VIOLA.   Madam, I come to whet your gentle thoughts
On his behalf.

OLIVIA.   O, by your leave, I pray you,
I bade you never speak again of him;
But, would you undertake another suit,   105
I had rather hear you to solicit that
Than music from the spheres.

VIOLA.   Dear lady,—

OLIVIA.   Give me leave, beseech you. I did send,
After the last enchantment you did here,
A ring in chase of you; so did I abuse   110
Myself, my servant, and, I fear me, you.
Under your hard construction must I sit,
To force that on you, in a shameful cunning,
Which you knew none of yours. What might you think?
Have you not set mine honor at the stake   115
And baited it with all th' unmuzzled thoughts
That tyrannous heart can think? To one of your receiving
Enough is shown. A cypress, not a bosom,
Hides my heart. So, let me hear you speak.

VIOLA.   I pity you.

OLIVIA.   That's a degree to love.   120

VIOLA.   No, not a grize; for 'tis a vulgar proof,
That very oft we pity enemies.

OLIVIA.   Why, then, methinks 'tis time to smile again.

---

96 lowly feigning *affected humility* / 107 music from the spheres *the stars were supposed to make harmonious music, inaudible to mortals* / 110 abuse *deceive* / 112 construction *judgment* / 115 at the stake . . . thoughts *i.e., like a chained bear attacked by dogs in the sport of bear-baiting* / 117 receiving *quick apprehension* / 118 cypress *black crepe* / 120 degree, grize *step* / 121 vulgar proof *common experience*

O world, how apt the poor are to be proud!
If one should be a prey, how much the better   125
To fall before the lion than the wolf!   *Clock strikes.*
The clock upbraids me with the waste of time.
Be not afraid, good youth, I will not have you;
And yet, when wit and youth is come to harvest,
Your wife is like to reap a proper man.   130
There lies your way, due west.
    VIOLA.   Then westward-ho!
Grace and good disposition attend your ladyship!
You'll nothing, madam, to my lord by me?
    OLIVIA.   Stay!
I prithee, tell me what thou think'st of me.   135
    VIOLA.   That you do think you are not what you are.
    OLIVIA.   If I think so, I think the same of you.
    VIOLA.   Then think you right. I am not what I am.
    OLIVIA.   I would you were as I would have you be!
    VIOLA.   Would it be better, madam, than I am?   140
I wish it might, for now I am your fool.
    OLIVIA.   O, what a deal of scorn looks beautiful
In the contempt and anger of his lip!
A murd'rous guilt shows not itself more soon
Than love that would seem hid. Love's night is noon.   145
Cesario, by the roses of the spring,
By maidhood, honor, truth, and everything,
I love thee so, that, maugre all thy pride,
Nor wit nor reason can my passion hide.
Do not extort thy reasons from this clause,   150
For that I woo, thou therefore hast no cause;
But rather reason thus with reason fetter,
Love sought is good, but given unsought is better.
    VIOLA.   By innocence I swear, and by my youth,
I have one heart, one bosom, and one truth,   155
And that no woman has; nor never nóne
Shall mistress be of it, save I alone.
And so adieu, good madam; nevermore
Will I my master's tears to you deplore.

---

124 apt *quick* / 148 maugre *despite* / 151 cause *i.e., cause to return it*
/ 152 fetter *join together*

OLIVIA.   Yet come again; for thou perhaps mayst move   160
That heart, which now abhors, to like his love.   *Exeunt.*

[ACT III · 2] *Olivia's house.*

Enter SIR TOBY, SIR ANDREW, *and* FABIAN.

SIR ANDREW.   No, faith, I'll not stay a jot longer.
SIR TOBY.   Thy reason, dear venom, give thy reason.
FABIAN.   You must needs yield your reason, Sir Andrew.
SIR ANDREW.   Marry, I saw your niece do more favors to
the Count's serving-man than ever she bestowed upon me. I   5
saw 't i' th' orchard.
SIR TOBY.   Did she see thee the while, old boy? Tell me
that.
SIR ANDREW.   As plain as I see you now.
FABIAN.   This was a great argument of love in her toward   10
you.
SIR ANDREW.   'Slight, will you make an ass o' me?
FABIAN.   I will prove it legitimate, sir, upon the oaths of
judgment and reason.
SIR TOBY.   And they have been grand-jurymen since be-   15
fore Noah was a sailor.
FABIAN.   She did show favor to the youth in your sight
only to exasperate you, to awake your dormouse valor, to put
fire in your heart, and brimstone in your liver. You should
then have accosted her; and with some excellent jests, fire-   20
new from the mint, you should have banged the youth into
dumbness. This was looked for at your hand, and this was
balked. The double gilt of this opportunity you let time wash
off, and you are now sailed into the north of my lady's opinion, where you will hang like an icicle on a Dutchman's   25
beard, unless you do redeem it by some laudable attempt
either of valor or policy.
SIR ANDREW.   An 't be any way, it must be with valor; for
policy I hate. I had as lief be a Brownist as a politician.
SIR TOBY.   Why, then, build me thy fortunes upon the   30
basis of valor. Challenge me the Count's youth to fight with

[ACT III · 2] 15 grand-jurymen *i.e., highly respected* / 18 dormouse
sleepy / 23 balked *missed* / 29 Brownist *a puritan extremist* / 29 politician *political trickster*

him; hurt him in eleven places; my niece shall take note of it;
and assure thyself, there is no love-broker in the world can
more prevail in man's commendation with woman than report
of valor.   35

FABIAN.   There is no way but this, Sir Andrew.

SIR ANDREW.   Will either of you bear me a challenge to
him?

SIR TOBY.   Go, write it in a martial hand. Be curst and
brief. It is no matter how witty, so it be eloquent and full of   40
invention. Taunt him with the license of ink. If thou *thou*'st him
some thrice, it shall not be amiss; and as many lies as will lie
in thy sheet of paper, although the sheet were big enough for
the bed of Ware in England, set 'em down. Go about it. Let
there be gall enough in thy ink, though thou write with a   45
goose-pen, no matter; about it.

SIR ANDREW.   Where shall I find you?

SIR TOBY.   We'll call thee at the cubiculo. Go.

Exit SIR ANDREW.

FABIAN.   This is a dear manikin to you, Sir Toby.

SIR TOBY.   I have been dear to him, lad, some two thou-   50
sand strong, or so.

FABIAN.   We shall have a rare letter from him. But you'll
not deliver 't?

SIR TOBY.   Never trust me, then; and by all means stir on
the youth to an answer. I think oxen and wainropes cannot   55
hale them together. For Andrew, if he were opened, and you
find so much blood in his liver as will clog the foot of a flea,
I'll eat the rest of th' anatomy.

FABIAN.   And his opposite, the youth, bears in his visage
no great presage of cruelty.   60

Enter MARIA.

SIR TOBY.   Look, where the youngest wren of nine comes.

MARIA.   If you desire the spleen, and will laugh yourselves into stitches, follow me. Yond gull Malvolio is turned
heathen, a very renegado; for there is no Christian that means

---

33 love-broker *marriage contractor* / 41 thou'st *i.e., insult him with familiar address* / 44 bed of Ware *built to accommodate fourteen people*
/ 48 cubiculo *writing room* / 55 wainropes *wagon ropes* / 64 renegado *renegade*

to be saved by believing rightly can ever believe such im-   65
possible passages of grossness. He's in yellow stockings.

SIR TOBY.   And cross-gartered?

MARIA.   Most villainously; like a pedant that keeps a school
i' the church. I have dogged him like his murderer. He does
obey every point of the letter that I dropped to betray him.   70
He does smile his face into more lines than is in the new map
with the augmentation of the Indies. You have not seen such
a thing as 'tis. I can hardly forbear hurling things at him. I
know my lady will strike him; if she do, he'll smile and take 't
for a great favor.   75

SIR TOBY.   Come, bring us, bring us where he is.

Exeunt.

[ACT III · 3] *A street.*

Enter SEBASTIAN *and* ANTONIO.

SEBASTIAN.   I would not by my will have troubled you;
But since you make your pleasure of your pains,
I will no further chide you.

ANTONIO.   I could not stay behind you. My desire,   5
More sharp than filed steel, did spur me forth,
And not all love to see you, though so much
As might have drawn one to a longer voyage,
But jealousy what might befall your travel,
Being skilless in these parts; which to a stranger,
Unguided and unfriended, often prove   10
Rough and unhospitable. My willing love,
The rather by these arguments of fear,
Set forth in your pursuit.

SEBASTIAN.   My kind Antonio,
I can no other answer make but thanks,
And thanks, and ever thanks; and oft good turns   15
Are shuffled off with such uncurrent pay;
But, were my worth as is my conscience firm,
You should find better dealing. What's to do?
Shall we go see the reliques of this town?

---

68 pedant *teacher*
[ACT III · 3] 8 jealousy *anxiety* / 16 shuffled off *inadequately re-*
warded / 17 worth *wealth* / 19 reliques *antiquities*

ANTONIO.   To-morrow, sir; best first go see your lodging.   20
SEBASTIAN.   I am not weary, and 'tis long to night.
I pray you, let us satisfy our eyes
With the memorials and the things of fame
That do renown this city.
ANTONIO.   Would you'd pardon me.
I do not without danger walk these streets.   25
Once, in a sea-fight, 'gainst the Count his galleys
I did some service; of such note indeed,
That were I ta'en here it would scarce be answer'd.
SEBASTIAN.   Belike you slew great number of his people.
ANTONIO.   Th' offense is not of such a bloody nature,   30
Albeit the quality of the time and quarrel
Might well have given us bloody argument.
It might have since been answer'd in repaying
What we took from them, which, for traffic's sake,
Most of our city did; only myself stood out,   35
For which, if I be lapsed in this place,
I shall pay dear.
SEBASTIAN.   Do not then walk too open.
ANTONIO.   It doth not fit me. Hold, sir, here's my purse.
In the south suburbs, at the Elephant
Is best to lodge. I will bespeak our diet,   40
Whiles you beguile the time and feed your knowledge
With viewing of the town. There shall you have me.
SEBASTIAN.   Why I your purse?
ANTONIO.   Haply your eye shall light upon some toy
You have desire to purchase; and your store,   45
I think, is not for idle markets, sir.
SEBASTIAN.   I'll be your purse-bearer and leave you for
An hour.
ANTONIO. To th' Elephant.
SEBASTIAN.   I do remember.   *Exeunt.*

---

28 scarce be answer'd *be difficult to justify* / 34 traffic's sake *sake of commerce* / 36 lapsed *surprised* / 39 Elephant *an inn* / 40 diet *dinner* / 46 idle markets *unnecessary purchases*

[ACT III · 4] *Olivia's garden.*

Enter OLIVIA *and* MARIA.

OLIVIA.   I have sent after him; he says he'll come.
How shall I feast him? What bestow of him?
For youth is bought more oft than begg'd or borrow'd.
I speak too loud.
Where's Malvolio? He is sad and civil,   5
And suits well for a servant with my fortunes.
Where is Malvolio?

MARIA.   He's coming, madam, but in very strange manner.
He is, sure, possessed, madam.

OLIVIA.   Why, what's the matter? Does he rave?   10

MARIA.   No, madam, he does nothing but smile. Your ladyship were best to have some guard about you, if he come;
for sure the man is tainted in's wits.

OLIVIA.   Go call him hither.   *Exit* MARIA.
                              I am as mad as he,
If sad and merry madness equal be.   15

Enter MALVOLIO, *with* MARIA.

How now, Malvolio!

MALVOLIO.   Sweet lady, ho, ho.

OLIVIA.   Smil'st thou?
I sent for thee upon a sad occasion.

MALVOLIO.   Sad, lady? I could be sad. This does make   20
some obstruction in the blood, this cross-gartering; but what
of that? If it please the eye of one, it is with me as the very
true sonnet is: "Please one, and please all."

OLIVIA.   Why, how dost thou, man? What is the matter ·
with thee?   25

MALVOLIO.   Not black in my mind, though yellow in my
legs. It did come to his hands, and commands shall be exe-
cuted. I think we do know the sweet Roman hand.

OLIVIA.   Wilt thou go to bed, Malvolio?

MALVOLIO.   To bed! Ay, sweet heart, and I'll come to thee.   30

[ACT III · 4] 5 sad and civil *sober and sedate* / 9 possessed *i.e.,
with the devil* / 23 sonnet *ballad* / 28 Roman hand *Italian style of
handwriting, fashionable with ladies*

OLIVIA.   God comfort thee! Why dost thou smile so and
kiss thy hand so oft?

MARIA.   How do you, Malvolio?

MALVOLIO.   At your request? Yes: nightingales answer
daws.   35

MARIA.   Why appear you with this ridiculous boldness before my lady?

MALVOLIO.   "Be not afraid of greatness:" 'twas well writ.

OLIVIA.   What mean'st thou by that, Malvolio?

MALVOLIO.   "Some are born great,"—   40

OLIVIA.   Ha?

MALVOLIO.   "Some achieve greatness,"—

OLIVIA.   What say'st thou?

MALVOLIO.   "And some have greatness thrust upon them."

OLIVIA.   Heaven restore thee!   45

MALVOLIO.   "Remember who commended thy yellow
stockings,"—

OLIVIA.   Thy yellow stockings!

MALVOLIO.   "And wish'd to see thee cross-gartered."

OLIVIA.   Cross-gartered!   50

MALVOLIO.   "Go to, thou art made, if thou desir'st to be
so;"—

OLIVIA.   Am I made?

MALVOLIO.   "If not, let me see thee a servant still."

OLIVIA.   Why, this is very midsummer madness.   55

Enter SERVANT.

SERVANT.   Madam, the young gentleman of the Count Orsino's is returned. I could hardly entreat him back. He attends
your ladyship's pleasure.

OLIVIA.   I'll come to him. [*Exit* SERVANT.] Good Maria, let
this fellow be looked to. Where's my cousin Toby? Let some   60
of my people have a special care of him. I would not have him
miscarry for the half of my dowry.

Exeunt OLIVIA *and* MARIA.

MALVOLIO.   O, ho! do you come near me now? No worse
man than Sir Toby to look to me! This concurs directly with
the letter: she sends him on purpose, that I may appear stub-   65

---

62 miscarry *come to harm*

born to him, for she incites me to that in the letter. "Cast thy
humble slough," says she; "be opposite with a kinsman, surly
with servants; let thy tongue tang with arguments of state; put
thyself into the trick of singularity;" and consequently sets
down the manner how; as, a sad face, a reverend carriage, a   70
slow tongue, in the habit of some sir of note, and so forth. I
have limed her; but it is Jove's doing, and Jove make me
thankful! And when she went away now, "Let this fellow be
looked to"; "fellow!" not Malvolio, nor after my degree, but
"fellow." Why everything adheres together, that no dram of   75
a scruple, no scruple of a scruple, no obstacle, no incredulous
or unsafe circumstance—What can be said? Nothing that
can be can come between me and the full prospect of my
hopes. Well, Jove, not I, is the doer of this, and he is to be
thanked.   80

Re-enter MARIA, *with* SIR TOBY *and* FABIAN.

SIR TOBY.   Which way is he, in the name of sanctity? If all
the devils of hell be drawn in little, and Legion himself possessed him, yet I'll speak to him.

FABIAN.   Here he is, here he is. How is 't with you, sir?
How is't with you, man?   85

MALVOLIO.   Go off; I discard you. Let me enjoy my private. Go off.

MARIA.   Lo, how hollow the fiend speaks within him! Did
not I tell you? Sir Toby, my lady prays you to have a care of
him.   90

MALVOLIO.   Ah, ha! Does she so?

SIR TOBY.   Go to, go to; peace, peace. We must deal gently
with him; let me alone. How do you Malvolio? How is't with
you? What man, defy the devil! Consider, he's an enemy to
mankind.   95

MALVOLIO.   Do you know what you say?

MARIA.   La you! and you speak ill of the devil, how he
takes it at heart! Pray God he be not bewitched!

FABIAN.   Carry his water to the wise woman.

---

71 sir of note *distinguished man* / 72 limed *caught* / 76 incredulous
incredible / 77 unsafe *dubious* / 82 in little *in a small space* / 82 Legion *all the devils* ("*My name is Legion*") / 86 private *privacy* / 99
water *i.e., for urinalysis*

MARIA.   Marry, and it shall be done to-morrow morning   100
if I live. My lady would not lose him for more than I'll say.

MALVOLIO.   How now, mistress!

MARIA.   O Lord!

SIR TOBY.   Prithee, hold thy peace; this is not the way. Do
you not see you move him? Let me alone with him.   105

FABIAN.   No way but gentleness; gently, gently. The fiend
is rough, and will not be roughly used.

SIR TOBY.   Why, how now, my bawcock! How dost thou,
chuck?

MALVOLIO.   Sir!   110

SIR TOBY.   Ay, biddy, come with me. What, man, 'tis not
for gravity to play at cherry-pit with Satan. Hang him, foul
collier!

MARIA.   Get him to say his prayers, good Sir Toby, get
him to pray.   115

MALVOLIO.   My prayers, minx!

MARIA.   No, I warrant you, he will not hear of godliness.

MALVOLIO.   Go, hang yourselves all! You are idle shallow
things; I am not of your element. You shall know more hereafter.   *Exit.*   120

SIR TOBY.   Is't possible?

FABIAN.   If this were played upon a stage now, I could
condemn it as an improbable fiction.

SIR TOBY.   His very genius hath taken the infection of the
device, man.   125

MARIA.   Nay, pursue him now, lest the device take air and
taint.

FABIAN.   Why, we shall make him mad indeed.

MARIA.   The house will be the quieter.

SIR TOBY.   Come, we'll have him in a dark room and   130
bound. My niece is already in the belief that he's mad. We
may carry it thus for our pleasure and his penance till our
very pastime, tired out of breath, prompt us to have mercy on
him; at which time we will bring the device to the bar and
crown thee for a finder of madmen. But see, but see.   135

---

108 bawcock *my fine rooster* / 109 chuck *chick* / 111 biddy *chicken* /
112 play at cherry-pit *i.e., make a playmate* / 113 collier *the Devil was
portrayed as black, like a coal man* / 124 genius *ruling personality* /
134 the bar *public judgment*

Enter SIR ANDREW.

FABIAN.   More matter for a May morning.

SIR ANDREW.   Here's the challenge, read it. I warrant
there's vinegar and pepper in't.

FABIAN.   Is't so saucy?

SIR ANDREW.   Ay, is't, I warrant him. Do but read.   140

SIR TOBY.   Give me. [*Reads.*] "Youth, whatsoever thou art,
thou art but a scurvy fellow."

FABIAN.   Good and valiant.

SIR TOBY.   [*Reads.*] "Wonder not, nor admire not in thy
mind, why I do call thee so, for I will show thee no reason   145
for 't."

FABIAN.   A good note. That keeps you from the blow of
the law.

SIR TOBY.   [*Reads.*] "Thou com'st to the lady Olivia, and
in my sight she uses thee kindly. But thou liest in thy throat;   150
that is not the matter I challenge thee for."

FABIAN.   Very brief, and to exceeding good sense—less.

SIR TOBY.   [*Reads.*] "I will waylay thee going home, where
if it be thy chance to kill me,"—

FABIAN.   Good.   155

SIR TOBY.   [*Reads.*] "Thou kill'st me like a rogue and a villain."

FABIAN.   Still you keep o' the windy side of the law; good.

SIR TOBY.   [*Reads.*] "Fare thee well, and God have mercy
upon one of our souls! He may have mercy upon mine; but   160
my hope is better, and so look to thyself. Thy friend, as thou
usest him, and thy sworn enemy,

ANDREW AGUECHEEK."

If this letter move him not, his legs cannot. I'll give 't him.

MARIA.   You may have very fit occasion for 't. He is now
in some commerce with my lady, and will by and by depart.   165

SIR TOBY.   Go, Sir Andrew, scout me for him at the corner
of the orchard like a bum-baily. So soon as ever thou seest
him, draw; and, as thou draw'st, swear horrible; for it comes
to pass oft that a terrible oath, with a swaggering accent

---

136 May morning *i.e., for the folk comedies enacted on May Day* /
144 admire *be amazed* / 157 windy *windward* (*protected*) / 167 bum-
bailly *sheriff's officer who made arrests*

sharply twanged off, gives manhood more approbation than   170
ever proof itself would have earned him. Away!

SIR ANDREW.   Nay, let me alone for swearing.   *Exit.*

SIR TOBY.   Now will not I deliver his letter; for the behavior
of the young gentleman gives him out to be of good capacity
and breeding; his employment between his lord and my niece   175
confirms no less; therefore this letter, being so excellently ignorant, will breed no terror in the youth; he will find it comes
from a clodpole. But, sir, I will deliver his challenge by word
of mouth, set upon Aguecheek a notable report of valor, and
drive the gentleman, as I know his youth will aptly receive it,   180
into a most hideous opinion of his rage, skill, fury, and im-
petuosity. This will so fright them both that they will kill one
another by the look, like cockatrices.

Re-enter OLIVIA *with* VIOLA.

FABIAN.   Here he comes with your niece. Give them way
till he take leave, and presently after him.   185

SIR TOBY.   I will meditate the while upon some horrid
message for a challenge.

Exeunt SIR TOBY, FABIAN, *and* MARIA.

OLIVIA.   I have said too much unto a heart of stone,
And laid mine honor too unchary out.
There's something in me that reproves my fault;   190
But such a headstrong potent fault it is
That it but mocks reproof.

VIOLA.   With the same 'havior that your passion bears
Goes on my master's grief.

OLIVIA.   Here, wear this jewel for me, 'tis my picture.   195
Refuse it not; it hath no tongue to vex you;
And I beseech you come again to-morrow.
What shall you ask of me that I'll deny,
That honor sav'd may upon asking give?

VIOLA.   Nothing but this—your true love for my master.   200

OLIVIA.   How with mine honor may I give him that
Which I have given to you?

VIOLA.   I will acquit you.

---

183 cockatrice *a fabulous serpent that killed with a glance of its eyes*
/ 189 unchary *carelessly* / 199 sav'd *without being sacrificed* / 202
acquit *release*

OLIVIA.   Well, come again to-morrow; fare thee well!
A fiend like thee might bear my soul to hell.   *Exit.*

Re-enter SIR TOBY *and* FABIAN.

SIR TOBY.   Gentleman, God save thee!   205
VIOLA.   And you, sir.
SIR TOBY.   That defense thou hast, betake thee to 't. Of
what nature the wrongs are thou hast done him, I know not;
but thy intercepter, full of despite, bloody as the hunter, attends thee at the orchard-end. Dismount thy tuck, be yare in   210
thy preparation, for thy assailant is quick, skilful, and deadly.
VIOLA.   You mistake, sir, I am sure; no man hath any
quarrel to me. My remembrance is very free and clear from
any image of offense done to any man.
SIR TOBY.   You'll find it otherwise, I assure you; therefore, 215
if you hold your life at any price, betake you to your guard;
for your opposite hath in him what youth, strength, skill, and
wrath can furnish man withal.
VIOLA.   I pray you, sir, what is he?
SIR TOBY.   He is knight, dubbed with unhatched rapier and   220
on carpet consideration; but he is a devil in private brawl.
Souls and bodies hath he divorced three; and his incensement
at this moment is so implacable, that satisfaction can be none
but by pangs of death and sepulchre. Hob, nob, is his word;
give 't or take 't.   225
VIOLA.   I will return again into the house and desire some
conduct of the lady. I am no fighter. I have heard of some
kind of men that put quarrels purposely on others, to taste
their valor. Belike this is a man of that quirk.
SIR TOBY.   Sir, no; his indignation derives itself out of a   230
very competent injury; therefore, get you on and give him his
desire. Back you shall not to the house, unless you undertake
that with me which with as much safety you might answer
him; therefore, on, or strip your sword stark naked; for
meddle you must, that's certain, or forswear to wear iron   235
about you.

---

209 despite *defiance* / 210 Dismount thy tuck *unsheathe thy rapier* /
210 yare *ready* / 218 withal *with* / 220 unhatched *unhacked* / 221
carpet consideration *affairs of peace* / 224 Hob, nob *blow for blow* /
227 conduct *escort* / 229 Belike *probably*

VIOLA. This is as uncivil as strange. I beseech you, do me this courteous office, as to know of the knight what my offense to him is. It is something of my negligence, nothing of my purpose. 240

SIR TOBY. I will do so. Signior Fabian, stay you by this gentleman till my return. *Exit.*

VIOLA. Pray you, sir, do you know of this matter?

FABIAN. I know the knight is incensed against you, even to a mortal arbitrement, but nothing of the circumstance more. 245

VIOLA. I beseech you, what manner of man is he?

FABIAN. Nothing of that wonderful promise, to read him by his form, as you are like to find him in the proof of his valor. He is, indeed, sir, the most skilful, bloody, and fatal opposite that you could possibly have found in any part of Illyria. Will you walk towards him? I will make your peace with him if I can. 250

VIOLA. I shall be much bound to you for 't. I am one that had rather go with sir priest than sir knight; I care not who knows so much of my mettle. *Exeunt.* 255

Re-enter SIR TOBY, *with* SIR ANDREW.

SIR TOBY. Why, man, he's a very devil; I have not seen such a firago. I had a pass with him, rapier, scabbard, and all, and he gives me the stuck-in with such a mortal motion, that it is inevitable; and on the answer, he pays you as surely as your feet hit the ground they step on. They say he has been fencer to the Sophy. 260

SIR ANDREW. Pox on 't, I'll not meddle with him.

SIR TOBY. Ay, but he will not now be pacified. Fabian can scarce hold him yonder. 265

SIR ANDREW. Plague on 't, an I thought he had been valiant and so cunning in fence, I'd have seen him damned ere I'd have challenged him. Let him let the matter slip, and I'll give him my horse, gray Capilet.

SIR TOBY. I'll make the motion. Stand here. Make a good 270

---

239 something . . . negligence *an oversight* / 245 mortal arbitrement *duel to the death* / 255 sir priest *sir was a priest's title* / 256 mettle *nature* / 258 firago *virago, a mannish woman* / 259 stuck-in *thrust* / 260 answer *return*

show on 't; this shall end without the perdition of souls.
[*Aside.*] Marry, I'll ride your horse as well as I ride you.

Re-enter FABIAN *and* VIOLA.

[*To* FABIAN.] I have his horse to take up the quarrel. I have
persuaded him the youth's a devil.

FABIAN.   He is as horribly conceited of him; and pants and   275
looks pale, as if a bear were at his heels.

SIR TOBY.   [*To* VIOLA.] There's no remedy, sir; he will fight
with you for 's oath sake. Marry, he hath better bethought him
of his quarrel, and he finds that now scarce to be worth talking of; therefore draw, for the supportance of his vow. He   280
protests he will not hurt you.

VIOLA.   [*Aside.*] Pray God defend me! A little thing would
make me tell them how much I lack of a man.

FABIAN.   Give ground, if you see him furious.

SIR TOBY.   Come, Sir Andrew, there's no remedy; the   285
gentleman will, for his honor's sake, have one bout with you.
He cannot by the duello avoid it; but he has promised me,
as he is a gentleman and a soldier, he will not hurt you.
Come on; to 't.

SIR ANDREW.   Pray God, he keep his oath!   290

Enter ANTONIO.

VIOLA.   I do assure you, 'tis against my will.

                                 They draw.

ANTONIO.   Put up your sword. If this young gentleman
Have done offense, I take the fault on me;
If you offend him, I for him defy you.

SIR TOBY.   You, sir! Why, what are you?   295

ANTONIO.   One sir, that for his love dares yet do more
Than you have heard him brag to you he will.

SIR TOBY.   Nay, if you be an undertaker, I am for you.

                                   They draw.

Enter OFFICERS.

FABIAN.   O good Sir Toby, hold! Here come the officers.

---

273 take up *settle* / 275 as . . . conceited *equally terrified* / 280 for
the supportance *to help him keep* / 287 duello *the code of duelling* /
298 undertaker *one who takes over responsibility*

SIR TOBY.   I'll be with you anon.   300

VIOLA.   Pray, sir, put your sword up, if you please.

SIR ANDREW.   Marry, will I, sir; and, for that I promised you, I'll be as good as my word. He will bear you easily and reins well.

FIRST OFFICER.   This is the man; do thy office.   305

SECOND OFFICER.   Antonio, I arrest thee at the suit
Of Count Orsino.

ANTONIO.   You do mistake me, sir.

FIRST OFFICER.   No, sir, no jot. I know your favor well.
Though now you have no sea-cap on your head.   310
Take him away; he knows I know him well.

ANTONIO.   I must obey. [*To* VIOLA.] This comes with seek-
        ing you.
But there's no remedy; I shall answer it.
What will you do, now my necessity
Makes me to ask you for my purse? It grieves me   315
Much more for what I cannot do for you
Than what befalls myself. You stand amaz'd,
But be of comfort.

SECOND OFFICER.   Come, sir, away.

ANTONIO.   I must entreat of you some of that money.

VIOLA.   What money, sir?   320
For the fair kindness you have show'd me here,
And, part, being prompted by your present trouble,
Out of my lean and low ability
I'll lend you something. My having is not much.
I'll make division of my present with you.   325
Hold, there's half my coffer.

ANTONIO.   Will you deny me now?
Is 't possible that my deserts to you
Can lack persuasion? Do not tempt my misery,
Lest that it make me so unsound a man
As to upbraid you with those kindnesses   330
That I have done for you.

VIOLA.   I know of none,
Nor know I you by voice or any feature.
I hate ingratitude more in a man

---

317 amaz'd *in a maze* / 322 present *cash in hand* / 326 coffer *purse*

Than lying, vainness, babbling drunkenness,
Or any taint of vice whose strong corruption 335
Inhabits our frail blood.

ANTONIO.   O heavens themselves!

SECOND OFFICER.   Come, sir, I pray you, go.

ANTONIO.   Let me speak a little. This youth that you see
    here
I snatch'd one half out of the jaws of death,
Reliev'd him with such sanctity of love, 340
And to his image, which methought did promise
Most venerable worth, did I devotion.

FIRST OFFICER.   What's that to us? The time goes by; away!

ANTONIO.   But, O, how vile an idol proves this god!

Thou hast, Sebastian, done good feature shame. 345
In nature there's no blemish but the mind;
None can be call'd deform'd but the unkind.
Virtue is beauty, but the beauteous evil
Are empty trunks o'erflourish'd by the devil.

FIRST OFFICER.   The man grows mad; away with him!
     Come, come, sir. 350

ANTONIO.   Lead me on.   *Exeunt with* OFFICERS.

VIOLA.   Methinks his words do from such passion fly,
That he believes himself; so do not I.
Prove true, imagination, O, prove true,
That I, dear brother, be now ta'en for you! 355

SIR TOBY.   Come hither, knight; come hither, Fabian; we'll
whisper o'er a couplet or two of most sage saws.

VIOLA.   He nam'd Sebastian. I my brother know
Yet living in my glass; even such and so
In favor was my brother, and he went 360
Still in this fashion, color, ornament,
For him I imitate. O, if it prove,
Tempests are kind and salt waves fresh in love.   *Exit.*

SIR TOBY.   A very dishonest paltry boy, and more a
coward than a hare. His dishonesty appears in leaving his 365
friend here in necessity and denying him; and, for his coward-
ship, ask Fabian.

---

341 image *i.e., the ideal that he seemed to represent* / 346 but the
mind *but in the mind* / 349 trunks *chests* / 349 o'erflourish'd *orna-
mented* / 357 saws *sayings* / 359 glass *mirror*

FABIAN.   A coward, a most devout coward, religious in it,

SIR ANDREW.   'Slid, I'll after him again and beat him.

SIR TOBY.   Do; cuff him soundly, but never draw thy   370
sword.

SIR ANDREW.   An I do not,—

FABIAN.   Come, let's see the event.

SIR TOBY.   I dare lay any money 'twill be nothing yet.

Exeunt.

[ACT IV · 1] *The street before Olivia's house.*

Enter SEBASTIAN *and* FESTE.

FESTE.   Will you make me believe that I am not sent for
you?

SEBASTIAN.   Go to, go to, thou art a foolish fellow; let me
be clear of thee.

FESTE.   Well held out, i' faith! No, I do not know you; nor   5
I am not sent to you by my lady, to bid you come speak with
her; nor your name is not Master Cesario; nor this is not my
nose neither. Nothing that is so is so.

SEBASTIAN.   I prithee, vent thy folly somewhere else. Thou
know'st not me.   10

FESTE.   Vent my folly! He has heard that word of some
great man and now applies it to a fool. Vent my folly! I am
afraid this great lubber, the world, will prove a cockney. I
prithee now, ungird thy strangeness and tell me what I shall
vent to my lady. Shall I vent to her that thou art coming?   15

SEBASTIAN.   I prithee, foolish Greek, depart from me.
There's money for thee. If you tarry longer,
I shall give worse payment.

FESTE.   By my troth, thou hast an open hand. These wise
men that give fools money get themselves a good report—   20
after fourteen years' purchase.

Enter SIR ANDREW, SIR TOBY, *and* FABIAN.

SIR ANDREW.   Now, sir, have I met you again? There's
for you.   *Striking* SEBASTIAN.

[ACT IV · 1] 9 vent *utter* / 13 lubber *clumsy mass* / 13 cockney
silly child / 16 Greek *jester* / 21 after . . . purchase *after a long
time, at excessive cost*

SEBASTIAN.   Why, there's for thee, and there, and there.
Are all the people mad?   *Beating* SIR ANDREW.   25
  SIR TOBY.   Hold, sir, or I'll throw your dagger o'er the
house.
  FESTE.   This will I tell my lady straight. I would not be in
some of your coats for two-pence.   *Exit.*
  SIR TOBY.   Come on, sir. Hold!   30
  SIR ANDREW.   Nay, let him alone. I'll go another way to
work with him; I'll have an action of battery against him, if
there be any law in Illyria. Though I struck him first, yet it's
no matter for that.
  SEBASTIAN.   Let go thy hand.   35
  SIR TOBY.   Come, sir, I will not let you go. Come, my
young soldier, put up your iron; you are well flesh'd. Come
on.
  SEBASTIAN.   I will be free from thee. What wouldst thou
            now?   40
If thou dar'st tempt me further, draw thy sword.

                                                    Draws.
  SIR TOBY.   What, what? Nay, then I must have an ounce or
two of this malapert blood from you.   *Draws.*

                    Enter OLIVIA.

  OLIVIA.   Hold, Toby! On thy life I charge thee, hold!
  SIR TOBY.   Madam—   45
  OLIVIA.   Will it be ever thus? Ungracious wretch,
Fit for the mountains and the barbarous caves,
Where manners ne'er were preach'd! Out of my sight!
Be not offended, dear Cesario.
Rudesby, be gone!
            Exeunt SIR TOBY, SIR ANDREW, *and* FABIAN.
                  I prithee, gentle friend,   50
Let thy fair wisdom, not thy passion, sway
In this uncivil and unjust extent
Against thy peace. Go with me to my house,
And hear thou there how many fruitless pranks
This ruffian hath botch'd up, that thou thereby   55

---

32 an action of *him brought to trial for* / 37 you are well flesh'd *you
have had a taste of fighting* / 43 malapert *saucy* / 50 Rudesby *ruffian*
/ 52 extent *despair*

Mayst smile at this. Thou shalt not choose but go.
Do not deny. Beshrew his soul for me,
He started one poor heart of mine in thee.

SEBASTIAN.   What relish is in this? How runs the stream?
Or I am mad, or else this is a dream.   60
Let fancy still my sense in Lethe steep.
If it be thus to dream, still let me sleep!

OLIVIA.   Nay, come, I prithee. Would thou'dst be rul'd
  by me!

SEBASTIAN.   Madam, I will

OLIVIA.   O, say so, and so be!

                                        Exeunt.

[ACT IV · 2] *Olivia's house.*

Enter MARIA *and* FESTE.

MARIA.   Nay, I prithee, put on this gown and this beard.
Make him believe thou art Sir Topas the curate. Do it quickly;
I'll call Sir Toby the whilst.   *Exit.*

FESTE.   Well, I'll put it on, and I will dissemble myself
in 't; and I would I were the first that ever dissembled in such   5
a gown. I am not tall enough to become the function well,
nor lean enough to be thought a good student; but to be said
an honest man and a good housekeeper goes as fairly as to
say a careful man and a great scholar. The competitors enter.

Enter SIR TOBY *and* MARIA.

SIR TOBY.   Jove bless thee, master Parson.   10

FESTE.   *Bonos dies,* Sir Toby: for, as the old hermit of
Prague, that never saw pen and ink, very wittily said to a
niece of King Gorboduc, "That that is is"; so I, being master
Parson, am master Parson; for, what is "that" but "that,"
and "is" but "is"?   15

SIR TOBY.   To him, Sir Topas.

FESTE.   What, ho, I say! Peace in this prison!

SIR TOBY.   The knave counterfeits well; a good knave.

MALVOLIO. [*Within.*]   Who calls there?

---

61 Lethe *river of forgetfulness*
  [ACT IV · 2] 9 competitors *associates*

FESTE.   Sir Topas the curate, who comes to visit Malvolio   20
the lunatic.

MALVOLIO.   Sir Topas, Sir Topas, good Sir Topas, go to
my lady.

FESTE.   Out, hyperbolical fiend! How vexest thou this
man! Talkest thou nothing but of ladies?   25

SIR TOBY.   Well said, master Parson.

MALVOLIO.   Sir Topas, never was man thus wronged. Good
Sir Topas, do not think I am mad. They have laid me here in
hideous darkness.

FESTE.   Fie, thou dishonest Satan! I call thee by the most   30
modest terms, for I am one of those gentle ones that will use
the devil himself with courtesy. Say'st thou that house is dark?

MALVOLIO.   As hell, Sir Topas.

FESTE.   Why, it hath bay windows transparent as barricadoes, and the clerestories toward the south north are as   35
lustrous as ebony; and yet complainest thou of obstruction?

MALVOLIO.   I am not mad, Sir Topas. I say to you, this
house is dark.

FESTE.   Madman, thou errest. I say, there is no darkness
but ignorance, in which thou art more puzzled than the   40
Egyptians in their fog.

MALVOLIO.   I say, this house is dark as ignorance, though
ignorance were as dark as hell; and I say, there was never
man thus abused. I am no more mad than you are; make the
trial of it in any constant question.   45

FESTE.   What is the opinion of Pythagoras concerning wild
fowl?

MALVOLIO.   That the soul of our grandam might haply
inhabit a bird.

FESTE.   What think'st thou of his opinion?   50

MALVOLIO.   I think nobly of the soul, and no way approve
his opinion.

FESTE.   Fare thee well! Remain thou still in darkness.
Thou shalt hold the opinion of Pythagoras ere I will allow of

---

24 hyperbolical *raging* / 34 barricadoes *barricades* / 35 clerestories
windows high in the wall / 41 fog *the ninth plague of Egypt* / 45 constant question *subject demanding rational speech* / 46 Pythagoras *Greek
philosopher, exponent of the doctrine of the transmigration of the soul*

thy wits, and fear to kill a woodcock, lest thou dispossess the   55
soul of thy grandam. Fare thee well.

MALVOLIO.   Sir Topas, Sir Topas!

SIR TOBY.   My most exquisite Sir Topas!

FESTE.   Nay, I am for all waters.

MARIA.   Thou mightst have done this without thy beard   60
and gown. He sees thee not.

SIR TOBY.   To him in thine own voice, and bring me word
how thou find'st him. I would we were well rid of his knavery. If he may be conveniently delivered, I would he were,
for I am now so far in offence with my niece that I cannot   65
pursue with any safety this sport to the upshot. Come by and
by to my chamber.   *Exit with* MARIA.

FESTE.   [*Singing.*]

>   "Hey, Robin, jolly Robin,
>   Tell me how thy lady does."

MALVOLIO.   Fool!   70

FESTE.   "My lady is unkind, perdy."

MALVOLIO.   Fool!

FESTE.   "Alas, why is she so?"

MALVOLIO.   Fool, I say!

FESTE.   "She loves another"—Who calls, ha?   75

MALVOLIO.   Good fool, as ever thou wilt deserve well at
my hand, help me to a candle, and pen, ink, and paper. As I
am a gentleman, I will live to be thankful to thee for 't.

FESTE.   Master Malvolio?

MALVOLIO.   Ay, good fool.   80

FESTE.   Alas, sir, how fell you besides your five wits?

MALVOLIO.   Fool, there was never man so notoriously   `
abused. I am as well in my wits, fool, as thou art.

FESTE.   But as well? Then you are mad indeed, if you be
no better in your wits than a fool.   85

MALVOLIO.   They have here propertied me, keep me in
darkness, send ministers to me, asses, and do all they can to
face me out of my wits.

---

55 woodcock *a particularly stupid bird* / 64 deliver'd *released* / 66 upshot *conclusion* / 71 perdy *assuredly* / 81 besides your five wits *out of
full possession of your senses* / 86 propertied me *treated me like a piece
of cast-off furniture*

FESTE.   Advise you what you say; the minister is here.
Malvolio, Malvolio, thy wits the heavens restore! Endeavor   90
thyself to sleep, and leave thy vain bibble-babble.

MALVOLIO.   Sir Topas!

FESTE.   Maintain no words with him, good fellow. Who,
I, sir? Not I, sir. God buy you, good Sir Topas. Marry, amen.
I will, sir, I will.   95

MALVOLIO.   Fool, fool, fool, I say!

FESTE.   Alas, sir, be patient. What say you, sir? I am shent
for speaking to you.

MALVOLIO.   Good fool, help me to some light and some
paper. I tell thee, I am as well in my wits as any man in   100
Illyria.

FESTE.   Well-a-day that you were, sir!

MALVOLIO.   By this hand, I am. Good fool, some ink,
paper, and light; and convey what I will set down to my lady.
It shall advantage thee more than ever the bearing of letter   105
did.

FESTE.   I will help you to 't. But tell me true, are you not
mad indeed, or do you but counterfeit?

MALVOLIO.   Believe me, I am not, I tell thee true.

FESTE.   Nay, I'll ne'er believe a madman till I see his   110
brains. I will fetch you light and paper and ink.

MALVOLIO.   Fool, I'll requite it in the highest degree. I
prithee, be gone.

FESTE.   [Singing.]

               I am gone, sir,
               And anon, sir,
            I'll be with you again,   115
               In a trice,
               Like to the old Vice,
            Your need to sustain;

               Who, with dagger of lath,
               In his rage and his wrath,   120
                  Cries, ah, ha! to the devil,

94 God buy you *Good-bye* / 97 shent *rebuked* / 117 Vice *a comic figure in the old morality plays, armed with a wooden dagger with which he
offers to manicure Satan* / 121 devil *i.e., Malvolio and the devil that
has possessed him*

> Like a mad lad.
> Pare thy nails, dad.
> Adieu, goodman devil.   *Exit.*

[ACT IV · 3] *Olivia's garden.*

Enter SEBASTIAN.

SEBASTIAN.   This is the air, that is the glorious sun,
This pearl she gave me, I do feel 't and see 't;
And though 'tis wonder that enwraps me thus,
Yet 'tis not madness. Where's Antonio, then?
I could not find him at the Elephant;   5
Yet there he was, and there I found this credit,
That he did range the town to seek me out.
His counsel now might do me golden service;
For though my soul disputes well with my sense,
That this may be some error, but no madness,   10
Yet doth this accident and flood of fortune
So far exceed all instance, all discourse,
That I am ready to distrust mine eyes
And wrangle with my reason that persuades me
To any other trust but that I am mad   15
Or else the lady's mad; yet, if 'twere so,
She could not sway her house, command her followers,
Take and give back affairs and their dispatch
With such a smooth, discreet, and stable bearing
As I perceive she does. There's something in 't   20
That is deceivable. But here the lady comes.

Enter OLIVIA *and* PRIEST.

OLIVIA.   Blame not this haste of mine. If you mean well,
Now go with me and with this holy man
Into the chantry by; there, before him,
And underneath that consecrated roof,   25
Plight me the full assurance of your faith,
That my most jealous and too doubtful soul

[ACT IV · 3] 6 credit *report* / 9 disputes well *agrees* / 12 instance
example / 12 discourse *reason* / 21 deceivable *misleading* / 24
chantry *chapel* / 26 faith *i.e., in a betrothal ceremony* / 27 jealous
suspicious

May live at peace. He shall conceal it
Whiles you are willing it shall come to note,
What time we will our celebration keep   30
According to my birth. What do you say?

SEBASTIAN. I'll follow this good man, and go with you;
And, having sworn truth, ever will be true.

OLIVIA. Then lead the way, good father; and heavens so
    shine
That they may fairly note this act of mine!   *Exeunt.*   35

[ACT V · 1] *Before Olivia's house.*

Enter FESTE *and* FABIAN.

FABIAN. Now, as thou lov'st me, let me see his letter.

FESTE. Good Master Fabian, grant me another request.

FABIAN. Anything.

FESTE. Do not desire to see this letter.

FABIAN. This is to give a dog and in recompense desire my
dog again.   5

Enter DUKE, VIOLA, CURIO, *and* LORDS.

DUKE. Belong you to the Lady Olivia, friends?

FESTE. Ay, sir! we are some of her trappings.

DUKE. I know thee well; how dost thou, my good fellow?

FESTE. Truly, sir, the better for my foes and the worse
for my friends.   10

DUKE. Just the contrary; the better for thy friends.

FESTE. No, sir, the worse.

DUKE. How can that be?

FESTE. Marry sir, they praise me and make an ass of me.
Now my foes tell me plainly I am an ass; so that by my foes,   15
sir, I profit in the knowledge of myself, and by my friends I
am abused; so that, conclusions to be as kisses, if your four
negatives make your two affirmatives, why then, the worse
for my friends and the better for my foes.

DUKE. Why, this is excellent.   20

FESTE. By my troth, sir, no; though it please you to be
one of my friends.

---

29 Whiles *until* / 30 celebration *marriage* / 35 fairly note *approve*
[ACT V · 1] 17 kisses *i.e., which stop lovers' arguments*

DUKE. Thou shalt not be the worse for me. There's gold.

FESTE. But that it would be double-dealing, sir, I would
you could make it another.   25

DUKE. O, you give me ill counsel.

FESTE. Put your grace in your pocket, sir, for this once,
and let your flesh and blood obey it.

DUKE. Well, I will be so much a sinner, to be a double-
dealer. There's another.   30

FESTE. Primo, secundo, tertio, is a good play; and the old
saying is, the third pays for all. The triplex, sir, is a good
tripping measure; or the bells of Saint Bennet, sir, may put
you in mind; one, two, three.

DUKE. You can fool no more money out of me at this   35
throw. If you will let your lady know I am here to speak with
her, and bring her along with you, it may awake my bounty
further.

FESTE. Marry, sir, lullaby to your bounty till I come
again. I go, sir, but I would not have you to think that my   40
desire of having is the sin of covetousness; but, as you say,
sir, let your bounty take a nap, I will awake it anon.

Exit.

Enter ANTONIO *and* OFFICERS.

VIOLA. Here comes the man, sir, that did rescue me.

DUKE. That face of his I do remember well,
Yet when I saw it last, it was besmear'd   45
As black as Vulcan in the smoke of war.
A baubling vessel was he captain of,
For shallow draught and bulk unprizable,
With which such scathful grapple did he make
With the most noble bottom of our fleet,   50
That very envy and the tongue of loss
Cried fame and honor on him. What's the matter?

FIRST OFFICER. Orsino, this is that Antonio
That took the *Phoenix* and her fraught from Candy,

---

33 Saint Bennet *the church of St. Benedict* / 46 Vulcan *blacksmith of
the gods* / 47 baubling *trifling* / 48 unprizable *of little value* / 49
scathful *destructive* / 50 bottom *ship* / 51 very *even* / 51 loss *of the
losers* / 54 fraught *cargo* / 54 Candy *Crete*

And this is he that did the *Tiger* board,   55
When your young nephew Titus lost his leg.
Here in the streets, desperate of shame and state,
In private brabble did we apprehend him.
  VIOLA.   He did me kindness, sir, drew on my side,
But in conclusion put strange speech upon me.   60
I know not what 'twas but distraction.
  DUKE.   Notable pirate! Thou salt-water thief!
What foolish boldness brought thee to their mercies
Whom thou, in terms so bloody and so dear,
Hast made thine enemies?
  ANTONIO.   Orsino, noble sir,   65
Be pleas'd that I shake off these names you give me.
Antonio never yet was thief or pirate,
Though I confess, on base and ground enough,
Orsino's enemy. A witchcraft drew me hither.
That most ingrateful boy there by your side,   70
From the rude sea's enrag'd and foamy mouth
Did I redeem; a wreck past hope he was.
His life I gave him, and did thereto add
My love, without retention or restraint,
All his in dedication. For his sake   75
Did I expose myself, pure for his love,
Into the danger of this adverse town;
Drew to defend him when he was beset;
Where being apprehended, his false cunning,
Not meaning to partake with me in danger,   80
Taught him to face me out of his acquaintance,
And grew a twenty years removed thing
While one would wink; denied me mine own purse,
Which I had recommended to his use
Not half an hour before.
  VIOLA.   How can this be?   85
  DUKE.   When came he to this town?
  ANTONIO.   To-day, my lord; and for three months before,
No interim, not a minute's vacancy,
Both day and night did we keep company.

---

57 desperate *disregarding* / 58 brabble *brawling* / 64 dear *intense* /
74 retention *holding back*

Enter OLIVIA *and* ATTENDANTS.

DUKE.   Here comes the countess; now heaven walks on
       earth.   90
But for thee, fellow; fellow, thy words are madness.
Three months this youth hath tended upon me;
But more of that anon. Take him aside.
OLIVIA.   What would my lord, but that he may not have,
Wherein Olivia may seem serviceable?   95
Cesario, you do not keep promise with me.
VIOLA.   Madam!
DUKE.   Gracious Olivia,—
OLIVIA.   What do you say, Cesario? Good my lord,—
VIOLA.   My lord would speak; my duty hushes me.   100
OLIVIA.   If it be aught to the old tune, my lord,
It is as fat and fulsome to mine ear
As howling after music.
DUKE.   Still so cruel!
OLIVIA.   Still so constant, lord.
DUKE.   What, to perverseness? You uncivil lady,   105
To whose ingrate and unauspicious altars
My soul the faithfull'st offerings have breath'd out
That e'er devotion tender'd! What shall I do?
OLIVIA.   Even what it please my lord, that shall become
       him.
DUKE.   Why should I not, had I the heart to do it,   110
Like to th' Egyptian thief at point of death,
Kill what I love?—a savage jealousy
That sometimes savors nobly. But hear me this:
Since you to non-regardance cast my faith,
And that I partly know the instrument   115
That screws me from my true place in your favor,
Live you the marble-breasted tyrant still;
But this your minion, whom I know you love,
And whom, by heaven I swear, I tender dearly,
Him will I tear out of that cruel eye,   120
Where he sits crowned in his master's spite.

---

102 fat and fulsome *distasteful* / 111 Egyptian thief *Thyamis, who killed
his supposed sweetheart when he was about to fall into the hands of his
enemies* / 118 minion *darling* / 121 his master's spite *in defiance of his
master*

Come, boy, with me; my thoughts are ripe in mischief.
I'll sacrifice the lamb that I do love,
To spite a raven's heart within a dove.

    VIOLA.   And I, most jocund, apt, and willingly,   125
To do you rest, a thousand deaths would die.

    OLIVIA.   Where goes Cesario?

    VIOLA.   After him I love
More than I love these eyes, more than my life,
More, by all mores, than e'er I shall love wife.
If I do feign, you witnesses above   130
Punish my life for tainting of my love!

    OLIVIA.   Ay me, detested! How am I beguil'd!

    VIOLA.   Who does beguile you? Who does do you wrong?

    OLIVIA.   Has thou forgot thyself? Is it so long?
Call forth the holy father.

    DUKE.   Come, away!   135

    OLIVIA.   Whither, my lord? Cesario, husband, stay.

    DUKE.   Husband?

    OLIVIA.   Ay, husband! Can he that deny?

    DUKE.   Her husband, sirrah?

    VIOLA.   No, my lord, not I.

    OLIVIA.   Alas, it is the baseness of thy fear
That makes thee strangle thy propriety.   140
Fear not, Cesario; take thy fortunes up.
Be that thou know'st thou art, and then thou art
As great as that thou fear'st.

Enter PRIEST.

                O, welcome, father!
Father, I charge thee by thy reverence,
Here to unfold, though lately we intended   145
To keep in darkness what occasion now
Reveals before 'tis ripe, what thou dost know
Hath newly pass'd between this youth and me.

    PRIEST.   A contract of eternal bond of love,
Confirm'd by mutual joinder of your hands,   150
Attested by the holy close of lips,
Strengthen'd by interchangement of your rings;

---

131 tainting of *hypocrisy in* / 143 that *i.e., the Duke*

And all the ceremony of this compact
Seal'd in my function, by my testimony;
Since when, my watch hath told me, toward my grave   155
I have travell'd but two hours.

    DUKE.   O thou dissembling cub! What wilt thou be
When time hath sow'd a grizzle on thy case?
Or will not else thy craft so quickly grow,
That thine own trip shall be thine overthrow?   160
Farewell, and take her; but direct thy feet
Where thou and I henceforth may never meet.

    VIOLA.   My lord, I do protest—
    OLIVIA.   O, do not swear!
Hold little faith, though thou hast too much fear.

Enter SIR ANDREW.

    SIR ANDREW.   For the love of God, a surgeon! Send one   165
presently to Sir Toby.

    OLIVIA.   What's the matter?

    SIR ANDREW.   Has broke my head across and has given
Sir Toby a bloody coxcomb too. For the love of God, your
help! I had rather than forty pound I were at home.   170

    OLIVIA.   Who has done this, Sir Andrew?

    SIR ANDREW.   The Count's gentleman, one Cesario. We
took him for a coward, but he's the very devil incardinate.

    DUKE.   My gentleman Cesario?

    SIR ANDREW.   'Ods lifelings, here he is! You broke my   175
head for nothing; and that that I did, I was set on to do't by
Sir Toby.

    VIOLA.   Why do you speak to me? I never hurt you.
You drew your sword upon me without cause;
But I bespake you fair, and hurt you not.   180

Enter SIR TOBY *and* FESTE.

    SIR ANDREW.   If a bloody coxcomb be a hurt, you have
hurt me; I think you set nothing by a bloody coxcomb. Here
comes Sir Toby halting. You shall hear more; but if he had

---

158 sow'd . . . case *mingled dark and gray hair on thy skin* / 160 trip
trickery / 164 little *some little* / 169 coxcomb *pate* / 173 incardinate
i.e., incarnate / 183 halting *limping*

not been in drink, he would have tickled you othergates than
he did.   185

DUKE.   How now, gentleman! How is't with you?

SIR TOBY.   That's all one. Has hurt me, and there's the
end on't. Sot, didst see Dick surgeon, sot?

FESTE.   O, he's drunk, Sir Toby, an hour agone. His eyes
were set at eight i' the morning.   190

SIR TOBY.   Then he's a rogue, and a passy measures pavin.
I hate a drunken rogue.

OLIVIA.   Away with him! Who hath made this havoc with
them?

SIR ANDREW.   I'll help you, Sir Toby, because we'll be   195
dressed together.

SIR TOBY.   Will you help?—an ass-head and a coxcomb
and a knave, a thin-faced knave, a gull!

OLIVIA.   Get him to bed, and let his hurt be look'd to.

        Exeunt FESTE, FABIAN, SIR TOBY, *and* SIR ANDREW.

                Enter SEBASTIAN.

SEBASTIAN.   I am sorry, madam, I have hurt your kinsman;   200
But, had it been the brother of my blood,
I must have done no less with wit and safety.
You throw a strange regard upon me, and by that
I do perceive it hath offended you.
Pardon me, sweet one, even for the vows   205
We made each other but so late ago.

DUKE.   One face, one voice, one habit, and two persons,
A natural perspective, that is and is not!

SEBASTIAN.   Antonio, O my dear Antonio!
How have the hours rack'd and tortur'd me,   210
Since I have lost thee!

ANTONIO.   Sebastian are you?

SEBASTIAN.   Fear'st thou that, Antonio?

ANTONIO.   How have you made division of yourself?
An apple, cleft in two, is not more twin
Than these two creatures. Which is Sebastian?   215

OLIVIA.   Most wonderful!

---

184 othergates *otherwise* / 189 agone *ago* / 190 set *dimmed by drink* /
191 passy measures pavin *a stately dance, hence a solemn humbug* /
196 dressed *treated* / 208 perspective *optical illusion*

SEBASTIAN.   Do I stand there? I never had a brother,
Nor can there be that deity in my nature
Of here and everywhere. I had a sister,
Whom the blind waves and surges have devour'd.   220
Of charity, what kin are you to me?
What countryman? What name? What parentage?
   VIOLA.   Of Messaline; Sebastian was my father;
Such a Sebastian was my brother too;
So went he suited to his watery tomb.   225
If spirits can assume both form and suit
You come to fright us.
   SEBASTIAN.   A spirit I am indeed:
But am in that dimension grossly clad
Which from the womb I did participate.
Were you a woman, as the rest goes even,   230
I should my tears let fall upon your cheek,
And say, "Thrice welcome, drowned Viola!"
   VIOLA.   My father had a mole upon his brow.
   SEBASTIAN.   And so had mine.
   VIOLA.   And died that day when Viola from her birth   235
Had number'd thirteen years.
   SEBASTIAN.   O, that record is lively in my soul!
He finished indeed his mortal act
That day that made my sister thirteen years.
   VIOLA.   If nothing lets to make us happy both   240
But this my masculine usurp'd attire,
Do not embrace me till each circumstance
Of place, time, fortune, do cohere and jump
That I am Viola; which to confirm,
I'll bring you to a captain in this town,   245
Where lie my maiden weeds; by whose gentle help
I was preserv'd to serve this noble count.
All the occurrence of my fortunes since
Hath been between this lady and this lord.
   SEBASTIAN. [To OLIVIA.]   So comes it, lady, you have been
        mistook;   250
But nature to her bias drew in that.

---

218 deity *divine quality* / 228 grossly clad *clothed in flesh* / 229 participate *inherit* / 240 lets *hinders* / 243 cohere and jump *agree* / 246
weeds *garments* / 251 her bias *inborn tendency*

You would have been contracted to a maid;
Nor are you therein, by my life, deceiv'd,
You are betroth'd both to a maid and man.

DUKE.   Be not amaz'd, right noble is his blood.   255
If this be so, as yet the glass seems true,
I shall have share in this most happy wreck.
[*To* VIOLA.] Boy, thou hast said to me a thousand times
Thou never shouldst love woman like to me.

VIOLA.   And all those sayings will I overswear;   260
And all those swearings keep as true in soul
As doth that orbed continent the fire
That severs day from night.

DUKE.   Give me thy hand,
And let me see thee in thy woman's weeds.

VIOLA.   The captain that did bring me first on shore   265
Hath my maid's garments. He upon some action
Is now in durance, at Malvolio's suit,
A gentleman, and follower of my lady's.

OLIVIA.   He shall enlarge him; fetch Malvolio hither.
And yet, alas, now I remember me,   270
They say, poor gentleman, he's much distract.

Re-enter FESTE *with a letter, and* FABIAN.

A most extracting frenzy of mine own
From my remembrance clearly banish'd his.
How does he, sirrah?

FESTE.   Truly, madam, he holds Belzebub at the stave's   275
end as well as a man in his case may do. Has here writ a letter
to you. I should have given 't you to day morning, but as a
madman's epistles are no gospels, so it skills not much when
they are delivered.

OLIVIA.   Open 't, and read it.   280

FESTE.   Look then to be well edified when the fool delivers the madman. [*Reads.*] "By the Lord, madam,"—

OLIVIA.   How now, art thou mad?

FESTE.   No, madam, I do but read madness; an your lady-

---

262 orbed continent *sun* / 267 durance *jail* / 269 enlarge *release* /
272 frenzy *madness* / 275 Belzebub *the devil* / 278 skills *matters* /
282 delivers *is messenger for*

ship will have it as it ought to be, you must allow Vox.   285
   OLIVIA.   Prithee, read i' thy right wits.
   FESTE.   So I do, madonna; but to read his right wits is to
read thus. Therefore perpend, my princess, and give ear.
   OLIVIA.   Read it you, sirrah. [*To* FABIAN.]
   FABIAN.   [*Reads.*]

"By the Lord, madam, you wrong me, and the world shall know   290
it. Though you have put me into darkness and given your drunken
cousin rule over me, yet have I the benefit of my senses as well as
your ladyship. I have your own letter that induced me to the sem-
blance I put on; with the which I doubt not but to do myself much
right, or you much shame. Think of me as you please. I leave my   295
duty a little unthought of and speak out of my injury.
                        "THE MADLY-USED MALVOLIO."

   OLIVIA.   Did he write this?
   FESTE.   Ay, madam.
   DUKE.   This savors not much of distraction.   300
   OLIVIA.   See him deliver'd, Fabian; bring him hither.
                                             Exit FABIAN.
My lord, so please you, these things further thought on,
To think me as well a sister as a wife,
One day shall crown the alliance on 't, so please you,
Here at my house and at my proper cost.   305
   DUKE.   Madam, I am most apt t' embrace your offer.
[*To* VIOLA.] Your master quits you; and for your service done
      him,
So much against the mettle of your sex,
So far beneath your soft and tender breeding,
And since you call'd me master for so long,   310
Here is my hand. You shall from this time be
Your master's mistress.
   OLIVIA.   A sister! You are she.

                 Enter MALVOLIO *and* FABIAN.

   DUKE.   Is this the madman?
   OLIVIA.   Ay, my lord, this same.
How now, Malvolio!

---

285 Vox *a loud voice* / 288 perpend *be attentive* / 305 proper *own* /
307 quits *releases*

MALVOLIO.   Madam, you have done me wrong,
Notorious wrong.

OLIVIA.   Have I, Malvolio? No.   315

MALVOLIO.   Lady, you have. Pray you, peruse that letter;
You must not now deny it is your hand.
Write from it, if you can, in hand or phrase;
Or say 'tis not your seal, not your invention.
You can say none of this. Well, grant it then   320
And tell me, in the modesty of honor,
Why you have givèn me such clear lights of favor,
Bade me come smiling and cross-garter'd to you,
To put on yellow stockings and to frown
Upon Sir Toby and the lighter people;   325
And, acting this in an obedient hope,
Why have you suffer'd me to be imprison'd,
Kept in a dark house, visited by the priest,
And made the most notorious geck and gull
That e'er invention played on? Tell me why.   330

OLIVIA.   Alas, Malvolio, this is not my writing,
Though, I confess, much like the character;
But out of question 'tis Maria's hand.
And now I do bethink me, it was she
First told me thou wast mad. Then cam'st in smiling,   335
And in such forms which here were presuppos'd
Upon thee in the letter. Prithee, be content.
This practice hath most shrewdly pass'd upon thee;
But when we know the grounds and authors of it,
Thou shalt be both the plaintiff and the judge   340
Of thine own cause.

FABIAN.   Good madam, hear me speak,
And let no quarrel nor no brawl to come
Taint the condition of this present hour,
Which I have wonder'd at. In hope it shall not,
Most freely I confess, myself and Toby   345
Set this device against Malvolio here,
Upon some stubborn and uncourteous parts
We had conceiv'd against him. Maria writ

318 from *in a different style from* / 329 geck and gull *dupe* / 332
character *handwriting* / 336 presuppos'd Upon *suggested to* / 338
practice *plot* / 348 conceiv'd against *perceived in*

The letter at Sir Toby's great importance,
In recompense whereof he hath married her.   350
How with a sportful malice it was follow'd
May rather pluck on laughter than revenge,
If that the injuries be justly weigh'd
That have on both sides pass'd.

    OLIVIA.   Alas, poor fool, how have they baffl'd thee!   355
    FESTE.   Why, "some are born great, some achieve great-
ness, and some have greatness thrown upon them." I was one,
sir, in this interlude; one Sir Topas, sir; but that's all one.
"By the Lord, fool, I am not mad." But do you remember?
"Madam, why laugh you at such a barren rascal? An you   360
smile not, he's gagged." And thus the whirligig of time brings
in his revenges.

    MALVOLIO.   I'll be reveng'd on the whole pack of you.

                                     Exit.

    OLIVIA.   He hath been most notoriously abus'd.
    DUKE.   Pursue him, and entreat him to a peace;   365
He hath not told us of the captain yet.
When that is known and golden time convents,
A solemn combination shall be made
Of our dear souls. Meantime, sweet sister,
We will not part from hence. Cesario, come;   370
For so you shall be, while you are a man;
But when in other habits you are seen,
Orsino's mistress and his fancy's queen.

                     Exeunt all, except FESTE.

    FESTE. [*Sings.*]
          When that I was and a little tiny boy,
             With hey, ho, the wind and the rain,   375
          A foolish thing was but a toy,
             For the rain it raineth every day.

          But when I came to man's estate,
             With hey, ho, etc.
          'Gainst knaves and thieves men shut their gate,   380
             For the rain, etc.

---

349 importance *urging* / 352 pluck on *provoke* / 355 baffl'd *shamed* /
367 convents *agrees* / 373 fancy's *love's* / 376 toy *trifle*

But when I came, alas! to wive,
   With hey, ho, etc.
By swaggering could I never thrive,
   For the rain, etc.   385

But when I came unto my beds,
   With hey, ho, etc.
With toss-pots still had drunken heads,
   For the rain, etc.

A great while ago the world begun,   390
   With hey, ho, etc.
But that's all one, our play is done,
   And we'll strive to please you every day.

                                         Exit.

---

388 toss-pots *drunkards*

Othello, the Moor of Venice

[ACT I · 1] *Venice. A street.*

Enter RODERIGO *and* IAGO.

RODERIGO.   Tush, never tell me! I take it much unkindly
That thou, Iago, who hast had my purse
As if the strings were thine, shouldst know of this.
 IAGO.   'Sblood, but you will not hear me.
If ever I did dream of such a matter,   5
Abhor me.
 RODERIGO.   Thou told'st me thou didst hold him in thy hate.
 IAGO.   Despise me, if I do not. Three great ones of the city,
In personal suit to make me his lieutenant,
Off-capp'd to him; and, by the faith of man,   10
I know my price; I am worth no worse a place.
But he, as loving his own pride and purposes,
Evades them with a bombast circumstance
Horribly stuff'd with epithets of war;
And, in conclusion,   15
Nonsuits my mediators; for, "Certes," says he,
"I have already chose my officer."
And what was he?
Forsooth, a great arithmetician,
One Michael Cassio, a Florentine,   20
(A fellow almost damn'd in a fair wife)
That never set a squadron in the field,
Nor the division of a battle knows
More than a spinster; unless the bookish theoric,
Wherein the toged consuls can propose   25
As masterly as he. Mere prattle without practice
Is all his soldiership. But he, sir, had the election;
And I, of whom his eyes had seen the proof
At Rhodes, at Cyprus, and on other grounds,

[ACT I · 1] 2 had *used* / 4 'Sblood *by Christ's blood* / 11 price
value / 13 bombast circumstance *circumlocutions padded out* / 16
Nonsuits *rejects the petitions of* / 16 Certes *certainly* / 19 arithmetician *i.e., student of books of military tactics (cf., Mercutio on Tybalt
as a fencer, Romeo, II, 3)* / 21 damn'd *married to* (?) / 23 division
. . . battle *organization of an army* / 24 bookish theoric *pedantic theory*
/ 25 toged *wearing a toga* / 25 propose *talk* / 27 had the election *was
chosen*

Christian and heathen, must be be-lee'd and calm'd   30
By debitor and creditor; this counter-caster,
He, in good time, must his lieutenant be,
And I—God bless the mark!—his Moorship's ancient.

RODERIGO. By heaven, I rather would have been
his hangman.

IAGO. Why, there's no remedy; 'tis the curse of service.   35
Preferment goes by letter and affection,
And not by old gradation, where each second
Stood heir to the first. Now, sir, be judge yourself
Whether I in any just term am affin'd
To love the Moor.

RODERIGO.   I would not follow him then.   40

IAGO. O, sir, content you.
I follow him to serve my turn upon him.
We cannot all be masters, nor all masters
Cannot be truly follow'd. You shall mark
Many a duteous and knee-crooking knave,   45
That, doting on his own obsequious bondage,
Wears out his time, much like his master's ass,
For nought but provender, and when he's old, cashier'd.
Whip me such honest knaves. Others there are
Who, trimm'd in forms and visages of duty,   50
Keep yet their hearts attending on themselves,
And, throwing but shows of service on their lords,
Do well thrive by 'em, and when they have lin'd their coats
Do themselves homage. These fellows have some soul;
And such a one do I profess myself. For, sir,   55
It is as sure as you are Roderigo,
Were I the Moor, I would not be Iago.
In following him, I follow but myself—
Heaven is my judge, not I for love and duty,
But seeming so, for my peculiar end.   60

---

30 be-lee'd *"have the wind taken out of my sails"* / 31 counter-caster *arithmetician* / 33 ancient *ensign, third officer (after Othello and Cassio)* / 36 Preferment *promotion* / 36 letter *influence* / 36 affection *favoritism* / 37 old gradation *the old way of promoting from one rank to the next* / 39 affin'd *bound by affection* / 48 cashier'd *dismissed* / 50 trimm'd *costumed* / 52 throwing but shows *bestowing only the appearance* / 54 Do . . . homage *serve themselves* / 60 peculiar *personal*

For when my outward action does demonstrate
The native act and figure of my heart
In compliment extern, 'tis not long after
But I will wear my heart upon my sleeve
For daws to peck at: I am not what I am.   65

    RODERIGO.   What a full fortune does the thick-lips owe,
If he can carry't thus!
    IAGO.   Call up her father.
Rouse him, make after him, poison his delight,
Proclaim him in the streets. Incense her kinsmen,
And, though he in a fortile climate dwell,   70
Plague him with flies; though that his joy be joy,
Yet throw such changes of vexation on 't,
As it may lose some color.
    RODERIGO.   Here is her father's house. I'll call aloud.
    IAGO   Do, with like timorous accent and dire yell   ·   75
As when, by night and negligence, the fire
Is spied in populous cities.
    RODERIGO.   What, ho, Brabantio! Signior Brabantio, ho!
    IAGO.   Awake! what, ho, Brabantio! thieves! thieves!
Look to your house, your daughter, and your bags!   80
Thieves! thieves!

       Enter BRABANTIO *above, at a window.*

    BRABANTIO.   What is the reason of this terrible summons?
What is the matter there?
    RODERIGO.   Signior, is all your family within?
    IAGO.   Are your doors lock'd?
    BRABANTIO.   Why, wherefore ask you this?   85
    IAGO.   'Zounds, sir, you're robb'd! For shame, put on
      your gown;
Your heart is burst, you have lost half your soul.
Even now, now, very now, an old black ram
Is tupping your white ewe. Arise, arise!
Awake the snorting citizens with the bell,   90

---

62 native *secret* / 62 figure *purpose* / 63 compliment extern *outward
appearance* / 65 daws *jackdaws, i.e., fools* / 72 changes *disturbances* /
75 timorous accent *voice of terror* / 86 'Zounds *by Christ's wounds* /
86 gown *dressing gown* / 90 snorting *snoring*

Or else the devil will make a grandsire of you.
Arise, I say!

BRABANTIO. What, have you lost your wits?

RODERIGO.   Most reverend signior, do you know my voice?

BRABANTIO.   Not I. What are you?

RODERIGO.   My name is Roderigo.

BRABANTIO.   The worser welcome.   95
I have charg'd thee not to haunt about my doors;
In honest plainness thou hast heard me say
My daughter is not for thee; and now, in madness,
Being full of supper and distempering draughts,
Upon malicious bravery dost thou come   100
To start my quiet.

RODERIGO.   Sir, sir, sir,—

BRABANTIO.   But thou must needs be sure
My spirits and my place have in them power
To make this bitter to thee.

RODERIGO.   Patience, good sir.

BRABANTIO.   What tell'st thou me of robbing?
      This is Venice;   105
My house is not a grange.

RODERIGO.   Most grave Brabantio,
In simple and pure soul I come to you.

IAGO.   'Zounds, sir, you are one of those that will not serve
God, if the devil bid you. Because we come to do you service and you think we are ruffians, you'll have your daughter   110
covered with a Barbary horse; you'll have your nephews neigh
to you; you'll have coursers for cousins, and gennets for germans.

BRABANTIO.   What profane wretch art thou?

IAGO.   I am one, sir, that comes to tell you your daughter   115
and the Moor are now making the beast with two backs.

BRABANTIO.   Thou art a villain.

IAGO.   You are—a senator.

BRABANTIO.   This thou shalt answer. I know thee,
      Roderigo.

---

99 distempering *uninhibiting* / 100 bravery *defiance* / 101 start *disturb*
/ 103 place *position* (*as Senator*) / 106 grange *isolated farm* / 112
gennets for germans *ponies for relatives* / 118 answer *be called to account for*

RODERIGO.   Sir, I will answer anything. But, I beseech you,
If 't be your pleasure and most wise consent,   120
(As partly I find it is) that your fair daughter,
At this odd-even and dull watch o' th' night,
Transported, with no worse nor better guard
But with a knave of common hire, a gondolier,
To the gross clasps of a lascivious Moor,—   125
If this be known to you and your allowance,
We then have done you bold and saucy wrongs;
But if you know not this, my manners tell me
We have your wrong rebuke. Do not believe
That, from the sense of all civility,   130
I thus would play and trifle with your reverence.
Your daughter, if you have not given her leave,
I say again, hath made a gross revolt;
Tying her duty, beauty, wit, and fortunes
In an extravagant and wheeling stranger   135
Of here and everywhere. Straight satisfy yourself.
If she be in her chamber or your house,
Let loose on me the justice of the state
For thus deluding you.
  BRABANTIO.   Strike on the tinder, ho!
Give me a taper! Call up all my people!   140
This accident is not unlike my dream.
Belief of it oppresses me already.
Light, I say! light!   *Exit.*
  IAGO.   Farewell; for I must leave you.
It seems not meet, nor wholesome to my place,
To be produc'd— as, if I stay, I shall—   145
Against the Moor; for, I do know, the state,
However this may gall him with some check,
Cannot with safety cast him, for he's embark'd
With such loud reason to the Cyprus wars,
Which even now stands in act, that, for their souls,   150
Another of his fathom they have none,

---

122 odd-even *around midnight* / 126 your allowance *a thing that you
approve* / 130 from *contrary to* / 135 extravagant *vagabond* / 140
taper *candle* / 144 meet *fitting* / 144 place *i.e., as Othello's ensign*
/ 147 check *rebuke* / 148 cast *discharge* / 149 loud *urgent* / 151
fathom *capacity*

To lead their business; in which regard,
Though I do hate him as I do hell-pains,
Yet, for necessity of present life,
I must show out a flag and sign of love,   155
Which is indeed but sign. That you shall surely find him,
Lead to the Sagittary the raised search;
And there will I be with him. So, farewell.   *Exit.*

Enter BRABANTIO *in his night-gown, and Servants with torches.*

BRABANTIO.   It is too true an evil. Gone she is;
And what's to come of my despised time   160
Is nought but bitterness. Now, Roderigo,
Where didst thou see her?—O unhappy girl!—
With the Moor, say'st thou?—Who would be a father!
How didst thou know 'twas she?—O, she deceives me
Past thought! What said she to you?—Get moe tapers;   165
Raise all my kindred.—Are they married, think you?
RODERIGO.   Truly, I think they are.
BRABANTIO.   O heaven! How got she out? O treason
      of the blood!
Fathers, from hence trust not your daughters' minds
By what you see them act. Is there not charms   170
By which the property of youth and maidhood
May be abus'd? Have you not read, Roderigo,
Of some such thing?
RODERIGO.   Yes, sir, I have indeed.
BRABANTIO.   Call up my brother.—O, would you had
      had her!
Some one way, some another.—Do you know   175
Where we may apprehend her and the Moor?
RODERIGO.   I think I can discover him, if you please
To get your guard and go along with me.
BRABANTIO.   Pray you, lead on. At every house I'll call;
I may command at most.—Get weapons, ho!   180
And raise some special officers of night.—
On, good Roderigo; I'll deserve your pains.   *Exeunt.*

---

157 Sagittary *an inn* (*at the sign of the Sagittarius, the Archer*) / s.d.
night-gown *dressing gown* / 160 despised time *rest of my life* / 165
moe *more* / 168 of the blood *against the family* / 171 property *nature* / 172 abus'd *deceived* / 180 command *find supporters*

[ACT I · 2] *Another street.*

Enter OTHELLO, IAGO, *and* ATTENDANTS *with torches.*

IAGO. Though in the trade of war I have slain men,
Yet do I hold it very stuff o' th' conscience
To do no contriv'd murder. I lack iniquity
Sometimes to do me service. Nine or ten times
I had thought to have yerk'd him here under the ribs.   5
   OTHELLO. 'Tis better as it is.
   IAGO.   Nay, but he prated,
And spoke such scurvy and provoking terms
Against your honor
That, with the little godliness I have,
I did full hard forbear him. But, I pray you, sir,   10
Are you fast married? Be assur'd of this,
That the magnifico is much belov'd,
And hath in his effect a voice potential
As double as the Duke's. He will divorce you;
Or put upon you what restraint or grievance   15
The law, with all his might to enforce it on,
Will give him cable.
   OTHELLO.   Let him do his spite;
My services which I have done the signiory
Shall out-tongue his complaints. 'Tis yet to know,—
Which, when I know that boasting is an honor,   20
I shall promulgate— I fetch my life and being
From men of royal siege, and my demerits
May speak unbonneted to as proud a fortune
As this that I have reach'd; for know, Iago,
But that I love the gentle Desdemona,   25
I would not my unhoused free condition
Put into circumscription and confine
For the sea's worth. But, look! what lights come yond?

[ACT I · 2] 2 very stuff'd *strict scruple* / 5 yerk'd *thrust* / 10 full
hard forbear *with difficulty spare* / 11 fast *securely* / 12 magnifico *i.e.,
senator* / 13 effect *ability to effect his wishes* / 13 voice potential *powerful voice* / 14 As . . . Duke's *like the Duke's double vote* / 15 grievance *obstacles* / 18 signiory *the government* / 19 yet to know *not yet known* / 22 royal siege *throne* / 22 demerits *deserts* / 23 unbonneted *i.e., on equal terms* / 26 unhoused *free from domestic cares*

Enter CASSIO *and* OFFICERS, *with torches*.

IAGO.   Those are the raised father and his friends.
You were best go in.

OTHELLO.   Not I; I must be found.   30
My parts, my title, and my perfect soul
Shall manifest me rightly. Is it they?

IAGO.   By Janus, I think no.

OTHELLO.   The servants of the Duke, and my lieutenant!
The goodness of the night upon you, friends!   35
What is the news?

CASSIO.   The Duke does greet you, general,
And he requires your haste-post-haste appearance,
Even on the instant.

OTHELLO.   What is the matter, think you?

CASSIO.   Something from Cyprus, as I may divine;
It is a business of some heat. The galleys   40
Have sent a dozen sequent messengers
This very night at one another's heels,
And many of the consuls, rais'd and met,
Are at the Duke's already. You have been hotly call'd for;
When, being not at your lodging to be found,   45
The Senate hath sent about three several quests
To search you out.

OTHELLO.   'Tis well I am found by you.
I will but spend a word here in the house,
And go with you.   *Exit.*

CASSIO.   Ancient, what makes he here?

IAGO.   Faith, he to-night hath boarded a land carack: 50
If it proves lawful prize, he's made for ever.

CASSIO.   I do not understand.

IAGO.   He's married.

CASSIO.   To who?

Re-enter OTHELLO.

IAGO.   Marry, to—Come, captain, will you go?

OTHELLO.   Have with you.

29 raised *aroused* / 31 parts *abilities* / 33 Janus *Roman god with two
faces* / 37 haste-post-haste *speediest* / 40 galleys *warships* / 41 sequent
one after another / 46 several *separate* / 49 makes he *is he doing* /
50 carack *merchant ship* / 53 Marry *a mild oath* / 53 captain *general*

CASSIO.   Here comes another troop to seek for you.

Enter BRABANTIO, RODERIGO, *and* OFFICERS *with torches
and weapons.*

IAGO.   It is Brabantio. General, be advis'd;   55
He comes to bad intent.
    OTHELLO.   Holla! stand there!
    RODERIGO.   Signior, it is the Moor.
    BRABANTIO.   Down with him, thief!
                    They draw on both sides.
    IAGO.   You, Roderigo! come, sir, I am for you.
    OTHELLO.   Keep up your bright swords, for the dew will
      rust them.
Good signior, you shall more command with years   60
Than with your weapons.
    BRABANTIO.   O thou foul thief, where hast thou
      stow'd my daughter?
Damn'd as thou art, thou hast enchanted her;
For I'll refer me to all things of sense,
If she in chains of magic were not bound,   65
Whether a maid so tender, fair, and happy,
So opposite to marriage that she shunn'd
The wealthy curled darlings of our nation,
Would ever have, t' incur a general mock,
Run from her guardage to the sooty bosom   70
Of such a thing as thou—to fear, not to delight.
Judge me the world, if 'tis not gross in sense
That thou hast practis'd on her with foul charms,
Abus'd her delicate youth with drugs or minerals
That weaken motion. I'll have't disputed on;   75
'Tis probable, and palpable to thinking.
I therefore apprehend and do attach thee
For an abuser of the world, a practiser
Of arts inhibited and out of warrant.
Lay hold upon him; if he do resist,   80
Subdue him at his peril.

---

55 advis'd *cautious* / 59 Keep up *sheathe* / 64 things of sense *rational
creatures* / 69 mock *ridicule* / 72 gross in sense *obvious to anyone's
perception* / 74 Abus'd *deluded* / 75 motion *perception* / 75 disputed
on *argued at law* / 77 attach *arrest* / 79 inhibited *illegal*

OTHELLO.   Hold your hands,
Both you of my inclining, and the rest.
Were it my cue to fight, I should have known it
Without a prompter. Where will you that I go
To answer this your charge?
BRABANTIO.   To prison, till fit time   85
Of law and course of direct session
Call thee to answer.
OTHELLO.   What if I do obey?
How may the Duke be therewith satisfied,
Whose messengers are here about my side
Upon some present business of the state   90
To bring me to him?
OFFICER.   'Tis true, most worthy signior.
The Duke's in council; and your noble self,
I am sure, is sent for.
BRABANTIO.   How? the Duke in council?
In this time of the night? Bring him away;
Mine's not an idle cause. The Duke himself,   95
Or any of my brothers of the state,
Cannot but feel this wrong as 'twere their own;
For if such actions may have passage free,
Bond-slaves and pagans shall our statesmen be.

                                    Exeunt.

[ACT I · 3] *A councilchamber.*

The DUKE *and* SENATORS *set at a table with lights;* OFFICERS
and ATTENDANTS.

· DUKE.   There is no composition in these news
That gives them credit.
FIRST SENATOR.   Indeed, they are disproportioned;
My letters say a hundred and seven galleys.
DUKE.   And mine, a hundred forty.
SECOND SENATOR.   And mine, two hundred!
But though they jump not on a just account,—   5

---

82 of my inclining *my supporters* / 86 direct *regular* / 90 present
immediate / 95 idle *trivial* / 98 passage free *free allowance*
   [ACT I · 3] 1 composition *consistency* / 5 jump *agree*

As in these cases, where the aim reports,
'Tis oft with difference—yet do they all confirm
A Turkish fleet, and bearing up to Cyprus.
    DUKE.   Nay, it is possible enough to judgment.
I do not so secure me in the error   10
But the main article I do approve
In fearful sense.
    SAILOR.   [*Within.*] What, ho! what, ho! what, ho!

Enter a SAILOR.

    OFFICER.   A messenger from the galleys.
    DUKE.   Now, what's the business?
    SAILOR.   The Turkish preparation makes for Rhodes;
So was I bid report here to the state   15
By Signior Angelo.
    DUKE.   How say you by this change?
    FIRST SENATOR.   This cannot be,
By no assay of reason. 'Tis a pageant,
To keep us in false gaze. When we consider
Th' importancy of Cyprus to the Turk,   20
And let ourselves again but understand
That, as it more concerns the Turk than Rhodes,
So may he with more facile question bear it,
For that it stands not in such warlike brace,
But altogether lacks th' abilities   25
That Rhodes is dress'd in; if we make thought of this,
We must not think the Turk is so unskilful
To leave that latest which concerns him first,
Neglecting an attempt of ease and gain
To wake and wage a danger profitless.   30
    DUKE.   Nay, in all confidence, he's not for Rhodes.
    OFFICER.   Here is more news.

Enter a MESSENGER.

    MESSENGER.   The Ottomites, reverend and gracious,

---

6 aim *guesswork* / 10 secure me in *free me from anxiety because of* /
11 main article *general statement* / 11 approve *believe* / 12 fearful *to
be feared* / 18 no assay *any test* / 18 pageant *a feint* / 19 in false gaze
looking in the wrong direction / 23 question *contest* / 23 bear *capture*
/ 24 brace *posture of defence* / 30 wage *risk*

Steering with due course toward the isle of Rhodes,
Have there injointed them with an after fleet.   35
   FIRST SENATOR.   Ay, so I thought. How many,
     as you guess?
   MESSENGER.   Of thirty sail; and now they do restem
Their backward course, bearing with frank appearance
Their purposes toward Cyprus. Signior Montano,
Your trusty and most valiant servitor,   40
With his free duty recommends you thus,
And prays you to believe him.
   DUKE.   'Tis certain, then, for Cyprus.
Marcus Lucchese, is not he in town?
   FIRST SENATOR.   He's now in Florence.   45
   DUKE.   Write from us to him; post-post-haste dispatch.
   FIRST SENATOR.   Here comes Brabantio and the
     valiant Moor.

     Enter BRABANTIO, OTHELLO, CASSIO, IAGO, RODERIGO,
         and OFFICERS.

   DUKE.   Valiant Othello, we must straight employ you
Against the general enemy Ottoman.
[*To* BRABANTIO.] I did not see you; welcome, gentle signior;   50
We lack'd your counsel and your help to-night.
   BRABANTIO.   So did I yours. Good your Grace, pardon me;
Neither my place nor aught I heard of business
Hath rais'd me from my bed, nor doth the general care
Take hold on me; for my particular grief   55
Is of so flood-gate and o'erbearing nature
That it engluts and swallows other sorrows
And it is still itself.
   DUKE.   Why, what's the matter?
   BRABANTIO.   My daughter! O, my daughter!
   SENATOR.   Dead?
   BRABANTIO.   Ay, to me;
She is abus'd, stol'n from me, and corrupted   60
By spells and medicines bought of mountebanks;
For nature so preposterously to err,

---

35 injointed *joined* / 35 after *second* / 37 restem *steer again* / 41 free
duty *due respect* / 55 particular *personal* / 57 engluts *swallows* / 61
mountebanks *quack doctors*

Being not deficient, blind, or lame of sense,
Sans witchcraft could not.

    DUKE.   Whoe'er he be that in this foul proceeding   65
Hath thus beguil'd your daughter of herself
And you of her, the bloody book of law
You shall yourself read in the bitter letter
After your own sense, yea, though our proper son
Stood in your action.

    BRABANTIO.   Humbly I thank your Grace.   70
Here is the man,—this Moor, whom now, it seems,
Your special mandate for the state affairs
Hath hither brought.

    ALL.   We are very sorry for 't.

    DUKE.   [*To* OTHELLO.] What, in your own part, can you
    say to this?

    BRABANTIO.   Nothing, but this is so.   75

    OTHELLO.   Most potent, grave, and reverend signiors,
My very noble and approv'd good masters,
That I have ta'en away this old man's daughter,
It is most true; true, I have married her:
The very head and front of my offending   80
Hath this extent, no more. Rude am I in my speech,
And little bless'd with the soft phrase of peace;
For since these arms of mine had seven years' pith
Till now, some nine moons wasted, they have us'd
Their dearest action in the tented field;   85
And little of this great world can I speak
More than pertains to feats of broils and battle;
And therefore little shall I grace my cause
In speaking for myself. Yet, by your gracious patience,
I will a round unvarnish'd tale deliver   90
Of my whole course of love—what drugs, what charms,
What conjuration, and what mighty magic,
(For such proceeding I am charg'd withal)
I won his daughter.

    BRABANTIO.   A maiden never bold;

---

64 Sans *without* / 69 proper *own* / 77 approv'd *tested* / 80 front *forehead* / 81 Rude *unpolished* / 83 pith *marrow, i.e., strength* / 84 moons wasted *months gone by* / 85 dearest *most intense* / 88 grace *make attractive* / 90 round *direct* / 93 withal *with*

Of spirit so still and quiet, that her motion   95
Blush'd at herself; and she, in spite of nature,
Of years, of country, credit, everything,
To fall in love with what she fear'd to look on!
It is a judgment maim'd and most imperfect
That will confess perfection so could err   100
Against all rules of nature, and must be driven
To find out practices of cunning hell,
Why this should be. I therefore vouch again
That with some mixtures powerful o'er the blood,
Or with some dram conjur'd to this effect,   105
He wrought upon her.

   DUKE.   To vouch this is no proof,
Without more wider and more overt test
Than these thin habits and poor likelihoods
Of modern seeming do prefer against him.

   FIRST SENATOR.   But, Othello, speak.   110
Did you by indirect and forced courses
Subdue and poison this young maid's affections?
Or came it by request and such fair question
As soul to soul affordeth?

   OTHELLO.   I do beseech you,
Send for the lady to the Sagittary,   115
And let her speak of me before her father.
If you do find me foul in her report,
The trust, the office I do hold of you,
Not only take away, but let your sentence
Even fall upon my life.

   DUKE.   Fetch Desdemona hither.   120

                      Exeunt two or three.

   OTHELLO.   Ancient, conduct them; you best know
     the place.   *Exit* IAGO.
And, till she come, as truly as to heaven
I do confess the vices of my blood,
So justly to your grave ears I'll present

---

95 her motion . . . herself *the slightest cause made her blush* / 97 credit
reputation / 102 practices *evil devices* / 105 conjur'd *compounded
with magic* / 108 habits *clothes, i.e., evidence* / 108 poor *unconvinc-
ing* / 109 modern seeming *slight suspicion* / 111 forced *unnatural*
/ 113 question *speech*

How I did thrive in this fair lady's love,   125
And she in mine.
     DUKE.   Say it, Othello.
     OTHELLO.   Her father lov'd me, oft invited me;
Still question'd me the story of my life
From year to year, the battles, sieges, fortunes,   130
That I have pass'd.
I ran it through, even from my boyish days,
To th' very moment that he bade me tell it.
Wherein I spoke of most disastrous chances,
Of moving accidents by flood and field,   135
Of hair-breadth scapes i' th' imminent deadly breach,
Of being taken by the insolent foe
And sold to slavery, of my redemption thence,
And portance in my travel's history;
Wherein of antres vast and deserts idle,   140
Rough quarries, rocks, and hills whose heads touch heaven,
It was my hint to speak,—such was my process,—
And of the Cannibals that each other eat,
The Anthropophagi, and men whose heads
Do grow beneath their shoulders. This to hear   145
Would Desdemona seriously incline;
But still the house-affairs would draw her thence,
Which ever as she could with haste dispatch,
She'd come again, and with a greedy ear
Devour up my discourse. Which I observing,   150
Took once a pliant hour, and found good means
To draw from her a prayer of earnest heart
That I would all my pilgrimage dilate,
Whereof by parcels she had something heard,
But not intentively. I did consent,   155
And often did beguile her of her tears
When I did speak of some distressful stroke
That my youth suffer'd. My story being done,

---

129 Still *continually* / 135 accidents *adventures* / 135 flood *sea* / 139 portance *my conduct* / 140 antres *caves* / 140 idle *uninhabited* / 142 hint *occasion* / 142 process *narrative* / 144 Anthropophagi *man-eaters* / 151 pliant *suitable* / 153 pilgrimage *wanderings (also, the Christian concept of man's life as a pilgrimage)* / 155 intentively *without distractions*

She gave me for my pains a world of sighs.
She swore, in faith, 'twas strange, 'twas passing strange,   160
'Twas pitiful, 'twas wondrous pitiful.
She wish'd she had not heard it; yet she wish'd
That Heaven had made her such a man. She thank'd me,
And bade me, if I had a friend that lov'd her,
I should but teach him how to tell my story,   165
And that would woo her. Upon this hint I spake.
She lov'd me for the dangers I had pass'd,
And I lov'd her that she did pity them.
This only is the witchcraft I have us'd.
Here comes the lady; let her witness it.   170

Enter DESDEMONA, IAGO, *and* ATTENDANTS.

DUKE.   I think this tale would win my daughter too.
Good Brabantio,
Take up this mangled matter at the best;
Men do their broken weapons rather use
Than their bare hands.
BRABANTIO.   I pray you, hear her speak.   175
If she confess that she was half the wooer,
Destruction on my head, if my bad blame
Light on the man! Come hither, gentle mistress.
Do you perceive in all this noble company
Where most you owe obedience?
DESDEMONA.   My noble father,   180
I do perceive here a divided duty.
To you I am bound for life and education;
My life and education both do learn me
How to respect you; you are lord of all my duty;
I am hitherto your daugher. But here's my husband;   185
And so much duty as my mother show'd
To you, preferring you before her father,
So much I challenge that I may profess
Due to the Moor, my lord.
BRABANTIO.   God be with you! I have done.

---

160 passing *surpassingly* / 166 hint *opportunity* (*not, direct suggestion*)
/ 173 mangled *confused* / 173 at the best *and make the best of it* /
183 learn *teach* / 187 preferring . . . before *placing you ahead of /*
188 challenge *claim the right*

Please it your Grace, on to the state-affairs.   190
I had rather to adopt a child than get it.
Come hither, Moor.
I here do give thee that with all my heart
Which, but thou hast already, with all my heart
I would keep from thee. For your sake, jewel,   195
I am glad at soul I have no other child;
For thy escape would teach me tyranny,
To hang clogs on them. I have done, my lord.
   DUKE.   Let me speak like yourself, and lay a sentence,
Which, as a grise or step, may help these lovers   200
Into your favor.
When remedies are past, the griefs are ended
By seeing the worst, which late on hopes depended.
To mourn a mischief that is past and gone
Is the next way to draw new mischief on.   205
What cannot be preserv'd when Fortune takes,
Patience her injury a mockery makes.
The robb'd that smiles steals something from the thief;
He robs himself that spends a bootless grief.
   BRABANTIO.   So let the Turk of Cyprus us beguile;   210
We lose it not, so long as we can smile.
He bears the sentence well that nothing bears
But the free comfort which from thence he hears,
But he bears both the sentence and the sorrow
That, to pay grief, must of poor patience borrow.   215
These sentences, to sugar, or to gall,
Being strong on both sides, are equivocal.
But words are words; I never yet did hear
That the bruis'd heart was pierced through the ear.
I humbly beseech you, proceed to th' affairs of state.   220
   DUKE.   The Turk with a most mighty preparation makes
for Cyprus. Othello, the fortitude of the place is best known
to you; and though we have there a substitute of most allowed

---

191 get *beget* / 198 clogs *weights* / 199 like yourself *as you ought* /
199 sentence *philosophical maxim* / 200 grise *step* / 203 depended *were
supported* / 205 next *nearest* / 209 bootless *unavailing* / 217 equivocal
ambiguous / 219 pierced *reached* / 223 substitute *deputy commander*
(*Montano*)

sufficiency, yet opinion, a sovereign mistress of effects, throws
a more safer voice on you. You must therefore be content to   225
slubber the gloss of your new fortunes with this more stubborn and boisterous expedition.

OTHELLO.   The tyrant custom, most grave senators,
Hath made the flinty and steel couch of war
My thrice-driven bed of down. I do agnize   230
A natural and prompt alacrity
I find in hardness, and do undertake
These present wars against the Ottomites.
Most humbly therefore bending to your state,
I crave fit disposition for my wife,   235
Due reference of place and exhibition,
With such accommodation and besort
As levels with her breeding.

DUKE.   If you please,
Be 't at her father's.

BRABANTIO.   I'll not have it so.

OTHELLO.   Nor I.

DESDEMONA.   Nor I; I would not there reside,   240
To put my father in impatient thoughts
By being in his eye. Most gracious duke,
To my unfolding lend your prosperous ear;
And let me find a charter in your voice,
T' assist my simpleness.   245

DUKE.   What would you, Desdemona?

DESDEMONA.   That I did love the Moor to live with him,
My downright violence and storm of fortunes
May trumpet to the world. My heart's subdued
Even to the very quality of my lord: 250
I saw Othello's visage in his mind,
And to his honors and his valiant parts
Did I my soul and fortunes consecrate.

---

224 sufficiency *ability* / 224 opinion *public opinion* / 224 effects *results* / 225 more safer voice *vote of greater confidence* / 226 slubber
tarnish / 230 driven *sifted* / 230 agnize *acknowledge* / 231 prompt
alacrity *spontaneous stimulus* / 232 hardness *hardship* / 236 exhibition *allowance (of money)* / 237 besort *attendants* / 238 levels with
suits / 243 unfolding *plan* / 243 prosperous *favorable* / 244 charter
permission / 248 storm of fortunes *taking my future in my own hands*
/ 250 quality *profession*

So that, dear lords, if I be left behind,
A moth of peace, and he go to the war,   255
The rites for why I love him are bereft me,
And I a heavy interim shall support
By his dear absence. Let me go with him.
     OTHELLO.   Let her have your voice.
Vouch for me, Heaven, I therefore beg it not   260
To please the palate of my appetite,
Nor to comply with heat the young affects—
In me defunct—and proper satisfaction;
But to be free and bounteous to her mind.
And Heaven defend your good souls, that you think   265
I will your serious and great business scant
When she is with me. No, when light-wing'd toys
Of feather'd Cupid seel with wanton dullness
My speculative and offic'd instruments
That my disports corrupt and taint my business,   270
Let housewives make a skillet of my helm,
And all indign and base adversities
Make head against my estimation!
     DUKE.   Be it as you shall privately determine,
Either for her stay or going. Th' affair cries haste,   275
And speed must answer it.
     FIRST SENATOR.   You must away to-night.
     DESDEMONA.   To-night, my lord!
     DUKE.   This night
     OTHELLO.   With all my heart.
     DUKE.   At nine i' th' morning here we'll meet again.
Othello, leave some officer behind,
And he shall our commission bring to you,   280
And such things else of quality and respect
As doth import you.
     OTHELLO.   So please your Grace, my ancient;
A man he is of honesty and trust.
To his conveyance I assign my wife,

---

255 moth *parasite* / 257 heavy interim *sad interval* / 262 young affects *youthful passions* / 263 defunct *mortified* / 263 proper *my own* / 265 defend *forbid* / 267 toys *trifles* / 268 seel *close up* / 269 speculative . . . instruments *power of sight and action* / 272 indign *unworthy* / 273 make head against *attack* / 284 conveyance *escort*

With what else needful your good Grace shall think   285
To be sent after me.
   DUKE.   Let it be so.
Good-night to every one. [*To* BRABANTIO.] And noble signior,
If virtue no delighted beauty lack,
Your son-in-law is far more fair than black.
   FIRST SENATOR.   Adieu, brave Moor; use Desdemona well.   290
   BRABANTIO.   Look to her, Moor, if thou hast eyes to see;
She has deceiv'd her father, and may thee.
           Exeunt DUKE, BRABANTIO, SENATORS, OFFICERS, *etc.*
   OTHELLO.   My life upon her faith! Honest Iago,
My Desdemona must I leave to thee.
I prithee, let thy wife attend on her;   295
And bring them after in the best advantage.
Come, Desdemona; I have but an hour
Of love, of worldly matters and direction,
To spend with thee. We must obey the time.
           Exeunt OTHELLO *and* DESDEMONA.
   RODERIGO.   Iago,—   300
   IAGO.   What say'st thou, noble heart?
   RODERIGO.   What will I do, think'st thou?
   IAGO.   Why, go to bed, and sleep.
   RODERIGO.   I will incontinently drown myself.
   IAGO.   If thou dost, I shall never love thee after. Why, thou   305
silly gentleman!
   RODERIGO.   It is silliness to live when to live is torment;
and then have we a prescription to die when Death is our
physician.
   IAGO.   O villainous! I have looked upon the world for four
times seven years; and since I could distinguish betwixt a   310
benefit and an injury, I never found man that knew how to
love himself. Ere I would say I would drown myself for the
love of a guinea-hen, I would change my humanity with a
baboon.   315
   RODERIGO.   What should I do? I confess it is my shame to
be so fond, but it is not in my virtue to amend it.
   IAGO.   Virtue! a fig! 'tis in ourselves that we are thus or
thus. Our bodies are our gardens, to the which our wills are

---

296 best advantage *first opportunity* / 298 of *stolen from* / 304 incontinently *straightway* / 314 change *exchange* / 317 fond *foolish*

gardeners; so that if we will plant nettles, or sow lettuce, set 320
hyssop and weed up thyme, supply it with one gender of
herbs, or distract it with many, either to have it sterile with
idleness, or manured with industry, why, the power and cor-
rigible authority of this lies in our wills. If the balance of our
lives had not one scale of reason to poise another of sensual- 325
ity, the blood and baseness of our natures would conduct us to
most preposterous conclusions. But we have reason to cool
our raging motions, our carnal stings, our unbitted lusts,
whereof I take this that you call love to be a sect or scion.

RODERIGO.   It cannot be. 330

IAGO.   It is merely a lust of the blood and a permission of
the will. Come, be a man. Drown thyself? drown cats and
blind puppies. I have professed me thy friend, and I confess
me knit to thy deserving with cables of perdurable tough-
ness; I could never better stead thee than now. Put money 335
in thy purse; follow thou the wars; defeat thy favor with an
usurped beard. I say, put money in thy purse. It cannot be
long that Desdemona should continue her love to the Moor,—
put money in thy purse,—nor he his to her. It was a violent
commencement in her, and thou shalt see an answerable se- 340
questration: put but money in thy purse. These Moors are
changeable in their wills;—fill thy purse with money;—the
food that to him now is as luscious as locusts, shall be to him
shortly as bitter as coloquintida. She must change for youth;
when she is sated with his body, she will find the error of 345
her choice—she must have change, she must—therefore put
money in thy purse. If thou wilt needs damn thyself, do it a
more delicate way than drowning. Make all the money thou
canst. If sanctimony and a frail vow betwixt an erring bar-
barian and a super-subtle Venetian be not too hard for my 350
wits and all the tribe of hell, thou shalt enjoy her; therefore
make money. A pox of drowning thyself! it is clean out of

---

321 gender *species* / 322 distract it with *divide it among* / 325 poise
balance / 327 conclusions *results* / 328 unbitted *uncontrolled* / 329
sect or scion *cutting or graft* / 334 perdurable *very hard* / 335 stead
serve / 336 defeat . . . beard *disguise your face by growing a beard* /
340 answerable sequestration *equally abrupt separation* / 343 locusts
some kind of fruit / 344 coloquintida *bitter medicine* / 348 Make all
change everything into

the way. Seek thou rather to be hanged in compassing thy joy
than to be drowned and go without her.

RODERIGO.   Wilt thou be fast to my hopes, if I depend on   355
the issue?

IAGO.   Thou art sure of me—go, make money—I have told
thee often, and I re-tell thee again and again, I hate the Moor.
My cause is hearted; thine hath no less reason. Let us be conjunctive in our revenge against him. If thou canst cuckold   360
him, thou dost thyself a pleasure, me a sport. There are many
events in the womb of time which will be delivered. Traverse!
go, provide thy money. We will have more of this to-morrow.
Adieu.

RODERIGO.   Where shall we meet i' th' morning?   365
IAGO.   At my lodging.
RODERIGO.   I'll be with thee betimes.
IAGO.   Go to; farewell. Do you hear, Roderigo?
RODERIGO.   What say you?
IAGO.   No more of drowning, do you hear?   370
RODERIGO.   I am chang'd; I'll go sell all my land.

                                                        Exit.

IAGO.   Thus do I ever make my fool my purse;
For I mine own gain'd knowledge should profane
If I would time expend with such a snipe
But for my sport and profit. I hate the Moor;   375
And it is thought abroad that 'twixt my sheets
He has done my office. I know not if 't be true;
But I, for mere suspicion in that kind,
Will do as if for surety. He holds me well;
The better shall my purpose work on him.   380
Cassio's a proper man. Let me see now:
To get his place and to plume up my will
In double knavery—How, how?—Let's see:—
After some time, to abuse Othello's ear
That he is too familiar with his wife.   385
He hath a person and a smooth dispose

---

353 hanged *i.e., for seduction* / 353 compassing *achieving* / 359 hearted
heartfelt / 359 conjunctive *united* / 362 Traverse *forward march!* /
367 betimes *early* / 374 snipe *silly fellow* / 376 thought abroad *ru-
mored* / 379 for surety *it were a proved fact* / 382 plume up *gratify* /
386 smooth dispose *easy way*

To be suspected, fram'd to make women false.
The Moor is of a free and open nature
That thinks men honest that but seem to be so,
And will as tenderly be led by th' nose   390
As asses are.
I have't. It is engender'd. Hell and night
Must bring this monstrous birth to the world's light.

Exit.

[ACT II · 1] *A sea-port in Cyprus. An open place.*

Enter MONTANO *and two* GENTLEMEN.

MONTANO.   What from the cape can you discern at sea?
FIRST GENTLEMAN.   Nothing at all; it is a high-wrought
    flood.
I cannot, 'twixt the heaven and the main,
Descry a sail.
MONTANO.   Methinks the wind hath spoke aloud at land;   5
A fuller blast ne'er shook our battlements,
If it hath ruffian'd so upon the sea,
What ribs of oak, when mountains melt on them,
Can hold the mortise? What shall we hear of this?
SECOND GENTLEMAN.   A segregation of the Turkish fleet.   10
For do but stand upon the foaming shore,
The chidden billow seems to pelt the clouds;
The wind-shak'd surge, with high and monstrous mane,
Seems to cast water on the burning Bear
And quench the Guards of th' ever-fixed pole.   15
I never did like molestation view
On the enchafèd flood.
MONTANO.   If that the Turkish fleet
Be not enshelter'd and embay'd, they are drown'd;
It is impossible to bear it out.

Enter a third GENTLEMAN.

---

390 tenderly *easily* / 392 engender'd *conceived*
   [ACT II · 1] 9 hold the mortise *remain joined together* / 10 segregation *dispersal* / 14 Bear *Ursa Major, a constellation* / 15 Guards *stars
in Ursa Major* / 17 enchafed *enraged* / 19 bear it out *weather the
storm*

THIRD GENTLEMAN.   News, lads! our wars are done.   20
The desperate tempest hath so bang'd the Turks,
That their designment halts. A noble ship of Venice
Hath seen a grievous wreck and sufferance
On most part of their fleet.
    MONTANO.   How? is this true?
    THIRD GENTLEMAN.   The ship is here put in,   25
A Veronesa. Michael Cassio,
Lieutenant to the warlike Moor Othello,
Is come on shore; the Moor himself at sea,
And is in full commission here for Cyprus.
    MONTANO.   I am glad on't; 'tis a worthy governor.   30
    THIRD GENTLEMAN.   But this same Cassio, though he
        speak of comfort
Touching the Turkish loss, yet he looks sadly,
And prays the Moor be safe; for they were parted
With foul and violent tempest.
    MONTANO.   Pray heavens he be;
For I have serv'd him, and the man commands   35
Like a full soldier. Let's to the seaside, ho!
As well to see the vessel that's come in
As to throw out our eyes for brave Othello,
Even till we make the main and th' aerial blue
An indistinct regard.
    THIRD GENTLEMAN.   Come, let's do so;   40
For every minute is expectancy
Of more arrivance.

Enter CASSIO.

    CASSIO.   Thanks, you the valiant of this warlike isle,
That so approve the Moor! O, let the heavens
Give him defense against the elements,   45
For I have lost him on a dangerous sea.
    MONTANO.   Is he well shipp'd?
    CASSIO.   His bark is stoutly timber'd, and his pilot
Of every expert and approv'd allowance;

---

22 designment halts *plan is checked* / 23 sufferance *disaster* / 29 in
. . . commission *with full powers* / 36 full *perfect* / 38 Even till . . .
regard *until we can no longer distinguish between the blue of the water
and the blue of the sky* / 42 arrivance *arrivals* / 49 approv'd allowance
tested skill

Therefore my hopes, not surfeited to death,   50
Stand in bold cure.
                    Within, "A sail, a sail, a sail!"

                        Enter a MESSENGER.

CASSIO.   What noise?
MESSENGER.   The town is empty; on the brow o' th' sea
Stand ranks of people, and they cry, "A sail!"
CASSIO.   My hopes do shape him for the governor.   55
                                                A shot.

SECOND GENTLEMAN.   They do discharge their shot
    of courtesy:
Our friends at least.
CASSIO.   I pray you, sir, go forth,
And give us truth who 'tis that is arriv'd.
SECOND GENTLEMAN.   I shall.   *Exit.*
MONTANO.   But, good lieutenant, is your general wiv'd?   60
CASSIO.   Most fortunately: he hath achiev'd a maid
That paragons description and wild fame;
One that excels the quirks of blazoning pens,
And in th' essential vesture of creation
Does tire the ingener.

                    Re-enter second GENTLEMAN.

                    How now? who has put in?   65
SECOND GENTLEMAN.   'Tis one Iago, ancient to the general.
CASSIO.   Has had most favorable and happy speed.
Tempests themselves, high seas, and howling winds,
The gutter'd rocks and congregated sands,
Traitors ensteep'd to clog the guiltless keel,   70
As having sense of beauty do omit
Their mortal natures, letting go safely by
The divine Desdemona.
MONTANO.   What is she?
CASSIO.   She that I spake of, our great captain's captain,

---

50 surfeited *sickened* / 51 bold *confident expectation of* / 62 paragons
surpasses / 63 quirks *elegant phrases* / 64 essential . . . of creation *her*
absolute perfection / 65 ingener *inventor, i.e., artist that could paint her*
as she truly is / 70 ensteep'd *submerged* / 71 omit *surrender temporar-*
ily / 72 mortal *deadly*

Left in the conduct of the bold Iago,   75
Whose footing here anticipates our thoughts
A se'nnight's speed. Great Jove, Othello guard,
And swell his sail with thine own powerful breath,
That he may bless this bay with his tall ship,
Make love's quick pants in Desdemona's arms,   80
Give renew'd fire to our extincted spirits,
And bring all Cyprus comfort!

> *Enter* DESDEMONA, EMILIA, IAGO, RODERIGO, *and* ATTENDANTS.

                      O, behold,
The riches of the ship is come on shore!
You men of Cyprus, let her have your knees.
Hail to thee, lady! and the grace of heaven,   85
Before, behind thee, and on every hand,
Enwheel thee round!
    DESDEMONA.   I thank you, valiant Cassio.
What tidings can you tell me of my lord?
    CASSIO.   He is not yet arriv'd; nor know I aught
But that he's well and will be shortly here.   90
    DESDEMONA.   O, but I fear—How lost you company?
    CASSIO.   The great contention of the sea and skies
Parted our fellowship.—But, hark! a sail.
                  Within, "A sail, a sail!" *Guns heard.*
    SECOND GENTLEMAN.   They give their greeting to
        the citadel:
This likewise is a friend.
    CASSIO.   See for the news.   95
                        Exit GENTLEMAN.
Good ancient, you are welcome. [*To* EMILIA.] Welcome,
    mistress.
Let it not gall your patience, good Iago,
That I extend my manners; 'tis my breeding
That gives me this bold show of courtesy.   *Kissing her.*
    IAGO.   Sir, would she give you so much of her lips   100
As of her tongue she oft bestows on me,
You'd have enough.
    DESDEMONA.   Alas, she has no speech.

---

76 footing *landing* / 77 se'nnight's *week's* / 81 extincted *extinguished*
/ 87 Enwheel *encompass* / 98 extend *show*

IAGO. In faith, too much;
I find it still, when I have list to sleep.
Marry, before your ladyship, I grant,   105
She puts her tongue a little in her heart,
And chides with thinking.
     EMILIA. You have little cause to say so.
     IAGO. Come on, come on; you are pictures out of doors,
Bells in your parlors, wild-cats in your kitchens,   110
Saints in your injuries, devils being offended,
Players in your housewifery, and housewives in your beds.
     DESDEMONA. O, fie upon thee, slanderer!
     IAGO. Nay, it is true, or else I am a Turk.
You rise to play and go to bed to work.   115
     EMILIA. You shall not write my praise.
     IAGO.   No, let me not.
     DESDEMONA. What wouldst thou write of me, if thou
         shouldst praise me?
     IAGO. O gentle lady, do not put me to 't;
For I am nothing, if not critical.   120
     DESDEMONA. Come on, assay.—There's one gone to
         the harbor?
     IAGO. Ay, madam.
     DESDEMONA. I am not merry; but I do beguile
The thing I am, by seeming otherwise.—
Come, how wouldst thou praise me?
     IAGO. I am about it; but indeed my invention   125
Comes from my pate as birdlime does from frieze;
It plucks out brains and all. But my Muse labors,
And thus she is deliver'd:

         If she be fair and wise, fairness and wit,
         The one's for use, the other useth it.   130

     DESDEMONA. Well prais'd! How if she be black and witty?
     IAGO.   If she be black, and thereto have a wit,
         She'll find a white that shall her blackness fit.

     DESDEMONA. Worse and worse.
     EMILIA. How if fair and foolish?   135

---

104 list *desire* / 110 Bells *sweet-voiced* / 112 housewives *hussies* / 120
critical *censorious* / 126 frieze *cloth with a nap* / 133 white *with a pun
on wight, man*

IAGO.   She never yet was foolish that was fair;
             For even her folly help'd her to an heir.

DESDEMONA.   These are old fond paradoxes to make fools
laugh i' th' alehouse. What miserable praise hast thou for her
that's foul and foolish?   140
IAGO.   There's none so foul and foolish thereunto,
             But does foul pranks which fair and wise ones
                 do.

DESDEMONA.   O heavy ignorance! thou praisest the worst
best. But what praise couldst thou bestow on a deserving
woman indeed, one that, in the authority of her merit, did   145
justly put on the vouch of very malice itself?
IAGO.   She that was ever fair and never proud,
             Had tongue at will and yet was never loud,
             Never lack'd gold and yet went never gay,
             Fled from her wish and yet said, "Now I   150
                 may";
             She that being anger'd, her revenge being
                 nigh,
             Bade her wrong stay and her displeasure fly;
             She that in wisdom never was so frail
             To change the cod's head for the salmon's
                 tail;
             She that could think and ne'er disclose her   155
                 mind
             See suitors following and not look behind,
             She was a wight, if ever such wights were,—

DESDEMONA.   To do what?
IAGO.   To suckle fools and chronicle small beer.

DESDEMONA.   O most lame and impotent conclusion! Do   160
not learn of him, Emilia, though he be thy husband. How say
you, Cassio? Is he not a most profane and liberal counsellor?
CASSIO.   He speaks home, madam. You may relish him

---

137 folly *foolishness and unchastity* / 138 fond *silly* / 140 foul *ugly* /
146 put on the vouch *demand praise* / 151 nigh *readily obtainable* /
154 To change . . . tail *to exchange the worthless part of a cheap fish
for the worthless part of an expensive one* / 159 chronicle small beer
keep household accounts / 162 liberal *licentious* / 163 home *to the
point* / 163 relish *like*

more in the soldier than in the scholar.

IAGO.   [*Aside*.] He takes her by the palm; ay, well said,   165
whisper. With as little a web as this will I ensnare as great a
fly as Cassio. Ay, smile upon her, do; I will gyve thee in thine
own courtship.—You say true; 'tis so, indeed.—If such tricks
as these strip you out of your lieutenantry, it had been better
you had not kissed your three fingers so oft, which now again   170
you are most apt to play the sir in. Very good; well kissed!
an excellent curtsy! 'Tis so, indeed. Yet again your fingers to
your lips? Would they were clyster-pipes for your sake!
[*Trumpet within*.]—The Moor! I know his trumpet.

CASSIO.   'Tis truly so.   175

DESDEMONA.   Let's meet him and receive him.

CASSIO.   Lo, where he comes!

Enter OTHELLO *and Attendants*.

OTHELLO.   O my fair warrior!

DESDEMONA.   My dear Othello!

OTHELLO.   It gives me wonder great as my content
To see you here before me. O my soul's joy!   180
If after every tempest come such calms,
May the winds blow till they have waken'd death!
And let the laboring bark climb hills of seas
Olympus-high, and duck again as low
As hell's from heaven! If it were now to die,   185
'Twere now to be most happy; for, I fear,
My soul hath her content so absolute
That not another comfort like to this
Succeeds in unknown fate.

DESDEMONA.   The heavens forbid
But that our loves and comforts should increase,   190
Even as our days do grow!

OTHELLO.   Amen to that, sweet powers!
I cannot speak enough of this content;
It stops me here; it is too much of joy.
And this, and this, the greatest discords be

They kiss.

---

167 gyve *handcuff* / 170 kissed your three fingers *a courtly gesture* /
173 clyster *enema* / 184 Olympus *mountain in Greece* / 193 here *in
the heart*

That e'er our hearts shall make!   195
    IAGO.   [*Aside.*] O, you are well tun'd now!
But I'll set down the pegs that make this music,
As honest as I am.
    OTHELLO.   Come, let us to the castle.
News, friends; our wars are done, the Turks are drown'd.
How does my old acquaintance of this isle?   200
Honey, you shall be well desir'd in Cyprus;
I have found great love amongst them. O my sweet,
I prattle out of fashion, and I dote
In mine own comforts. I prithee, good Iago,
Go to the bay and disembark my coffers.   205
Bring thou the master to the citadel;
He is a good one, and his worthiness
Does challenge much respect. Come, Desdemona,
Once more, well met at Cyprus.
        Exeunt OTHELLO, DESDEMONA *and* ATTENDANTS.
    IAGO.   Do thou meet me presently at the harbor. Come   210
hither. If thou be'st valiant,—as, they say, base men being in
love have then a nobility in their natures more than is native
to them,—list me. The lieutenant tonight watches on the
court of guard;—first, I must tell thee this: Desdemona is directly in love with him.   215
    RODERIGO.   With him? Why, 'tis not possible.
    IAGO.   Lay thy finger thus, and let thy soul be instructed.
Mark me with what violence she first loved the Moor, but for
bragging and telling her fantastical lies. To love him still for
prating,—let not thy discreet heart think it. Her eye must be 220
fed; and what delight shall she have to look on the devil?
When the blood is made dull with the act of sport, there
should be, again to inflame it, and to give satiety a fresh
appetite, loveliness in favor, sympathy in years, manners, and
beauties; all which the Moor is defective in. Now, for want of 225
these required conveniences, her delicate tenderness will find
itself abused, begin to heave the gorge, disrelish and abhor the

---

197 set down the pegs *untune the strings of a musical instrument* / 204
In *on account of* / 206 master *ship's captain* / 210 presently *immediately* / 214 court *headquarters* / 217 thus *i.e., on the lips* (*be silent*) /
219 still *forever* / 221 devil *in popular art the devil was represented as
black* / 224 favor *features* / 227 heave the gorge *retch*

Moor; very nature will instruct her in it and compel her to
some second choice. Now, sir, this granted,—as it is a most
pregnant and unforced position—who stands so eminent in   230
the degree of this fortune as Cassio does? a knave very vol-
uble; no further conscionable than in putting on the mere
form of civil and humane seeming, for the better compassing
of his salt and most hidden loose affection? Why, none; why,
none; a slipper and subtle knave, a finder of occasion, that   235
has an eye can stamp and counterfeit advantages, though true
advantage never present itself; a devilish knave. Besides, the
knave is handsome, young, and hath all those requisites in
him that folly and green minds look after; a pestilent com-
plete knave, and the woman hath found him already.   240

RODERIGO. I cannot believe that in her; she's full of most
blessed condition.

IAGO. Blessed fig's-end! The wine she drinks is made of
grapes. If she had been blessed, she would never have loved
the Moor. Blessed pudding! Didst thou not see her paddle   245
with the palm of his hand? Didst not mark that?

RODERIGO. Yes, that I did; but that was but courtesy.

IAGO. Lechery, by this hand; an index and obscure pro-
logue to the history of lust and foul thoughts. They met so
near with their lips that their breaths embraced together, Vil- 250
lainous thoughts, Roderigo! When these mutualities so mar-
shal the way, hard at hand comes the master and main exercise, th' incorporate conclusion. Pish! But, sir, be you ruled
by me; I have brought you from Venice. Watch you to-night;
for the command, I'll lay 't upon you. Cassio knows you not. 255
I'll not be far from you. Do you find some occasion to anger
Cassio, either by speaking too loud, or tainting his discipline,
or from what other course you please, which the time shall
more favorably minister.

RODERIGO. Well?   260

IAGO. Sir, he's rash and very sudden in choler, and haply

---

230 pregnant *obvious* / 232 conscionable *conscientious* / 234 salt *lustful* / 235 slipper *slippery* / 236 stamp *devise by craft* / 239 green *un-
sophisticated* / 242 blessed condition *heavenly qualities* / 248 index
forerunner / 251 mutualities *reciprocal familiarities* / 253 incorporate
bodily / 255 the command *your orders* / 259 minister *provide* / 261
choler *anger* / 261 haply *perhaps*

may strike at you. Provoke him, that he may; for even out
of that will I cause these of Cyprus to mutiny, whose qualification shall come into no true taste again but by the dis-
planting of Cassio. So shall you have a shorter journey to your   265
desires by the means I shall then have to prefer them; and
the impediment most profitably removed, without the which
there were no expectation of our prosperity.

    RODERIGO.   I will do this, if you can bring it to any oppor-
tunity.   270

    IAGO.   I warrant thee. Meet me by and by at the citadel;
I must fetch his necessaries ashore. Farewell.

    RODERIGO.   Adieu.   *Exit.*

    IAGO.   That Cassio loves her, I do well believe 't;
That she loves him, 'tis apt and of great credit;   275
The Moor, howbeit that I endure him not,
Is of a constant, loving, noble nature,
And I dare think he'll prove to Desdemona
A most dear husband. Now, I do love her too;
Not out of absolute lust, though peradventure   280
I stand accountant for as great a sin,
But partly led to diet my revenge,
For that I do suspect the lusty Moor
Hath leap'd into my seat; the thought whereof
Doth, like a poisonous mineral, gnaw my inwards;   285
And nothing can or shall content my soul
Till I am even'd with him, wife for wife;
Or failing so, yet that I put the Moor
At least into a jealousy so strong
That judgment cannot cure. Which thing to do,   290
If this poor trash of Venice, whom I trash
For his quick hunting, stand the putting on,
I'll have our Michael Cassio on the hip,
Abuse him to the Moor in the rank garb—
For I fear Cassio with my night-cap too—   295
Make the Moor thank me, love me, and reward me,

---

263 qualification *appeasement* / 264 come . . . taste *not be attained*
/ 266 prefer *promote* / 275 apt . . . credit *probable and credible* /
281 accountant *accountable* / 282 diet *feed* / 290 judgment *reason* /
291 trash For *hold back from* / 294 rank garb *coarse fashion*

For making him egregiously an ass
And practicing upon his peace and quiet
Even to madness. 'Tis here, but yet confus'd;
Knavery's plain face is never seen till us'd.   *Exit.*   300

[ACT II · 2] *A street.*

Enter Othello's HERALD, *with a proclamation.*
People following.

HERALD.   It is Othello's pleasure, our noble and valiant
general, that, upon certain tidings now arrived importing the
mere perdition of the Turkish fleet, every man put himself
into triumph; some to dance, some to make bonfires, each
man to what sport and revels his addiction leads him; for, be-   5
side these beneficial news, it is the celebration of his nuptial.
So much was his pleasure should be proclaimed. All offices
are open, and there is full liberty of feasting from this present
hour of five till the bell have told eleven. Heaven bless the isle
of Cyprus and our noble general Othello!   *Exeunt.*   10

[ACT II · 3] *A hall in the castle.*

Enter OTHELLO, DESDEMONA, CASSIO, *and* ATTENDANTS.

OTHELLO.   Good Michael, look you to the guard to-night.
Let's teach ourselves that honorable stop,
Not to outsport discretion.
CASSIO.   Iago hath direction what to do;
But, notwithstanding, with my personal eye   5
Will I look to 't.
OTHELLO.   Iago is most honest.
Michael, good-night; to-morrow with your earliest
Let me have speech with you. [*To* DESDEMONA.] Come, my
        dear love,
The purchase made, the fruits are to ensue;
That profit's yet to come 'tween me and you.   10
Good-night.

---

297 egregiously *notably* / 298 practising upon *plotting against* / 299
here *i.e., in Iago's brain*
    [ACT II · 2] 3 mere *complete* / 7 offices *places to supply food **and**
drink* / 9 told *counted*
    [ACT II · 3] 3 outsport discretion *overdo revelry*

Exeunt OTHELLO, DESDEMONA, *and* ATTENDANTS.

Enter IAGO.

CASSIO.   Welcome, Iago; we must to the watch.

IAGO.   Not this hour, lieutenant; 'tis not yet ten o' th'
clock. Our general cast us thus early for the love of his Desdemona; who let us not therefore blame: he hath not yet   15
made wanton the night with her; and she is sport for Jove.

CASSIO.   She's a most exquisite lady.

IAGO.   And, I'll warrant her, full of game.

CASSIO.   Indeed, she's a most fresh and delicate creature.

IAGO.   What an eye she has! Methinks it sounds a parley   20
to provocation.

CASSIO.   An inviting eye; and yet methinks right modest.

IAGO.   And when she speaks, is it not an alarum to love?

CASSIO.   She is indeed perfection.

IAGO.   Well, happiness to their sheets! Come, lieutenant, I   25
have a stoup of wine; and here without are a brace of Cyprus
gallants that would fain have a measure to the health of black
Othello.

CASSIO.   Not to-night, good Iago. I have very poor and unhappy brains for drinking; I could well wish courtesy would   30
invent some other custom of entertainment.

IAGO.   O, they are our friends: but one cup; I'll drink for
you.

CASSIO.   I have drunk but one cup to-night, and that was
craftily qualified too, and, behold, what innovation it makes   35
here. I am unfortunate in the infirmity, and dare not task my
weakness with any more.

IAGO.   What, man! 'tis a night of revels.
The gallants desire it.

CASSIO.   Where are they?   40

IAGO.   Here at the door; I pray you, call them in.

CASSIO.   I'll do 't; but it dislikes me.   *Exit.*

IAGO.   If I can fasten but one cup upon him,
With that which he hath drunk to-night already,
He'll be as full of quarrel and offense   45

---

14 cast *dismissed* / 23 alarum *call to arms, summons* / 26 stoup *large
goblet* / 27 fain *gladly* / 35 craftily qualified *diluted on the sly* / 36
here *i.e., in his face*

As my young mistress' dog. Now, my sick fool Roderigo,
Whom love hath turn'd almost the wrong side out,
To Desdemona hath to-night carous'd
Potations pottle-deep; and he's to watch.
Three lads of Cyprus, noble swelling spirits   50
That hold their honors in a wary distance,
The very elements of this warlike isle,
Have I to-night fluster'd with flowing cups,
And they watch too. Now, 'mongst this flock of drunkards
Am I to put our Cassio in some action   55
That may offend the isle. But here they come.

     Re-enter CASSIO, *with him* MONTANO *and* GENTLEMEN.
             Servants follow with wine.

If consequence do but approve my dream,
My boat sails freely, both with wind and stream.
    CASSIO.   'Fore God, they have given me a rouse already.
    MONTANO.   Good faith, a little one; not past a pint, as I   60
am a soldier.
    IAGO.   Some wine, ho!
Sings.   And let me the canakin clink, clink;
              And let me the canakin clink.
              A soldier's a man;   65
              O, man's life's but a span;
              Why, then, let a soldier drink.

Some wine, boys!
    CASSIO.   'Fore God, an excellent song.
    IAGO.   I learned it in England, where, indeed, they are most 70
potent in pottling; your Dane, your German, and your swag-
bellied Hollander —Drink, ho!—are nothing to your English.
    CASSIO.   Is your Englishman so exquisite in his drinking?
    IAGO.   Why, he drinks you, with facility, your Dane dead
drunk; he sweats not to overthrow your Almain; he gives your 75
Hollander a vomit ere the next pottle can be filled.
    CASSIO.   To the health of our general!

---

48 carous'd *drunk off* / 49 pottle-deep *bottoms-up* / 51 in a wary distance *i.e., are supersensitive* (*about their personal honor*) / 57 consequence *what follows* / 59 rouse *deep drink* / 63 canakin *small drinking
pot* / 71 swag-bellied *"beer-bellied"* / 75 sweats not *does not have to
exert himself* / 75 Almain *German*

MONTANO.   I am for it, lieutenant; and I'll do you justice.
IAGO.   O sweet England!

> King Stephen was and-a worthy peer,   80
> His breeches cost him but a crown;
> He held them sixpence all too dear,
> With that he call'd the tailor lown.

> He was a wight of high renown,
> And thou art but of low degree.   85
> 'Tis pride that pulls the country down;
> And take thy auld cloak about thee.

Some wine, ho!
CASSIO.   Why, this is a more exquisite song than the other.
IAGO.   Will you hear 't again?   90
CASSIO.   No; for I hold him to be unworthy of his place
that does those things. Well, God's above all; and there be
souls must be saved, and there be souls must not be saved.
IAGO.   It's true, good lieutenant.
CASSIO.   For mine own part,—no offense to the general,   95
nor any man of quality—I hope to be saved.
IAGO.   And so do I too, lieutenant.
CASSIO.   Ay, but, by your leave, not before me; the lieu-
tenant is to be saved before the ancient. Let's have no more
of this; let's to our affairs.—God forgive us our sins!—Gen- 100
tlemen, let's look to our business. Do not think, gentlemen, I
am drunk. This is my ancient; this is my right hand, and this
is my left. I am not drunk now; I can stand well enough, and
I speak well enough.
GENTLEMEN.   Excellent well.   105
CASSIO.   Why, very well then; you must not think then that
I am drunk.   *Exit.*
MONTANO.   To th' platform, masters. Come, let's set the
watch.
IAGO.   You see this fellow that is gone before: 110
He is a soldier fit to stand by Caesar
And give direction; and do but see his vice.

---

83 lown *lout* / 86 pride *extravagant dress* / 87 auld *old* / 108 platform *paved court where the guard is mustered*

'Tis to his virtue a just equinox,
The one as long as the other; 'tis pity of him.
I fear the trust Othello puts him in,   115
On some odd time of his infirmity,
Will shake this island.

    MONTANO.   But is he often thus?

    IAGO.   'Tis evermore his prologue to his sleep.
He'll watch the horologe a double set,
If drink rock not his cradle.

    MONTANO.   It were well   120
The general were put in mind of it.
Perhaps he sees it not; or his good nature
Prizes the virtue that appears in Cassio,
And looks not on his evils. Is not this true?

              Enter RODERIGO.

    IAGO.   [*Aside to him.*] How now, Roderigo!   125
I pray you, after the lieutenant; go.

                    Exit RODERIGO.

    MONTANO.   And 'tis great pity that the noble Moor
Should hazard such a place as his own second
With one of an ingraft infirmity:
It were an honest action to say   130
So to the Moor.

    IAGO.   Not I, for this fair island.
I do love Cassio well; and would do much
To cure him of this evil. But, hark! what noise?

            Cry within: "Help! help!"

      Re-enter CASSIO, *pursuing* RODERIGO.

    CASSIO.   'Zounds, you rogue! you rascal!

    MONTANO.   What's the matter, lieutenant?

    CASSIO.   A knave teach me my duty! I'll beat the knave   135
into a twiggen bottle.

    RODERIGO.   Beat me?

    CASSIO.   Dost thou prate, rogue?

             Striking RODERIGO.

---

113 just equinox *exact equivalent* / 116 odd time *time or other* / 119
watch . . . double set *stay awake twenty-four hours* / 129 ingraft *firmly
fixed* / 136 twiggen *wicker-covered*

MONTANO.   Nay, good lieutenant; [*Staying him.*] I pray
you, sir, hold your hand.   140
    CASSIO.   Let me go, sir,
Or I'll knock you o'er the mazzard.
    MONTANO.   Come, come, you're drunk.
    CASSIO.   Drunk!   *They fight.*
    IAGO.   [*Aside to* RODERIGO.] Away, I say; go out, and cry
    a mutiny.   145

Exit RODERIGO.

Nay, good lieutenant,—God's will, gentlemen;—
Help, ho!—Lieutenant,—sir,—Montano,—sir;—
Help, masters!—Here's a goodly watch indeed!

A bell rings.

Who's that which rings the bell?—Diablo, ho!   150
The town will rise. God's will, lieutenant, hold!
You will be sham'd for ever.

Re-enter OTHELLO *and* ATTENDANTS.

    OTHELLO.   What is the matter here?
    MONTANO.   'Zounds, I bleed still; I am hurt to th' death.
    He dies!
    OTHELLO.   Hold, for your lives!
    IAGO.   Hold, ho! Lieutenant,—sir,—Montano,—
    gentlemen,—   155
Have you forgot all sense of place and duty?
Hold! the general speaks to you; hold, for shame!
    OTHELLO.   Why, how now, ho! from whence ariseth this?
Are we turn'd Turks, and to ourselves do that
Which Heaven hath forbid the Ottomites?   160
For Christian shame, put by this barbarous brawl.
He that stirs next to carve for his own rage
Holds his soul light; he dies upon his motion.
Silence that dreadful bell; it frights the isle
From her propriety. What is the matter, masters?   165
Honest Iago, that looks dead with grieving,
Speak, who began this? On thy love, I charge thee.
    IAGO.   I do not know: friends all but now, even now,
In quarter, and in terms like bride and groom

---

141 mazzard *head* / 150 bell *alarm bell* / 150 Diablo *the devil* / 162
carve for *indulge* / 165 propriety *natural behavior* / 169 quarter *amity*

Divesting them for bed; and then, but now—   170
As if some planet had unwitted men—
Swords out, and tilting one at other's breast,
In opposition bloody. I cannot speak
Any beginning to this peevish odds;
And would in action glorious I had lost   175
Those legs that brought me to a part of it!

    OTHELLO.   How comes it, Michael, you are thus forgot?

    CASSIO.   I pray you, pardon me; I cannot speak.

    OTHELLO.   Worthy Montano, you were wont to be civil;
The gravity and stillness of your youth   180
The world hath noted, and your name is great
In mouths of wisest censure. What's the matter,
That you unlace your reputation thus,
And spend your rich opinion for the name
Of a night-brawler? Give me answer to it.   185

    MONTANO.   Worthy Othello, I am hurt to danger.
Your officer, Iago, can inform you—
While I spare speech, which something now offends me—
Of all that I do know; nor know I aught
By me that's said or done amiss this night,   190
Unless self-charity be sometimes a vice,
And to defend ourselves it be a sin
When violence assails us.

    OTHELLO.   Now, by heaven,
My blood begins my safer guides to rule;
And passion, having my best judgment collied,   195
Assays to lead the way. If I once stir
Or do but lift this arm, the best of you
Shall sink in my rebuke. Give me to know
How this foul rout began, who set it on;
And he that is approv'd in this offense,   200
Though he had twinn'd with me, both at a birth,
Shall lose me. What! in a town of war,
Yet wild, the people's hearts brimful of fear,
To manage private and domestic quarrel,

---

171 unwitted men *struck men with madness* / 174 peevish odds *child-ish quarrel* / 177 forgot *forgetful of yourself* / 182 censure *judgment* / 184 spend *lose* / 191 self-charity *care of one's self* / 195 collied *darkened* / 204 manage *engage in*

In night, and on the court and guard of safety!   205
'Tis monstrous. Iago, who began 't?
   MONTANO.   If partially affin'd, or leagued in office,
Thou dost deliver more or less than truth,
Thou art no soldier.
   IAGO.   Touch me not so near.
I had rather have this tongue cut from my mouth   210
Than it should do offense to Michael Cassio;
Yet, I persuade myself, to speak the truth
Shall nothing wrong him. Thus it is, general:
Montano and myself being in speech,
There comes a fellow crying out for help;   215
And Cassio following him with determin'd sword
To execute upon him. Sir, this gentleman
Steps in to Cassio and entreats his pause;
Myself the crying fellow did pursue,
Lest by his clamor—as it so fell out—   220
The town might fall in fright. He, swift of foot,
Outran my purpose; and I return'd the rather
For that I heard the clink and fall of swords,
And Cassio high in oath; which till to-night
I ne'er might say before. When I came back—   225
For this was brief—I found them close together,
At blow and thrust; even as again they were
When you yourself did part them.
More of this matter cannot I report.
But men are men; the best sometimes forget.   230
Though Cassio did some little wrong to him,
As men in rage strike those that wish them best,
Yet surely Cassio, I believe, receiv'd
From him that fled some strange indignity
Which patience could not pass.
   OTHELLO.   I know, Iago,   235
Thy honesty and love doth mince this matter,
Making it light to Cassio. Cassio, I love thee;
But never more be officer of mine.

             Re-enter DESDEMONA, *attended.*

---

207 partially affin'd *influenced by partiality* / **222** rather *sooner* / **235**
patience *self-control* / **235** pass *endure* / **236** mince *extenuate*

Look, if my gentle love be not rais'd up!
I'll make thee an example.

DESDEMONA.   What's the matter, dear?   240

OTHELLO.   All's well now, sweeting; come away to bed.

Sir, [*To* MONTANO], for your hurts, myself will be your sur-
        geon.—

Lead him off.   MONTANO *is led off*.

Iago, look with care about the town,

And silence those whom this vile brawl distracted.   245

Come, Desdemona; 'tis the soldiers' life

To have their balmy slumbers wak'd with strife.

                        Exeunt all but IAGO *and* CASSIO.

IAGO.   What, are you hurt, lieutenant?

CASSIO.   Ay, past all surgery.

IAGO.   Marry, God forbid!   250

CASSIO.   Reputation, reputation, reputation! O, I have lost
my reputation! I have lost the immortal part of myself, and
what remains is bestial. My reputation, Iago, my reputation!

IAGO.   As I am an honest man, I thought you had received
some bodily wound; there is more sense in that than in reputa-   255
tion. Reputation is an idle and most false imposition; oft got
without merit, and lost without deserving. You have lost no
reputation at all, unless you repute yourself such a loser. What,
man! there are more ways to recover the general again. You
are but now cast in his mood, a punishment more in policy   260
than in malice; even so as one would beat his offenseless dog
to affright an imperious lion. Sue to him again, and he's yours.

CASSIO.   I will rather sue to be despised than to deceive so
good a commander with so slight, so drunken, and so indis-
creet an officer. Drunk? and speak parrot? and squabble?   265
swagger? swear? and discourse fustian with one's own
shadow? O thou invisible spirit of wine, if thou hast no name
to be known by, let us call thee devil!

IAGO.   What was he that you followed with your sword?
What had he done to you?   270

CASSIO.   I know not.

---

255 sense *feeling* / 256 imposition *characteristic conferred by others* /
259 recover *win back* / 260 cast in his mood *dismissed because of his
anger* / 265 parrot *without knowing what one says* / 266 fustian *nonsense*

IAGO. Is't possible?

CASSIO. I remember a mass of things, but nothing distinctly; a quarrel, but nothing wherefore. O God, that men should put an enemy in their mouths to steal away their   275
brains! That we should, with joy, pleasance, revel, and applause, transform ourselves into beasts!

IAGO. Why, but you are now well enough. How came you thus recovered?

CASSIO. It hath pleased the devil drunkenness to give place   280
to the devil wrath. One unperfectness shows me another, to make me frankly despise myself.

IAGO. Come, you are too severe a moraler. As the time, the place, and the condition of this country stands, I could heartily wish this had not befallen; but since it is as it is,   285
mend it for your own good.

CASSIO. I will ask him for my place again; he shall tell me I am a drunkard! Had I as many mouths as Hydra, such an answer would stop them all. To be now a sensible man, by and by a fool, and presently a beast! O strange! Every in-   290
ordinate cup is unblessed and the ingredient is a devil.

IAGO. Come, come, good wine is a good familiar creature, if it be well used; exclaim no more against it. And, good lieutenant, I think you think I love you.

CASSIO. I have well approved it, sir. I drunk!   295

IAGO. You or any man living may be drunk at a time, man. I'll tell you what you shall do. Our general's wife is now the general;—I may say so in this respect, for that he hath devoted and given up himself to the contemplation, mark, and denotement of her parts and graces;—confess yourself   300
freely to her; importune her help to put you in your place again. She is of so free, so kind, so apt, so blessed a disposition, she holds it a vice in her goodness not to do more than she is requested. This broken joint between you and her husband entreat her to splinter; and, my fortunes against any lay   305
worth naming, this crack of your love shall grow stronger than it was before.

---

276 pleasance *merry-making* / 283 moraler *moralizer* / 287 shall *inevitably will* / 288 Hydra *a many-headed monster* / 290 inordinate *excessive* / 292 familiar *serviceable* / 300 denotement *observation* / 305 splinter *bind up with splints* / 305 lay *wager*

CASSIO.   You advise me well.

IAGO.   I protest, in the sincerity of love and honest kind-
ness.   310

CASSIO.   I think it freely; and betimes in the morning I will
beseech the virtuous Desdemona to undertake for me. I am
desperate of my fortunes if they check me here.

IAGO.   You are in the right. Good-night, lieutenant; I must
to the watch.   315

CASSIO.   Good-night, honest Iago.   *Exit.*

IAGO.   And what's he then that says I play the villain?
When this advice is free I give and honest,
Probal to thinking and indeed the course
To win the Moor again? For 'tis must easy   320
The inclining Desdemona to subdue
In any honest suit; she's fram'd as fruitful
As the free elements. And then for her
To win the Moor, were't to renounce his baptism,
All seals and symbols of redeemed sin,   325
His soul is so enfetter'd to her love,
That she may make, unmake, do what she list,
Even as her appetite shall play the god
With his weak function. How am I then a villain
To counsel Cassio to this parallel course,   330
Directly to his good? Divinity of hell!
When devils will the blackest sins put on,
They do suggest at first with heavenly shows,
As I do now; for whiles this honest fool
Plies Desdemona to repair his fortunes   335
And she for him pleads strongly to the Moor,
I'll pour this pestilence into his ear,
That she repeals him for her body's lust;
And by how much she strives to do him good,
She shall undo her credit with the Moor.   340
So will I turn her virtue into pitch,
And out of her own goodness make the net
That shall enmesh them all.

---

313 desperate *hopeless* / 313 check me *hold me back* / 319 Probal to
thinking *approved by men of judgment* / 322 fruitful *generous* / 329
weak function *feeble powers* / 333 suggest *tempt* / 338 repeals *would
call back*

Re-enter RODERIGO.

How now, Roderigo!

RODERIGO.   I do follow here in the chase, not like a hound
that hunts, but one that fills up the cry. My money is almost   345
spent; I have been to-night exceedingly well cudgelled; and I
think the issue will be, I shall have so much experience for
my pains; and so, with no money at all and a little more wit,
return again to Venice.

IAGO.   How poor are they that have not patience!   350
What wound did ever heal but by degrees?
Thou know'st we work by wit, and not by witchcraft;
And wit depends on dilatory Time.
Does't not go well? Cassio hath beaten thee,
And thou, by that small hurt, hast cashier'd Cassio.   355
Though other things grow fair against the sun,
Yet fruits that blossom first will first be ripe.
Content thyself a while. By the mass, 'tis morning;
Pleasure and action make the hours seem short.
Retire thee; go where thou art billeted.   360
Away, I say; thou shalt know more hereafter.
Nay, get thee gone. [*Exit* RODERIGO.] Two things are to
     be done:
My wife must move for Cassio to her mistress;
I'll set her on;
Myself the while to draw the Moor apart,   365
And bring him jump when he may Cassio find
Soliciting his wife. Ay, that's the way;
Dull not device by coldness and delay.   *Exit.*

[ACT III · 1] *Before the castle.*

Enter CASSIO, *with* MUSICIANS.

CASSIO.   Masters, play here; I will content your pains;
Something that's brief; and bid "Good morrow, General."

                                             They play.

---

345 cry *pack* / 348 wit *common sense* / 352 wit *clever planning* / 353
dilatory Time *Time, who cannot be hastened* / 355 cashier'd *brought
about the dismissal of* / 363 move *petition* / 366 jump *just* / 368 coldness *lack of energy*

Enter CLOWN.

CLOWN. Why, masters, have your instruments been in
Naples, that they speak i' th' nose thus?

FIRST MUSICIAN. How, sir, how?   5

CLOWN. Are these, I pray you, wind-instruments?

FIRST MUSICIAN. Ay, marry, are they, sir.

CLOWN. O, thereby hangs a tail.

FIRST MUSICIAN. Whereby hangs a tale, sir?

CLOWN. Marry, sir, by many a wind-instrument that I   10
know. But, masters, here's money for you; and the General
so likes your music, that he desires you, of all loves, to make
no more noise with it.

FIRST MUSICIAN. Well, sir, we will not.

CLOWN. If you have any music that may not be heard,   15
to 't again; but, as they say, to hear music the General does
not greatly care.

FIRST MUSICIAN. We have none such, sir.

CLOWN. Then put up your pipes in your bag, for I'll away.
Go, vanish into air, away!   *Exeunt* MUSICIANS.   20

CASSIO. Dost thou hear, mine honest friend?

CLOWN. No, I hear not your honest friend; I hear you.

CASSIO. Prithee, keep up thy quillets. There's a poor piece
of gold for thee. If the gentlewoman that attends the general's
wife be stirring, tell her there's one Cassio entreats her a   25
little favor of speech. Wilt thou do this?

CLOWN. She is stirring, sir: if she will stir hither, I shall
seem to notify unto her.

CASSIO. Do, good my friend.   *Exit* CLOWN.

Enter IAGO.

In happy time, Iago.

IAGO. You have not been a-bed, then?   30

CASSIO. Why, no; the day had broke
Before we parted. I have made bold, Iago,
To send in to your wife. My suit to her
Is that she will to virtuous Desdemona

[ACT III · 1] 4 Naples *i.e., have they acquired the Neapolitan*
(*venereal*) *disease* / 23 keep up thy quillets *keep your jokes to yourself*
/ 29 in happy time *well met*

Procure me some access.

IAGO.   I'll send her to you presently;   35
And I'll devise a mean to draw the Moor
Out of the way, that your converse and business
May be more free.

CASSIO.   I humbly thank you for 't. [*Exit* IAGO.]
    I never knew
A Florentine more kind and honest.   40

Enter EMILIA.

EMILIA.   Good morrow, good lieutenant: I am sorry
For your displeasure; but all will sure be well.
The General and his wife are talking of it,
And she speaks for you stoutly. The Moor replies,
That he you hurt is of great fame in Cyprus   45
And great affinity, and that in wholesome wisdom
He might not but refuse you; but he protests he loves you,
And needs no other suitor but his likings
To take the safest occasion by the front
To bring you in again.

CASSIO.   Yet, I beseech you   50
If you think fit, or that it may be done,
Give me advantage of some brief discourse
With Desdemon alone.

EMILIA.   Pray you, come in;
I will bestow you where you shall have time
To speak your bosom freely.

CASSIO.   I am much bound to you.   55
Exeunt.

[ACT III · 2] *A room in the castle.*

Enter OTHELLO, IAGO, *and* GENTLEMEN.

OTHELLO.   These letters give, Iago, to the pilot;
And by him do my duties to the Senate.
That done, I will be walking on the works;

---

42 displeasure *disfavor* / 46 affinity *kindred* / 48 likings *affection* / 49 take . . . by the front *"take Time by the forelock,"* seize the **first good opportunity** / 55 bosom *inmost thoughts*
  [ACT III · 2] 3 works *fortifications*

Repair there to me.

IAGO.   Well, my good lord, I'll do 't.

OTHELLO.   This fortification, gentlemen, shall we see 't?   5

GENTLEMEN.   We'll wait upon your lordship.

                                                Exeunt.

[ACT III · 3] *The garden of the castle.*

Enter DESDEMONA, CASSIO, *and* EMILIA.

DESDEMONA.   Be thou assur'd, good Cassio, I will do
All my abilities in thy behalf.

EMILIA.   Good madam, do. I warrant it grieves
     my husband
As if the cause were his.

DESDEMONA.   O, that's an honest fellow. Do not
     doubt, Cassio,   5
But I will have my lord and you again
As friendly as you were.

CASSIO.   Bounteous madam,
Whatever shall become of Michael Cassio,
He's never anything but your true servant.

DESDEMONA.   I know 't; I thank you. You do love my lord;   10
You have known him long; and be you well assur'd
He shall in strangeness stand no farther off
Than in a politic distance.

CASSIO.   Ay, but, lady,
That policy may either last so long,
Or feed upon such nice and waterish diet,   15
Or breed itself so out of circumstances,
That, I being absent and my place suppli'd,
My general will forget my love and service.

DESDEMONA.   Do not doubt that; before Emilia here
I give thee warrant of thy place. Assure thee,   20
If I do vow a friendship, I'll perform it
To the last article. My lord shall never rest;
I'll watch him tame, and talk him out of patience;

[ACT III · 3] 12 strangeness *estrangement* / 13 than in . . . distance *than policy requires* / 15 nice and waterish *trivial and insignificant* / 16 out of *by (further)* / 19 doubt *fear* / 23 watch him *keep awake until he is*

His bed shall seem a school, his board a shrift;
I'll intermingle everything he does   25
With Cassio's suit. Therefore be merry, Cassio;
For thy solicitor shall rather die
Than give thy cause away.

Enter OTHELLO *and* IAGO.

EMILIA.   Madam, here comes my lord.
CASSIO.   Madam, I'll take my leave.   30
DESDEMONA.   Why, stay, and hear me speak.
CASSIO.   Madam, not now; I am very ill at ease,
Unfit for mine own purposes.
DESDEMONA.   Well, do your discretion.

Exit CASSIO.

IAGO   Ha! I like not that.
OTH LLO.   What dost thou say?   35
IAGO.   Nothing, my lord; or if—I know not what.
OTHELLO.   Was not that Cassio parted from my wife?
IAGO.   Cassio, my lord! No, sure, I cannot think it,
That he would steal away so guilty-like,
Seeing your coming.
OTHELLO.   I do believe 'twas he.   40
DESDEMONA.   How now, my lord!
I have been talking with a suitor here,
A man that languishes in your displeasure.
OTHELLO.   Who is 't you mean?
DESDEMONA.   Why, your lieutenant, Cassio. Good my lord,   45
If I have any grace or power to move you,
His present reconciliation take;
For if he be not one that truly loves you,
That errs in ignorance and not in cunning,
I have no judgment in an honest face.   50
I prithee, call him back.
OTHELLO.   Went he hence now?
DESDEMONA.   Yes, faith; so humbled
That he hath left part of his grief with me
To suffer with him. Good love, call him back.

---

24 shrift *place of admonition* / 28 away *up* / 33 purposes *best interests*
/ 47 his present reconciliation take *accept his apology and become rec-
onciled* / 51 prithee *pray you*

OTHELLO.   Not now, sweet Desdemon; some other time.   55
DESDEMONA.   But shall 't be shortly?
OTHELLO.   The sooner, sweet, for you.
DESDEMONA.   Shall 't be to-night at supper?
OTHELLO.   No, not to-night.
DESDEMONA.   To-morrow dinner, then?
OTHELLO.   I shall not dine at home;
I meet the captains at the citadel.
DESDEMONA.   Why, then, to-morrow night; on
        Tuesday morn;   60
On Tuesday morn, or night; on Wednesday morn.
I prithee, name the time, but let it not
Exceed three days. In faith, he's penitent;
And yet his trespass, in our common reason—
Save that, they say, the wars must make example   65
Out of their best—is not almost a fault
T' incur a private check. When shall he come?
Tell me, Othello. I wonder in my soul,
What you would ask me, that I should deny,
Or stand so mamm'ring on. What! Michael Cassio,   70
That came a-wooing with you, and so many a time,
When I have spoke of you dispraisingly,
Hath ta'en your part, —to have so much to do
To bring him in! Trust me, I could do much,—
OTHELLO.   Prithee, no more; let him come when he will!   75
I will deny thee nothing.
DESDEMONA.   Why, this is not a boon.
'Tis as I should entreat you wear your gloves,
Or feed on nourishing dishes, or keep you warm,
Or sue to you to do a peculiar profit
To your own person. Nay, when I have a suit   80
Wherein I mean to touch your love indeed,
It shall be full of poise and difficult weight
And fearful to be granted.
OTHELLO.   I will deny thee nothing;
Whereon, I do beseech thee, grant me this,
To leave me but a little to myself.   85

---

64 reason *sense* / 65 wars *i.e., military discipline* / 66 not almost **hardly**
/ 70 mamm'ring on *hesitating over* / 76 boon *great favor to me*

DESDEMONA.   Shall I deny you? No. Farewell, my lord.

OTHELLO.   Farewell, my Desdemona; I'll come to
thee straight.

DESDEMONA.   Emilia, come.—Be as your fancies
teach you;

Whate'er you be, I am obedient.

Exeunt DESDEMONA *and* EMILIA.

OTHELLO.   Excellent wretch! Perdition catch my soul,   90
But I do love thee! and when I love thee not,
Chaos is come again.

IAGO.   My noble lord,—

OTHELLO.   What dost thou say, Iago?

IAGO.   Did Michael Cassio, when you woo'd my lady,
Know of your love?   95

OTHELLO.   He did, from first to last. Why dost thou ask?

IAGO.   But for a satisfaction of my thought;
No further harm.

OTHELLO.   Why of thy thought, Iago?

IAGO.   I did not think he had been acquainted with her.

OTHELLO.   O, yes; and went between us very oft.   100

IAGO.   Indeed!

OTHELLO.   Indeed! ay, indeed. Discern'st thou
aught in that?

Is he not honest?

IAGO.   Honest, my lord?

OTHELLO.   Honest! ay, honest.

IAGO.   My lord, for aught I know.

OTHELLO.   What dost thou think?

IAGO.   Think, my lord?

OTHELLO.   Think, my lord!   105
By heaven, he echoes me,
As if there were some monster in his thought
Too hideous to be shown.—Thou dost mean something:
I heard thee say but now, thou lik'st not that,
When Cassio left my wife. What didst not like?   110
And when I told thee he was of my counsel
In my whole course of wooing, thou criedst, "Indeed!"

---

92 Chaos *the utter confusion that existed before the order of the universe
was established and that will accompany the end of time /* 111 of my
counsel *in my confidence*

And didst contract and purse thy brow together,
As if thou then hadst shut up in thy brain
Some horrible conceit. If thou dost love me,   115
Show me thy thought.
    IAGO.   My lord, you know I love you.
    OTHELLO.   I think thou dost;
And, for I know thou'rt full of love and honesty,
And weigh'st thy words before thou giv'st them breath,
Therefore these stops of thine fright me the more;   120
For such things in a false disloyal knave
Are tricks of custom; but in a man that's just
They're close dilations, working from the heart
That passion cannot rule.
    IAGO.   For Michael Cassio,
I dare be sworn I think that he is honest.   125
    OTHELLO.   I think so too.
    IAGO.   Men should be what they seem;
Or those that be not, would they might seem none!
    OTHELLO.   Certain, men should be what they seem.
    IAGO.   Why, then, I think Cassio's an honest man.
    OTHELLO.   Nay, yet there's more in this.   130
I prithee, speak to me as to thy thinkings,
As thou dost ruminate, and give thy worst of thoughts
The worst of words.
    IAGO.   Good my lord, pardon me.
Though I am bound to every act of duty,
I am not bound to that all slaves are free to.   135
Utter my thoughts? Why, say they are vile and false;
As where's that palace whereinto foul things
Sometimes intrude not? Who has a breast so pure
But some uncleanly apprehensions
Keep leets and law-days and in sessions sit   140
With meditations lawful?
    OTHELLO.   Thou dost conspire against thy friend, Iago,
If thou but think'st him wrong'd and mak'st his ear
A stranger to thy thoughts.

---

113 purse *draw* / 115 conceit *notion* / 122 tricks of custom *habitual tricks* / 123 close dilations *hidden emotions that make the heart swell* / 127 none *i.e., not men, but monsters* / 139 apprehensions *thoughts* / 140 leets *court sessions* / 140 sit With *sit on the bench beside*

IAGO.   I do beseech you—
Though I perchance am vicious in my guess,   145
As, I confess, it is my nature's plague
To spy into abuses, and oft my jealousy
Shapes faults that are not—that your wisdom yet,
From one that so imperfectly conceits,
Would take no notice, nor build yourself a trouble   150
Out of his scattering and unsure observance.
It were not for your quiet nor your good,
Nor for my manhood, honesty, and wisdom,
To let you know my thoughts.
OTHELLO.   What dost thou mean?
IAGO.   Good name in man and woman, dear my lord,   155
Is the immediate jewel of their souls.
Who steals my purse steals trash; 'tis something, nothing;
'Twas mine, 'tis his, and has been slave to thousands;
But he that filches from me my good name
Robs me of that which not enriches him   160
And makes me poor indeed.
OTHELLO.   By heaven, I'll know thy thoughts.
IAGO.   You cannot, if my heart were in your hand;
Nor shall not, whilst 'tis in my custody.
OTHELLO.   Ha!
IAGO.   O, beware, my lord, of jealousy;   165
It is the green-ey'd monster which doth mock
The meat it feeds on. That cuckold lives in bliss
Who, certain of his fate, loves not his wronger;
But, O, what damned minutes tells he o'er
Who dotes, yet doubts, suspects, yet strongly loves!   170
OTHELLO.   O misery!
IAGO.   Poor and content is rich and rich enough,
But riches fineless is as poor as winter
To him that ever fears he shall be poor.
Good heaven, the souls of all my tribe defend   175
From jealousy!
OTHELLO.   Why, why is this?

---

145 vicious *mistaken* / 147 jealousy *suspicious nature* / 149 imperfectly conceits *has such vague ideas* / 151 scattering *casual* / 151 observance *observations* / 166 mock *play cat and mouse with* / 168
wronger *faithless wife* / 169 tells *counts* / 173 fineless *boundless*

Think'st thou I'd make a life of jealousy,
To follow still the changes of the moon
With fresh suspicions? No! to be once in doubt
Is once to be resolv'd. Exchange me for a goat   180
When I shall turn the business of my soul
To such exsufflicate and blown surmises,
Matching thy inference. 'Tis not to make me jealous
To say my wife is fair, feeds well, loves company,
Is free of speech, sings, plays, and dances well;   185
Where virtue is, these are more virtuous;
Nor from mine own weak merits will I draw
The smallest fear or doubt of her revolt;
For she had eyes, and chose me. No, Iago;
I'll see before I doubt; when I doubt, prove;   190
And on the proof, there is no more but this,—
Away at once with love or jealousy!

    IAGO.   I am glad of this, for now I shall have reason
To show the love and duty that I bear you
With franker spirit; therefore, as I am bound,   195
Receive it from me. I speak not yet of proof.
Look to your wife; observe her well with Cassio;
Wear your eyes thus, not jealous nor secure.
I would not have your free and noble nature,
Out of self-bounty, be abus'd; look to 't.   200
I know our country disposition well;
In Venice they do let God see the pranks
They dare not show their husbands. Their best conscience
Is not to leave 't undone, but keep 't unknown.
    OTHELLO.   Dost thou say so?   205
    IAGO.   She did deceive her father, marrying you;
And when she seem'd to shake and fear your looks,
She lov'd them most.
    OTHELLO.   And so she did.
    IAGO.   Why, go to then.
She that, so young, could give out such a seeming,
To seel her father's eyes up close as oak—   210
He thought 'twas witchcraft—but I am much to blame.

---

180 to be resolv'd *to discover the truth* / 182 exsufflicate *odious* / 182
blown *flyspecked* / 200 self-bounty *innate goodness* / 210 as oak *as the
grain of oak*

I humbly do beseech you of your pardon
For too much loving you.

OTHELLO.   I am bound to thee for ever.

IAGO.   I see this hath a little dash'd your spirits.

OTHELLO.   Not a jot, not a jot.

IAGO.   I' faith, I fear it has.   215
I hope you will consider what is spoke
Comes from my love. But I do see you're mov'd.
I am to pray you not to strain my speech
To grosser issues nor to larger reach
Than to suspicion.   220

OTHELLO.   I will not.

IAGO.   Should you do so, my lord,
My speech should fall into such vile success
Which my thoughts aim'd not at. Cassio's my worthy friend,—
My lord, I see you're mov'd.

OTHELLO.   No, not much mov'd.
I do not think but Desdemona's honest.   225

IAGO.   Long live she so; and long live you to think so!

OTHELLO.   And yet, how nature erring from itself,—

IAGO.   Ay, there's the point; as—to be bold with you—
Not to affect many proposed matches
Of her own clime, complexion, and degree,   230
Whereto we see in all things nature tends—
Foh! one may smell in such, a will most rank,
Foul disproportions, thoughts unnatural.
But pardon me; I do not in position
Distinctly speak of her; though I may fear   235
Her will, recoiling to her better judgment,
May fall to match you with her country forms,
And happily repent.

OTHELLO.   Farewell, farewell!
If more thou dost perceive, let me know more;
Set on thy wife to observe. Leave me, Iago.   240

IAGO. [*Going.*]   My lord, I take my leave.

---

213 bound *indebted* / 219 grosser issues *worse conclusions* / 229 affect *care for, be inclined to* / 234 position *this principle* / 235 Distinctly *specifically* / 237 match *compare* / 237 her country forms *men of her own country*

OTHELLO.   Why did I marry? This honest
    creature doubtless
Sees and knows more, much more, than he unfolds.
    IAGO. [*Returning*.]´ My lord, I would I might entreat
    your honor
To scan this thing no farther; leave it to time.   245
Although 'tis fit that Cassio have his place,
For, sure, he fills it up with great ability,
Yet, if you please to hold him off a while,
You shall by that perceive him and his means.
Note if your lady strain his entertainment   250
With any strong or vehement importunity;
Much will be seen in that. In the mean time,
Let me be thought too busy in my fears—
As worthy cause I have to fear I am—
And hold her free, I do beseech your honor.   255
    OTHELLO.   Fear not my government.
    IAGO.   I once more take my leave.   *Exit.*
    OTHELLO.   This fellow's of exceeding honesty,
And knows all qualities, with a learned spirit,
Of human dealings. If I do prove her haggard,   260
Though that her jesses were my dear heartstrings,
I'd whistle her off and let her down the wind
To prey at fortune. Haply, for I am black
And have not those soft parts of conversation
That chamberers have, or for I am declin'd   265
Into the vale of years,— yet that's not much—
She's gone. I am abus'd; and my relief
Must be to loathe her. O curse of marriage,
That we can call these delicate creatures ours,
And not their appetites! I had rather be a toad   270
And live upon the vapor of a dungeon,
Than keep a corner in the thing I love
For others' uses. Yet, 'tis the plague of great ones;
Prerogativ'd are they less than the base:
'Tis destiny unshunnable, like death.   275

---

250 his entertainment *that you reinstate him* / 256 government *self-control* / 260 haggard *a wild hawk and an unchaste woman* / 261 jesses *straps on a falcon's legs* / 265 chamberers *gallants* / 274 Prerogativ'd *privileged*

Even then this forked plague is fated to us
When we do quicken. Look where she comes.

Re-enter DESDEMONA *and* EMILIA.

If she be false, O, then heaven mocks itself!
I'll not believe 't.

    DESDEMONA.   How now, my dear Othello!

Your dinner, and the generous islanders   280
By you invited, do attend your presence.

    OTHELLO.   I am to blame.

    DESDEMONA.   Why do you speak so faintly?

Are you not well?

    OTHELLO.   I have a pain upon my forehead here.

    DESDEMONA.   Faith, that's with watching; 'twill
       away again.   285

Let me but bind it hard, within this hour
It will be well.

    OTHELLO.   Your napkin is too little;
       He puts the handkerchief from him; and it drops.

Let it alone. Come, I'll go in with you.

    DESDEMONA.   I am very sorry that you are not well.

                  Exeunt OTHELLO *and* DESDEMONA.

    EMILIA.   I am glad I have found this napkin;   290
This was her first remembrance from the Moor.
My wayward husband hath a hundred times
Woo'd me to steal it; but she so loves the token,
For he conjur'd her she should ever keep it,
That she reserves it evermore about her   295
To kiss and talk to. I'll have the work ta'en out,
And give 't Iago. What he will do with it
Heaven knows, not I;
I nothing but to please his fantasy.

Re-enter IAGO.

    IAGO.   How now! what do you here alone?   300
    EMILIA.   Do not you chide; I have a thing for you.
    IAGO.   A thing for me? It is a common thing—

---

276 forked *horned* / 277 do quicken *are born* / 287 napkin *handker-chief* / 292 wayward *capricious* / 296 work *embroidery* / 296 ta'en out *copied* / 299 fantasy *whim*

EMILIA.   Ha!

IAGO.   To have a foolish wife.

EMILIA.   O, is that all? What will you give me now   305
For that same handkerchief?

IAGO.   What handkerchief?

EMILIA.   What handkerchief!
Why, that the Moor first gave to Desdemona;
That which so often you did bid me steal.

IAGO.   Hast stol'n it from her?   310

EMILIA.   No, faith; she let it drop by negligence,
And, to th' advantage, I, being here, took 't up.
Look, here it is.

IAGO.   A good wench; give it me.

EMILIA.   What will you do with 't, that you have
     been so earnest
To have me filch it?   315

IAGO. [*Snatching it.*]   Why, what is that to you?

EMILIA.   If it be not for some purpose of import,
Give 't me again. Poor lady, she'll run mad
When she shall lack it.

IAGO.   Be not you acknown on 't; I have use for it.   320
Go, leave me.   *Exit* EMILIA.
I will in Cassio's lodging lose this napkin
And let him find it. Trifles light as air
Are to the jealous confirmations strong
As proofs of holy writ; this may do something.   325
The Moor already changes with my poison.
Dangerous conceits are, in their nature, poisons,
Which at the first are scarce found to distaste,
But with a little act upon the blood,
Burn like the mines of sulphur. I did say so.   330

Re-enter OTHELLO.

Look, where he comes! Not poppy, nor mandragora,
Nor all the drowsy syrups of the world
Shall ever medicine thee to that sweet sleep

---

312 to th' advantage *opportunity* / 313 wench *girl* / 317 import *importance* / 319 lack *miss* / 320 Be not . . . on't *don't admit any knowledge of it* / 328 distaste *taste bad* / 329 with a little act *having acted a little while* / 332 drowsy syrups *sleeping potions*

Which thou ow'dst yesterday.

OTHELLO.　　　　　　　　Ha! ha! false to me?

IAGO.　Why, how now, General! no more of that.　　　335

OTHELLO.　Avaunt! be gone! thou hast set me on the rack.
I swear 'tis better to be much abus'd
Than but to know 't a little.

IAGO.　　　　　　　　How now, my lord!

OTHELLO.　What sense had I of her stol'n hours of lust?
I saw 't not, thought it not, it harm'd not me.　　　340
I slept the next night well, fed well, was free and merry;
I found not Cassio's kisses on her lips.
He that is robb'd, not wanting what is stol'n,
Let him not know 't, and he's not robb'd at all.

IAGO.　I am sorry to hear this.　　　345

OTHELLO.　I had been happy, if the general camp,
Pioners and all, had tasted her sweet body,
So I had nothing known. O, now, for ever
Farewell the tranquil mind! farewell content!
Farewell the plumed troop, and the big wars,　　　350
That makes ambition virtue! O, farewell!
Farewell the neighing steed, and the shrill trump,
The spirit-stirring drum, th' ear-piercing fife,
The royal banner, and all quality,
Pride, pomp, and circumstance of glorious war!　　　355
And, O you mortal engines, whose rude throats
Th' immortal Jove's dread clamors counterfeit,
Farewell! Othello's occupation's gone!

IAGO.　Is't possible, my lord?

OTHELLO.　Villain, be sure thou prove my love a whore,　　　360
Be sure of it; give me the ocular proof;
Or, by the worth of mine eternal soul,
Thou hadst been better have been born a dog
Than answer my wak'd wrath!

IAGO.　　　　　　　　Is't come to this?

OTHELLO.　Make me to see 't; or, at the least, so prove it,　　　365
That the probation bear no hinge nor loop

---

334 ow'dst *possessed* / 336 Avaunt *Get out!* / 343 wanting *missing* /
347 Pioners *soldiers of the lowest rank* / 350 big *stately* / 354 quality
characteristics / 355 circumstance *pageantry* / 356 mortal engines
deadly machines / 357 counterfeit *imitate* / 364 answer *be exposed to*
/ 366 probation *proof*

To hang a doubt on; or woe upon thy life!

IAGO.   My noble lord,—

OTHELLO.   If thou dost slander her and torture me,
Never pray more; abandon all remorse;   370
On horror's head horrors accumulate;
Do deeds to make heaven weep, all earth amaz'd;
For nothing canst thou to damnation add
Greater than that.

IAGO.   O grace! O Heaven forgive me!
Are you a man? Have you a soul or sense?   375
God buy you; take mine office. O wretched fool,
That lov'st to make thine honesty a vice!
O monstrous world! Take note, take note, O world,
To be direct and honest is not safe.
I thank you for this profit; and from hence   380
I'll love no friend, sith love breeds such offence.

OTHELLO.   Nay, stay. Thou shouldst be honest.

IAGO.   I should be wise, for honesty's a fool
And loses that it works for.

OTHELLO.   By the world,
I think my wife be honest and think she is not;   385
I think that thou art just and think thou art not.
I'll have some proof. Her name, that was as fresh
As Dian's visage, is now begrim'd and black
As mine own face. If there be cords, or knives,
Poison, or fire, or suffocating streams,   390
I'll not endure it. Would I were satisfied!

IAGO.   I see, sir, you are eaten up with passion;
I do repent me that I put it to you.
You would be satisfied?

OTHELLO.   Would! nay, I will.

IAGO.   And may; but, how? How satisfied, my lord?   395
Would you, the supervisor, grossly gape on—
Behold her tupp'd?

OTHELLO.   Death and damnation! O!

IAGO.   It were a tedious difficulty, I think,

---

370 remorse *compassion* / 372 amaz'd *paralyzed with horror* / 376
God buy you *good-bye* / 380 profit *profitable lesson* / 384 that *i.e.,
trust* / 388 Dian *Diana, goddess of chastity* / 396 supervisor *as an
eyewitness*

To bring them to that prospect; damn them then,
If ever mortal eyes do see them bolster   400
More than their own! What then? How then?
What shall I say? Where's satisfaction?
It is impossible you should see this,
Were they as prime as goats, as hot as monkeys,
As salt as wolves in pride, and fools as gross   405
As ignorance made drunk. But yet, I say,
If imputation and strong circumstances,
Which lead directly to the door of truth,
Will give you satisfaction, you might have 't.

    OTHELLO.   Give me a living reason she's disloyal.   410
    IAGO.   I do not like the office;
But, sith I am enter'd in this cause so far,
Prick'd to 't by foolish honesty and love,
I will go on. I lay with Cassio lately;
And, being troubled with a raging tooth,   415
I could not sleep.
There are a kind of men so loose of soul
That in their sleeps will mutter their affairs;
One of this kind is Cassio.
In sleep I heard him say, "Sweet Desdemona,   420
Let us be wary, let us hide our loves";
And then, sir, would he gripe and wring my hand,
Cry, "O sweet creature!" and then kiss me hard,
As if he pluck'd up kisses by the roots
That grew upon my lips; then laid his leg   425
Over my thigh, and sigh'd and kiss'd; and then
Cried, "Cursed fate that gave thee to the Moor!"

    OTHELLO.   O monstrous! monstrous!
    IAGO.   Nay, this was but his dream.
    OTHELLO.   But this denoted a foregone conclusion.
'Tis a shrewd doubt, though it be but a dream.   430
    IAGO.   And this may help to thicken other proofs
That do demonstrate thinly.
    OTHELLO.   I'll tear her all to pieces.

---

400 bolster *lie together on a bolster (i.e., bed)* / 401 More than *other than* / 404 prime *lustful* / 405 pride *lust* / 407 imputation . . . circumstances *strong circumstantial evidence* / 412 sith *since* / 429 foregone conclusion *something already completed* / 430 shrewd *cursed*

IAGO. Nay, but be wise; yet we see nothing done.
She may be honest yet. Tell me but this,
Have you not sometimes seen a handkerchief   435
Spotted with strawberries in your wife's hand?

OTHELLO. I gave her such a one; 'twas my first gift.

IAGO. I know not that; but such a handkerchief—
I am sure it was your wife's—did I to-day
See Cassio wipe his beard with.

OTHELLO.   If it be that,—   440

IAGO. If it be that, or any that was hers,
It speaks against her with the other proofs.

OTHELLO. O, that the slave had forty thousand lives!
One is too poor, too weak for my revenge.
Now do I see 'tis true. Look here, Iago;   445
All my fond love thus do I blow to Heaven.
'Tis gone.
Arise, black Vengeance, from the hollow hell!
Yield up, O love, thy crown and hearted throne
To tyrannous hate! Swell, bosom, with thy fraught,   450
For 'tis of aspics' tongues!

IAGO.   Yet be content.

OTHELLO. O, blood, blood, blood!

IAGO. Patience, I say; your mind perhaps may change.

OTHELLO. Never, Iago. Like to the Pontic Sea,
Whose icy current and compulsive course   455
Ne'er feels retiring ebb, but keeps due on
To the Propontic and the Hellespont,
Even so my bloody thoughts, with violent pace,
Shall ne'er look back, ne'er ebb to humble love,
Till that a capable and wide revenge   460
Swallow them up. Now, by yond marble heaven,
In the due reverence of a sacred vow
I here engage my words.   *Kneels.*

IAGO.   Do not rise yet.
Witness, you ever-burning lights above.

---

436 spotted with *with a pattern of* / 443 slave *i.e., Cassio* / 449 hearted throne *throne in my heart* / 450 fraught *burden* / 451 aspic *asp, poisonous snake* / 454 Pontic *Black* / 457 Propontic *Sea of Marmora* / 457 Hellespont *Bosporus* / 460 capable *all embracing*

You elements that clip us round about,   *Kneels.*   465
Witness that here Iago doth give up
The execution of his wit, hands, heart,
To wrong'd Othello's service! Let him command,
And to obey shall be in me remorse,
What bloody business ever.   *They rise.*
  OTHELLO.   I greet thy love,   470
Not with vain thanks, but with acceptance bounteous,
And will upon the instant put thee to 't.
Within these three days let me hear thee say
That Cassio's not alive.
  IAGO. My friend is dead; 'tis done at your request.   475
But let her live.
  OTHELLO. Damn her, lewd minx! O, damn her!
Come, go with me apart; I will withdraw
To furnish me with some swift means of death
For the fair devil. Now art thou my lieutenant.
  IAGO. I am your own for ever.   *Exeunt.*   480

[ACT III · 4] *Before the castle.*

Enter DESDEMONA, EMILIA, *and* CLOWN.

  DESDEMONA. Do you know, sirrah, where Lieutenant Cassio lies?
  CLOWN. I dare not say he lies anywhere.
  DESDEMONA. Why, man?
  CLOWN. He's a soldier, and for me to say a soldier lies,   5
'tis stabbing.
  DESDEMONA. Go to! Where lodges he?
  CLOWN. To tell you where he lodges, is to tell you where
I lie.
  DESDEMONA. Can anything be made of this?   10
  CLOWN. I know not where he lodges, and for me to devise a lodging and say he lies here or he lies there, were to
lie in mine own throat.
  DESDEMONA. Can you inquire him out, and be edified by
report?   15

---

465 clip *embrace* ⟨ 467 The execution *all that can be done by* ⟨ 469 remorse *as if only an act of pity*
 [ACT III · 4] 14 edified *instructed*

CLOWN.   I will catechize the world for him; that is, make
questions, and by them answer.

DESDEMONA.   Seek him, bid him come hither. Tell him
I have moved my lord on his behalf, and hope all will be well.

CLOWN.   To do this is within the compass of man's wit;   20
and therefore I will attempt the doing it.   *Exit.*

DESDEMONA.   Where should I lose the handkerchief,
Emilia?

EMILIA.   I know not, madam.

DESDEMONA.   Believe me, I had rather have lost my purse   25
Full of crusadoes; and, but my noble Moor
Is true of mind and made of no such baseness
As jealous creatures are, it were enough
To put him to ill thinking.

EMILIA.   Is he not jealous?

DESDEMONA.   Who, he? I think the sun where he was born   30
Drew all such humors from him.

EMILIA.   Look, where he comes.

Enter OTHELLO.

DESDEMONA.   I will not leave him now till Cassio
Be call'd to him.—How is't with you, my lord?

OTHELLO.   Well, my good lady. [*Aside.*] O, hardness to
          dissemble!—

How do you, Desdemona?

DESDEMONA.   Well, my good lord.   35

OTHELLO.   Give me your hand. This hand is moist,
          my lady.

DESDEMONA.   It yet hath felt no age nor known no sorrow.

OTHELLO.   This argues fruitfulness and liberal heart;
Hot, hot, and moist. This hand of yours requires
A sequester from liberty, fasting and prayer,   40
Much castigation, exercise devout;
For here's a young and sweating devil here,
That commonly rebels. 'Tis a good hand,
A frank one.

DESDEMONA.   You may, indeed, say so;
For 'twas that hand that gave away my heart.   45

---

26 crusadoes *gold coins* / 31 humors *whims* / 40 sequester *retirement*
/ 42 devil *i.e., sensual desire*

OTHELLO.   A liberal hand. The hearts of old gave hands;
But our new heraldry is hands, not hearts.

DESDEMONA.   I cannot speak of this. Come now,
    your promise.

OTHELLO.   What promise, chuck?

DESDEMONA.   I have sent to bid Cassio come speak
    with you.   50

OTHELLO.   I have a salt and sorry rheum offends me;
Lend me thy handkerchief.

DESDEMONA.   Here, my lord.

OTHELLO.   That which I gave you.

DESDEMONA.   I have it not about me.

OTHELLO.   Not?

DESDEMONA.   No, faith, my lord.

OTHELLO.   That's a fault. That handkerchief   55
Did an Egyptian to my mother give;
She was a charmer, and could almost read
The thoughts of people. She told her, while she kept it
'Twould make her amiable and subdue my father
Entirely to her love, but if she lost it,   60
Or made a gift of it, my father's eye
Should hold her loathed and his spirits should hunt
After new fancies. She, dying, gave it me;
And bid me, when my fate would have me wiv'd,
To give it her. I did so; and take heed on't;   65
Make it a darling like your precious eye.
To lose't or give't away were such perdition
As nothing else could match.

DESDEMONA.   Is't possible?

OTHELLO.   'Tis true; there's magic in the web of it.
A sibyl, that had number'd in the world   70
The sun to course two hundred compasses,
In her prophetic fury sew'd the work;
The worms were hallowed that did breed the silk;
And it was dy'd in mummy which the skilful
Conserv'd of maidens' hearts.

---

47 heraldry *symbolism* (*hand joined to hand, rather than hand with a heart in it*) / 49 chuck *chick* / 51 rheum *head cold* / 56 Egyptian *gypsy* / 70 sibyl *prophetess* / 74 mummy *a concoction made of dried flesh* / 75 Conserv'd *prepared*

DESDEMONA.   Indeed! is't true?   75
OTHELLO.   Most veritable; therefore look to't well.
DESDEMONA.   Then would to God that I had never seen 't
OTHELLO.   Ha! wherefore?
DESDEMONA.   Why do you speak so startingly and rash?
OTHELLO.   Is't lost? Is't gone? Speak, is't out o' the way?   80
DESDEMONA.   Heaven bless us!
OTHELLO.   Say you?
DESDEMONA.   It is not lost; but what an if it were?
OTHELLO.   How?
DESDEMONA.   I say, it is not lost.
OTHELLO.   Fetch 't, let me see 't.
DESDEMONA.   Why, so I can, sir, but I will not now.   85
This is a trick to put me from my suit;
Pray you, let Cassio be receiv'd again.
OTHELLO.   Fetch me the handkerchief; my mind misgives.
DESDEMONA.   Come, come;
You'll never meet a more sufficient man.   90
OTHELLO.   The handkerchief!
DESDEMONA.   I pray, talk me of Cassio.
OTHELLO.   The handkerchief!
DESDEMONA.   A man that all his time
Hath founded his good fortunes on your love,
Shar'd dangers with you,—
OTHELLO.   The handkerchief!   95
DESDEMONA.   I' faith, you are to blame.
OTHELLO.   'Zounds!   *Exit* OTHELLO.
EMILIA.   Is not this man jealous?
DESDEMONA.   I ne'er saw this before.
Sure, there's some wonder in this handkerchief;   100
I am most unhappy in the loss of it.
EMILIA.   'Tis not a year or two shows us a man:
They are all but stomachs, and we all but food;
They eat us hungerly, and when they are full
They belch us.

             Enter CASSIO *and* IAGO.

       Look you, Cassio and my husband!   105

---

79 startingly *by fits and starts* / 82 an if *if* / 103 all *nothing*

IAGO.　There is no other way, 'tis she must do 't;
And, lo, the happiness! Go, and importune her.
　　DESDEMONA.　How now, good Cassio! what's the news
　　　　with you?
　　CASSIO.　Madam, my former suit. I do beseech you
That by your virtuous means I may again　　　　　　　110
Exist, and be a member of his love
Whom I with all the office of my heart
Entirely honor. I would not be delay'd.
If my offense be of such mortal kind
That nor my service past, nor present sorrows,　　　115
Nor purpos'd merit in futurity
Can ransom me into his love again,
But to know so must be my benefit;
So shall I clothe me in a forc'd content,
And shut myself up in some other course,　　　　　120
To Fortune's alms.
　　DESDEMONA.　　　Alas, thrice-gentle Cassio!
My advocation is not now in tune;
My lord is not my lord, nor should I know him
Were he in favor as in humor alter'd.
So help me every spirit sanctified　　　　　　　　125
As I have spoken for you all my best
And stood within the blank of his displeasure
For my free speech! You must a while be patient.
What I can do I will; and more I will
Than for myself I dare. Let that suffice you.　　　130
　　IAGO.　Is my lord angry?
　　EMILIA.　　　　　　　He went hence but now,
And certainly in strange unquietness.
　　IAGO.　Can he be angry? I have seen the cannon
When it hath blown his ranks into the air,
And, like the devil, from his very arm　　　　　　135
Puff'd his own brother—and can he be angry?
Something of moment then. I will go meet him.
There's matter in 't indeed, if he be angry.　　　*Exit* IAGO.

---

110 virtuous means *by means of virtue* / 112 office *devotion* / 118 But
only / 118 my benefit *a favor to me* / 121 To Fortune's alms *to take
what Fortune may give me* / 127 blank *direct aim* / 137 Something
some business

DESDEMONA.   I prithee, do so. Something, sure, of state,
Either from Venice, or some unhatch'd practice   140
Made demonstrable here in Cyprus to him,
Hath puddled his clear spirit; and in such cases
Men's natures wrangle with inferior things,
Though great ones are their object. 'Tis even so;
For let our finger ache, and it indues   145
Our other healthful members even to a sense
Of pain. Nay, we must think men are not gods,
Nor of them look for such observancy
As fits the bridal. Beshrew me much, Emilia,
I was, unhandsome warrior as I am,   150
Arraigning his unkindness with my soul;
But now I find I had suborn'd the witness,
And he's indicted falsely.
   EMILIA.   Pray Heaven it be state matters, as you think,
And no conception nor no jealous toy   155
Concerning you.
   DESDEMONA.   Alas the day! I never gave him cause.
   EMILIA.   But jealous souls will not be answer'd so;
They are not ever jealous for the cause,
But jealous for they're jealous. It is a monster   160
Begot upon itself, born on itself.
   DESDEMONA.   Heaven keep that monster from
      Othello's mind!
   EMILIA.   Lady, amen.
   DESDEMONA.   I will go seek him. Cassio, walk hereabout;
If I do find him fit, I'll move your suit   165
And seek to effect it to my uttermost.
   CASSIO.   I humbly thank your ladyship.
                              Exeunt DESDEMONA *and* EMILIA.

                         Enter BIANCA.

   BIANCA.   Save you, friend Cassio!
   CASSIO.   What make you from home?
How is it with you, my most fair Bianca?

---

140 unhatch'd practice *plot not yet matured* / 145 indues *brings into
accord* / 148 observancy *attention* / 150 unhandsome *unfair* / 152
suborn'd *corrupted*

I' faith, sweet love, I was coming to your house.   170
   BIANCA.   And I was going to your lodging, Cassio.
What, keep a week away? seven days and nights?
Eightscore eight hours? and lovers' absent hours,
More tedious than the dial eightscore times?
O weary reck'ning!
   CASSIO.   Pardon me, Bianca.   175
I have this while with leaden thoughts been press'd;
But I shall, in a more continuate time,
Strike off this score of absence. Sweet Bianca,
             Giving her DESDEMONA'S *handkerchief.*
Take me this work out.
   BIANCA.   O Cassio, whence came this?
This is some token from a newer friend;   180
To the felt absence now I feel a cause.
Is't come to this? Well, well.
   CASSIO.   Go to, woman!
Throw your vile guesses in the devil's teeth,
From whence you have them. You are jealous now
That this is from some mistress, some remembrance.   185
No, by my faith, Bianca.
   BIANCA.   Why, whose is it?
   CASSIO.   I know not, sweet; I found it in my chamber.
I like the work well; ere it be demanded—
As like enough it will—I'd have it copied.
Take it, and do't; and leave me for this time.   190
   BIANCA.   Leave you! Wherefore?
   CASSIO.   I do attend here on the General;
And think it no addition, nor my wish,
To have him see me woman'd.
   BIANCA.   Why, I pray you?
   CASSIO.   Not that I love you not.
   BIANCA.   But that you do not love me.   195
I pray you, bring me on the way a little,
And say if I shall see you soon at night.
   CASSIO.   'Tis but a little way that I can bring you,

---

174 dial *the whole round of the clock's hands* / 177 more continuate
less interrupted / 180 friend *mistress* / 185 remembrance *keepsake* /
192 attend . . . on *wait for* / 193 addition *credit* / 194 woman'd *with
a woman*

For I attend here; but I'll see you soon.

BIANCA.   'Tis very good; I must be circumstanc'd.   200

Exeunt.

[ACT IV · 1] *Cyprus. Before the castle.*

Enter OTHELLO *and* IAGO.

IAGO.   Will you think so?

OTHELLO.   Think so, Iago!

IAGO.   What,
To kiss in private?

OTHELLO.   An unauthoriz'd kiss.

IAGO.   Or to be naked with her friend in bed
An hour or more, not meaning any harm?

OTHELLO.   Naked in bed, Iago, and not mean harm!   5
It is hypocrisy against the devil:
They that mean virtuously, and yet do so,
The devil their virtue tempts, and they tempt heaven.

IAGO.   So they do nothing, 'tis a venial slip;
But if I give my wife a handkerchief,—   10

OTHELLO.   What then?

IAGO.   Why, then, 'tis hers, my lord; and, being hers,
She may, I think, bestow 't on any man.

OTHELLO.   She is protectress of her honor too;
May she give that?   15

IAGO.   Her honor is an essence that's not seen;
They have it very oft that have it not;
But, for the handkerchief,—

OTHELLO.   By heaven, I would most gladly have forgot it.
Thou said'st—O, it comes o'er my memory,   20
As doth the raven o'er the infected house,
Boding to all—he had my handkerchief.

IAGO.   Ay, what of that?

OTHELLO.   That's not so good now.

IAGO.   What

---

200 be circumstanc'd *submit to circumstances*

[ACT IV · 1] 6 hypocrisy against the devil *appearing to do evil without "meaning any harm"* / 8 heaven *i.e., heaven's power to keep them from harm* / 9 venial *pardonable* / 17 have it *are reputed to have it* / 22 Boding *ominous*

If I had said I had seen him do you wrong?
Or heard him say,—as knaves be such abroad,   25
Who having, by their own importunate suit,
Or voluntary dotage of some mistress,
Convinced or supplied them, cannot choose
But they must blab—

    OTHELLO.   Hath he said anything?

    IAGO.   He hath, my lord; but be you well assur'd,   30
No more than he'll unswear.

    OTHELLO.   What hath he said?

    IAGO.   Faith, that he did—I know not what he did.

    OTHELLO.   What? what?

    IAGO.   Lie—

    OTHELLO.   With her?

    IAGO.   With her, on her; what you will.   35

    OTHELLO.   Lie with her! lie on her! We say lie on her,
when they belie her. Lie with her! 'Zounds, that's fulsome!—
Handkerchief—confessions—handkerchief!—To confess, and
be hanged for his labor;—first, to be hanged, and then to
confess.—I tremble at it. Nature would not invest herself in   40
such shadowing passion without some destruction. It is not
words that shakes me thus. Pish! Noses, ears, and lips.—Is't
possible?—Confess—handkerchief!—O devil!

                                        Falls in a trance.

    IAGO.   Work on,
My medicine, work! Thus credulous fools are caught;   45
And many worthy and chaste dames even thus,
All guiltless, meet reproach.—What, ho! my lord!
My lord, I say! Othello!

                    Enter CASSIO.

                  How now, Cassio!

    CASSIO.   What's the matter?

    IAGO.   My lord is fall'n into an epilepsy.   50
This is his second fit; he had one yesterday.

    CASSIO.   Rub him about the temples.

    IAGO.   No, forbear;
The lethargy must have his quiet course;

---

28 convinced or supplied *seduced or complied with* / 40 invest herself
fill me with / 41 destruction *actual cause* / 52 forbear *let him alone* /
53 lethargy *fit*

If not, he foams at mouth and by and by
Breaks out to savage madness. Look, he stirs.   55
Do you withdraw yourself a little while,
He will recover straight. When he is gone,
I would on great occasion speak with you.

Exit CASSIO.

How is it, general? Have you not hurt your head?
  OTHELLO.   Dost thou mock me?
  IAGO.   I mock you not, by heaven.   60
Would you would bear your fortune like a man!
  OTHELLO.   A horned man's a monster and a beast.
  IAGO.   There's many a beast then in a populous city,
And many a civil monster.
  OTHELLO.   Did he confess it?
  IAGO.   Good sir, be a man;   65
Think every bearded fellow that's but yok'd
May draw with you. There's millions now alive
That nightly lie in those unproper beds
Which they dare swear peculiar; your case is better.
O, 'tis the spite of hell, the fiend's arch-mock,   70
To lip a wanton in a secure couch,
And to suppose her chaste! No, let me know;
And knowing what I am, I know what she shall be.
  OTHELLO.   O, thou art wise; 'tis certain.
  IAGO.   Stand you a while apart;
Confine yourself but in a patient list.   75
Whilst you were here o'erwhelmed with your grief—
A passion most unsuiting such a man—
Cassio came hither. I shifted him away,
And laid good 'scuse upon your ecstasy;
Bade him anon return and here speak with me,   80
The which he promis'd. Do but encave yourself,
And mark the fleers, the gibes, and notable scorns,
That dwell in every region of his face;
For I will make him tell the tale anew,

---

60 mock *Othello instantly thinks of the horns of a cuckold* / 64 civil
citizen / 66 yok'd *married* / 67 draw with *share your fate* / 68 unproper *not exclusively theirs* / 69 peculiar *theirs alone* / 71 secure *free
from suspicion* / 75 patient list *in the bounds of self-control* / 81 encave
conceal

Where, how, how oft, how long ago, and when   85
He hath, and is again to cope your wife.
I say, but mark his gesture. Marry, patience;
Or I shall say you're all in all in spleen,
And nothing of a man.
    OTHELLO.   Dost thou hear, Iago?
I will be found most cunning in my patience;   90
But—dost thou hear?—most bloody.
    IAGO.   That's not amiss;
But yet keep time in all. Will you withdraw?
                     OTHELLO *retires*.

Now will I question Cassio of Bianca,
A housewife that by selling her desires
Buys herself bread and clothes. It is a creature   95
That dotes on Cassio;—as 'tis the strumpet's plague
To beguile many and be beguil'd by one;—
He, when he hears of her, cannot refrain
From the excess of laughter. Here he comes:

               Re-enter CASSIO.

As he shall smile, Othello shall go mad;   100
And his unbookish jealousy must construe
Poor Cassio's smiles, gestures, and light behaviors
Quite in the wrong. How do you, lieutenant?
    CASSIO.   The worser that you give me the addition
Whose want even kills me.   105
    IAGO.   Ply Desdemona well, and you are sure on't.
Now, if this suit lay in Bianca's power,
How quickly should you speed!
    CASSIO.   Alas, poor caitiff!
    OTHELLO.   Look, how he laughs already!
    IAGO.   I never knew a woman love man so.   110
    CASSIO.   Alas, poor rogue! I think, i' faith, she loves me.
    OTHELLO.   Now he denies it faintly, and laughs it out.
    IAGO.   Do you hear, Cassio?
    OTHELLO.   Now he importunes him
To tell it o'er. Go to; well said, well said.

---

86 cope *meet* / 88 all in all in spleen *totally governed by impulses* / 92
keep time *act reasonably* / 94 housewife *hussy, harlot* / 101 unbookish
ignorant / 104 addition *title* / 108 caitiff *wretch*

IAGO.   She gives it out that you shall marry her.   115
Do you intend it?

CASSIO.   Ha, ha, ha!

OTHELLO.   Do ye triumph, Roman? Do you triumph?

CASSIO.   I marry her! What? a customer! Prithee, bear
some charity to my wit; do not think it so unwholesome. Ha,   120
ha, ha!

OTHELLO.   So, so, so, so; Laugh that wins.

IAGO.   Faith, the cry goes that you shall marry her.

CASSIO.   Prithee, say true.

IAGO.   I am a very villain else.   125

OTHELLO.   Have you scor'd me? Well.

CASSIO.   This is the monkey's own giving out. She is persuaded I will marry her, out of her own love and flattery, not
out of my promise.

OTHELLO.   Iago beckons me; now he begins the story,   130

CASSIO.   She was here even now; she haunts me in every
place. I was the other day talking on the sea-bank with certain Venetians; and thither comes the bauble, and, by this
hand, she falls me thus about my neck—

OTHELLO.   Crying, "O dear Cassio!" as it were; his gesture   135
imports it.

CASSIO.   So hangs, and lolls, and weeps upon me; so shakes
and pulls me. Ha, ha, ha!

OTHELLO.   Now he tells how she plucked him to my chamber. O, I see that nose of yours, but not that dog I shall throw   140
it to.

CASSIO.   Well, I must leave her company.

IAGO.   Before me! look, where she comes.

Enter BIANCA.

CASSIO.   'Tis such another fitchew! Marry, a perfumed
one.—What do you mean by this haunting of me?   145

BIANCA.   Let the devil and his dam haunt you! What did
you mean by that same handkerchief you gave me even now?
I was a fine fool to take it. I must take out the work?—A
likely piece of work, that you should find it in your chamber,

---

118 Roman *i.e., proud fellow* / 119 customer *harlot* / 126 scor'd me
summed me up / 133 bauble *plaything* / 144 fitchew *polecat* / 146
dam *mother*

and know not who left it there! This is some minx's token, and 150
I must take out the work? There; give it your hobby-horse.
Wheresoever you had it, I'll take out no work on't.

CASSIO.   How now, my sweet Bianca! how now! how now!

OTHELLO.   By heaven, that should be my handkerchief!

BIANCA.   If you'll come to supper to-night, you may; if you 155
will not, come when you are next prepared for.   *Exit.*

IAGO.   After her, after her.

CASSIO.   Faith, I must; she'll rail in the streets else.

IAGO.   Will you sup there?

CASSIO.   Faith, I intend so.   160

IAGO.   Well, I may chance to see you; for I would very fain
speak with you.

CASSIO.   Prithee, come; will you?

IAGO.   Go to; say no more.   .   *Exit* CASSIO.

OTHELLO.   [*Advancing.*] How shall I murder him, Iago? 165

IAGO.   Did you perceive how he laughed at his vice?

OTHELLO.   O Iago!

IAGO.   And did you see the handkerchief?

OTHELLO.   Was that mine?

IAGO.   Yours, by this hand: and to see how he prizes the 170
foolish woman your wife! She gave it him, and he hath given
it his whore.

OTHELLO.   I would have him nine years a-killing.
A fine woman! a fair woman! a sweet woman!

IAGO.   Nay, you must forget that.   175

OTHELLO.   Ay, let her rot, and perish, and be damned to-
night; for she shall not live. No, my heart is turned to stone;
I strike it, and it hurts my hand. O, the world hath not a
sweeter creature! She might lie by an emperor's side and command him tasks.   180

IAGO.   Nay, that's not your way.

OTHELLO.   Hang her! I do but say what she is. So delicate
with her needle! an admirable musician! O! she will sing the
savageness out of a bear: of so high and plenteous wit and
invention!   185

---

151 hobby-horse *plaything* / 181 Nay . . . way *you must not soften
in your purpose* / 185 invention *originality*

IAGO.   She's the worse for all this.

OTHELLO.   O, a thousand thousand times! And then, of so gentle a condition!

IAGO.   Ay, too gentle.

OTHELLO.   Nay, that's certain. But yet the pity of it, Iago!   190
O Iago, the pity of it, Iago!

IAGO.   If you are so fond over her iniquity, give her patent to offend; for, if it touch not you, it comes near nobody.

OTHELLO.   I will chop her into messes. Cuckold me!

IAGO.   O, 'tis foul in her.   195

OTHELLO.   With mine officer!

IAGO.   That's fouler.

OTHELLO.   Get me some poison, Iago, this night. I'll not expostulate with her, lest her body and beauty unprovide my mind again. This night, Iago.   200

IAGO.   Do it not with poison; strangle her in her bed, even the bed she hath contaminated.

OTHELLO.   Good, good; the justice of it pleases; very good.

IAGO.   And for Cassio, let me be his undertaker: you shall hear more by midnight.   205

OTHELLO.   Excellent good!   *A trumpet.*

           What trumpet is that same?

IAGO.   Something from Venice sure.

     Enter LODOVICO, DESDEMONA, and Attendants.

                'Tis Lodovico
Come from the Duke; and, see, your wife is with him.

LODOVICO.   God save you, worthy General!

OTHELLO.   With all my heart, sir.

LODOVICO.   The Duke and senators of Venice greet you.   210

                Gives him a letter.

OTHELLO.   I kiss the instrument of their pleasures.

                Opens the letter and reads.

DESDEMONA.   And what's the news, good cousin Lodovico?

IAGO.   I am very glad to see you, signior; Welcome to Cyprus.

---

188 condition *disposition* / 192 patent *a charter* / 204 be his undertaker *manage his business* / 211 kiss *welcome*

LODOVICO.   I thank you. How does Lieutenant Cassio?   215
IAGO.   Lives, sir.
DESDEMONA.   Cousin, there's fall'n between him and
    my lord
An unkind breach; but you shall make all well.
OTHELLO.   Are you sure of that?
DESDEMONA.   My lord!   220
OTHELLO.   [*Reads.*] "This fail you not to do, as you will"—
LODOVICO.   He did not call; he's busy in the paper.
Is there division 'twixt my lord and Cassio?
DESDEMONA.   A most unhappy one. I would do much
T'atone them, for the love I bear to Cassio.   225
OTHELLO.   Fire and brimstone!
DESDEMONA.   My lord?
OTHELLO.   Are you wise?
DESDEMONA.   What, is he angry?
LODOVICO.   May be the letter mov'd him;
For, as I think, they do command him home,
Deputing Cassio in his government.
DESDEMONA.   Trust me, I am glad on 't.
OTHELLO.   Indeed!
DESDEMONA.   My lord?   230
OTHELLO.   I am glad to see you mad.
DESDEMONA.   Why, sweet Othello,—
OTHELLO.   [*Striking her.*] Devil!
DESDEMONA.   I have not deserv'd this.
LODOVICO.   My lord, this would not be believ'd in Venice
Though I should swear I saw't. 'Tis very much.   235
Make her amends: she weeps.
OTHELLO.   O devil, devil!
If that the earth could teem with a woman's tears,
Each drop she falls would prove a crocodile.
Out of my sight!
DESDEMONA.   I will not stay to offend you.

                                    Going.

LODOVICO.   Truly, an obedient lady,   240
I do beseech your lordship, call her back.

---

225 T'atone *to reconcile* / 226 wise *i.e., sane* / 237 teem *bear offspring*
/ 238 crocodile *the crocodile was supposed to trap victims by weeping,
and then devouring any who came to pity it*

OTHELLO.   Mistress!

DESDEMONA.   My lord?

OTHELLO.   What would you with her, sir?

LODOVICO.   Who, I, my lord?

OTHELLO.   Ay; you did wish that I would make her turn.

Sir, she can turn, and turn, and yet go on,   245

And turn again; and she can weep, sir, weep;

And she's obedient, as you say, obedient,

Very obedient. Proceed you in your tears.

Concerning this, sir,—O well-painted passion!—

I am commanded home.—Get you away;   250

I'll send for you anon.—Sir, I obey the mandate,

And will return to Venice.—Hence, avaunt!—

                    Exit DESDEMONA.

Cassio shall have my place. And, sir, to-night,

I do entreat that we may sup together.

You are welcome, sir, to Cyprus.— Goats and monkeys!   255

   LODOVICO.   Is this the noble Moor whom our full Senate

Call all in all sufficient? Is this the nature

Whom passion could not shake? whose solid virtue

The shot of accident nor dart of chance

Could neither graze nor pierce?

   IAGO.   He is much chang'd.   260

   LODOVICO.   Are his wits safe? Is he not light of brain?

   IAGO.   .He's that he is; I may not breathe my censure

What he might be. If what he might he is not,

I would to heaven he were!

   LODOVICO.   What, strike his wife!

   IAGO.   Faith, that was not so well; yet would I knew   265

That stroke would prove the worst!

   LODOVICO.   Is it his use?

Or did the letters work upon his blood,

And new-create this fault?

   IAGO.   Alas, alas!

It is not honesty in me to speak

What I have seen and known. You shall observe him,   270

And his own courses will denote him so

---

249 well-painted *cleverly imitated* / 258 passion *emotion* / 262 censure *opinion* / 266 use *habit* / 271 courses *behavior*

That I may save my speech. Do but go after,
And mark how he continues.

  LODOVICO. I am sorry that I am deceiv'd in him.   275

                     Exeunt.

[ACT IV · 2] *A room in the castle.*

Enter OTHELLO *and* EMILIA.

  OTHELLO. You have seen nothing then?
  EMILIA. Nor ever heard, nor ever did suspect.
  OTHELLO. Yes, you have seen Cassio and she together.
  EMILIA. But then I saw no harm, and then I heard
Each syllable that breath made up between them.   5
  OTHELLO. What, did they never whisper?
  EMILIA.   Never, my lord.
  OTHELLO. Nor send you out o' th' way?
  EMILIA. Never.
  OTHELLO. To fetch her fan, her gloves, her mask, nor
   nothing?
  EMILIA. Never, my lord.   10
  OTHELLO. That's strange.
  EMILIA. I durst, my lord, to wager she is honest,
Lay down my soul at stake. If you think other,
Remove your thought; it doth abuse your bosom.
If any wretch have put this in your head,   15
Let Heaven requite it with the serpent's curse!
For, if she be not honest, chaste, and true,
There's no man happy; the purest of their wives
Is foul as slander.
  OTHELLO.   Bid her come hither; go.

                 Exit EMILIA.

She says enough yet she's a simple bawd   20
That cannot say as much. This is a subtle whore,
A closet lock and key of villanous secrets;
And yet she'll kneel and pray; I have seen her do 't.

[ACT IV · 2] 9 mask *often worn by Elizabethan ladies in public places* / 13 at stake *as a wager* / 13 other *otherwise* / 16 curse *i.e., always to crawl on his belly; cf., the Snake in the Garden of Eden* / 20 bawd *proprietor of a brothel* / 22 closet *private room* / 22 lock and key *i.e., keeper*

Enter DESDEMONA *with* EMILIA.

DESDEMONA.   My lord, what is your will?
OTHELLO.   Pray, chuck, come hither.
DESDEMONA.   What is your pleasure?
OTHELLO.   Let me see your eyes;   25
Look in my face.
DESDEMONA.   What horrible fancy's this?
OTHELLO.   [*To* EMILIA.] Some of your function, mistress;
Leave procreants alone and shut the door;
Cough, or cry "hem," if anybody come.
Your mystery, your mystery; nay, dispatch.   30
                                    Exit EMILIA.
DESDEMONA.   Upon my knees, what doth your
        speech import?
I understand a fury in your words,
But not the words.
    OTHELLO.   Why, what art thou?
DESDEMONA.   Your wife, my lord; your true
And loyal wife.
    OTHELLO.   Come, swear it, damn thyself.   35
Lest, being like one of heaven, the devils themselves
Should fear to seize thee; therefore be double damn'd,
Swear thou art honest.
    DESDEMONA.   Heaven doth truly know it.
    OTHELLO.   Heaven truly knows that thou art false as hell.
DESDEMONA.   To whom, my lord? With whom? How
        am I false?   40
OTHELLO.   Ah, Desdemon! Away! away! away!
DESDEMONA.   Alas the heavy day! Why do you weep?
Am I the motive of these tears, my lord?
If haply you my father do suspect
An instrument of this your calling back,   45
Lay not your blame on me. If you have lost him,
Why, I have lost him too.
    OTHELLO.   Had it pleas'd Heaven
To try me with affliction; had they rain'd
All kinds of sores and shames on my bare head,

---

27 Some *perform some* / 27 function *office* (*of bawd*) / 30 mystery
trade / 42 heavy *sorrowful*

Steep'd me in poverty to the very lips   50
Given to captivity me and my utmost hopes,
I should have found in some place of my soul
A drop of patience; but, alas, to make me
The fixed figure for the time of scorn
To point his slow unmoving finger at!   55
Yet could I bear that too, well, very well;
But there, where I have garner'd up my heart,
Where either I must live, or bear no life;
The fountain from the which my current runs,
Or else dries up to be discarded thence!   60 ·
Or keep it as a cistern for foul toads
To knot and gender in! Turn thy complexion there,
Patience, thou young and rose-lipp'd cherubin,
Ay, there look grim as hell!
    DESDEMONA.   I hope my noble lord esteems me honest.   65
    OTHELLO.   O, ay; as summer flies are in the shambles,
That quicken even with blowing. O thou weed,
Who art so lovely fair and smell'st so sweet
That the sense aches at thee, would thou hadst
      ne'er been born!
    DESDEMONA.   Alas, what ignorant sin have I committed?   70
    OTHELLO.   Was this fair paper, this most goodly book,
Made to write "whore" upon? What committed?
Committed! O thou public commoner!
I should make very forges of my cheeks,
That would to cinders burn up modesty,   75
Did I but speak thy deeds. What committed?
Heaven stops the nose at it, and the moon winks,
The bawdy wind that kisses all it meets,
Is hush'd within the hollow mine of earth,
And will not hear it. What committed!   80
Impudent strumpet!

---

54 time of scorn *scornful world* / 55 to point . . . finger at *i.e., the
finger is slow in "coming to point," but once fixed, is immoveable* / 57
garnered up *stored the harvest of* / 59 fountain *spring* / 60 discarded
thence *rejected from it* (*i.e., her love*) / 61 cistern *cesspool* / 62 gender
mate / 66 shambles *slaughterhouse* / 67 quicken *spring to life* / 67
blowing *laying of the eggs* / 73 commoner *prostitute* / 77 winks *shuts
her eyes* / 79 mine of earth *cave whence the winds issued in classical
legend*

DESDEMONA.   By heaven, you do me wrong.
OTHELLO.   Are not you a strumpet?
DESDEMONA.   No, as I am a Christian.
If to preserve this vessel for my lord
From any other foul unlawful touch
Be not to be a strumpet, I am none.   85
OTHELLO.   What, not a whore?
DESDEMONA.   No, as I shall be sav'd.
OTHELLO.   Is 't possible?
DESDEMONA.   O, Heaven forgive us!
OTHELLO.   I cry you mercy, then.
I took you for that cunning whore of Venice
That married with Othello. You, mistress,   90

Re-enter EMILIA.

That have the office opposite to Saint Peter,
And keeps the gate of hell! You, you, ay, you!
We have done our course; there's money for your pains.
I pray you, turn the key and keep our counsel.   *Exit.*
EMILIA.   Alas, what does this gentleman conceive?   95
How do you, madam? How do you, my good lady?
DESDEMONA.   Faith, half asleep.
EMILIA.   Good madam, what's the matter with my lord?
DESDEMONA.   With who?
EMILIA.   Why, with my lord, madam.   100
DESDEMONA.   Who is thy lord?
EMILIA,   He that is yours, sweet lady.
DESDEMONA.   I have none. Do not talk to me, Emilia;
I cannot weep, nor answers have I none
But what should go by water. Prithee, to-night
Lay on my bed my wedding sheets—remember;   105
And call thy husband hither.
EMILIA.   Here's a change indeed!
                                                        Exit.
DESDEMONA.   'Tis meet I should be us'd so, very meet.
How have I been behav'd, that he might stick
The small'st opinion on my least misuse?

---

91 Saint Peter *gatekeeper of heaven* / 94 counsel *secret* / 104 go by
water *be expressed by tears* / 107 meet *proper* / 109 misuse *slightest
misconduct*

Re-enter EMILIA *with* IAGO.

IAGO.   What is your pleasure, madam? How is 't with you?   110
DESDEMONA.   I cannot tell. Those that do teach
    young babes
Do it with gentle means and easy tasks.
He might have chid me so; for, in good faith,
I am a child to chiding.
IAGO.   What's the matter, lady?
EMILIA.   Alas, Iago, my lord hath so bewhor'd her,   115
Thrown such despite and heavy terms upon her,
That true hearts cannot bear.
DESDEMONA.   Am I that name, Iago?
IAGO.   What name, fair lady?
DESDEMONA.   Such as she said my lord did say I was.
EMILIA.   He call'd her whore. A beggar in his drink   120
Could not have laid such terms upon his callet.
IAGO.   Why did he so?
DESDEMONA.   I do not know; I am sure I am none such.
IAGO.   Do not weep, do not weep. Alas the day!
EMILIA.   Hath she forsook so many noble matches,   125
Her father and her country and her friends,
To be call'd whore? Would it not make one weep?
DESDEMONA.   It is my wretched fortune.
IAGO.   Beshrew him for 't!
How comes this trick upon him?
DESDEMONA.   Nay, Heaven doth know.
EMILIA.   I will be hang'd, if some eternal villain,   130
Some busy and insinuating rogue,
Some cogging, cozening slave, to get some office,
Have not devis'd this slander; I'll be hang'd else.
IAGO.   Fie, there is no such man; it is impossible.
DESDEMONA.   If any such there be, Heaven pardon him!   135
EMILIA.   A halter pardon him and hell gnaw his bones!
Why should he call her whore? Who keeps her company?
What place? what time? what form? what likelihood?
The Moor's abus'd by some most villainous knave,
Some base notorious knave, some scurvy fellow.   140

---

121 callet *trull, "moll"* / 129 trick *freak* / 131 busy *meddlesome* / 132
cogging *cheating* / 136 halter *hangman's noose* / 140 notorious *notable*

O heaven, that such companions thou 'dst unfold,
And put in every honest hand a whip
To lash the rascals naked through the world
Even from the east to th' west!

    IAGO.   Speak within door.

    EMILIA.   O, fie upon them! Some such squire he was   145
That turn'd your wit the seamy side without,
And made you to suspect me with the Moor.

    IAGO.   You are a fool; go to.

    DESDEMONA.   Alas, Iago,
What shall I do to win my lord again?
Good friend, go to him; for, by this light of heaven,   150
I know not how I lost him. Here I kneel:
If e'er my will did trespass 'gainst his love,
Either in discourse of thought or actual deed,
Or that mine eyes, mine ears, or any sense
Delighted them in any other form;   155
Or that I do not yet, and ever did,
And ever will—though he do shake me off
To beggarly divorcement—love him dearly,
Comfort forswear me! Unkindness may do much;
And his unkindness may defeat my life,   160
But never taint my love. I cannot say "whore."
It does abhor me now I speak the word;
To do the act that might the addition earn
Not the world's mass of vanity could make me.

    IAGO.   I pray you, be content; 'tis but his humor.   165
The business of the state does him offense,
And he does chide with you.

    DESDEMONA.   If 'twere no other,—

    IAGO.   It is but so, I warrant.
                             Trumpets within.

Hark, how these instruments summon to supper!
The messengers of Venice stay the meat.   170
Go in, and weep not; all things shall be well.
                    Exeunt DESDEMONA *and* EMILIA.

---

141 companions *knaves* / 141 unfold *reveal* / 144 within door *more
quietly* / 146 seamy *wrong* / 153 discourse *process* / 155 them *themselves* / 155 form *man* / 164 vanity *vain delights* / 170 meat *supper*

Enter RODERIGO.

How now, Roderigo!

RODERIGO.   I do not find that thou deal'st justly with me.

IAGO.   What in the contrary?

RODERIGO.   Every day thou daff'st me with some device,   175
Iago; and rather, as it seems to me now, keep'st from me all
conveniency than suppliest me with the least advantage of
hope. I will indeed no longer endure it, nor am I yet persuaded to put up in peace what already I have foolishly suf-
fered.   180

IAGO.   Will you hear me, Roderigo?

RODERIGO.   Faith, I have heard too much, for your words
and performances are no kin together.

IAGO.   You charge me most unjustly.

RODERIGO.   With nought but truth. I have wasted myself   185
out of my means. The jewels you have had from me to deliver Desdemona would half have corrupted a votarist. You
have told me she hath received them and returned me expec-
tations and comforts of sudden respect and acquaintance, but
I find none.   190

IAGO.   Well; go to; very well.

RODERIGO.   Very well! go to! I cannot go to, man; nor 'tis
not very well. By this hand, I say 'tis scurvy, and begin to find
myself fopped in it.

IAGO.   Very well.   195

RODERIGO.   I tell you 'tis not very well. I will make myself
known to Desdemona: if she will return me my jewels, I will
give over my suit and repent my unlawful solicitation; if not,
assure yourself I will seek satisfaction of you.

IAGO.   You have said now.   200

RODERIGO.   Ay, and said nothing but what I protest in-
tendment of doing.

IAGO.   Why, now I see there's mettle in thee, and even
from this instant do build on thee a better opinion than ever
before. Give me thy hand, Roderigo. Thou hast taken against 205
me a most just exception; but yet, I protest, I have dealt most
directly in thy affair.

---

175 daff'st me *put me off* / 177 conveniency *opportunity* / 187 votarist
nun / 189 sudden *immediate* / 194 fopped *made a fool of* / 203 mettle
spirit

RODERIGO.   It hath not appeared.

IAGO.   I grant indeed it hath not appeared, and your sus- 210
picion is not without wit and judgment. But, Roderigo, if thou
hast that in thee indeed, which I have greater reason to believe now than ever—I mean purpose, courage, and valor—
this night show it. If thou the next night following enjoy not
Desdemona, take me from this world with treachery and devise engines for my life. 215

RODERIGO.   Well, what is it? Is it within reason and compass?

IAGO.   Sir, there is especial commission come from Venice
to depute Cassio in Othello's place.

RODERIGO.   Is that true? Why, then Othello and Desde- 220
mona return again to Venice.

IAGO.   O, no; he goes into Mauretania and takes away with
him the fair Desdemona, unless his abode be lingered here
by some accident; wherein none can be so determinate as the
removing of Cassio. 225

RODERIGO.   How do you mean, removing him?

IAGO.   Why, by making him uncapable of Othello's place;
knocking out his brains.

RODERIGO.   And that you would have me to do?

IAGO.   Ay, if you dare do yourself a profit and a right. He 230
sups to-night with a harlotry, and thither will I go to him; he
knows not yet of his honorable fortune. If you will watch
his going thence, which I will fashion to fall out between
twelve and one, you may take him at your pleasure. I will
be near to second your attempt, and he shall fall between us. 235
Come, stand not amazed at it, but go along with me; I will
show you such a necessity in his death that you shall think
yourself bound to put it on him. It is now high suppertime,
and the night grows to waste. About it.

RODERIGO.   I will hear further reason for this. 240

IAGO.   And you shall be satisfied.   *Exeunt.*

---

215 engines for *plots against* / 223 abode be lingered *stay be length-
ened* / 224 determinate *decisive* / 227 uncapable of *unable to succeed
to* / 231 harlotry *harlot* / 238 high *exactly*

[ACT IV · 3] *Another room in the castle.*

Enter OTHELLO, LODOVICO, DESDEMONA, EMILIA, *and* ATTENDANTS.

LODOVICO.   I do beseech you, sir, trouble yourself no
further.

OTHELLO.   O, pardon me; 'twill do me good to walk.

LODOVICO.   Madam, good-night; I humbly thank
your ladyship.

DESDEMONA.   Your honor is most welcome.

OTHELLO.   Will you walk, sir?
O, Desdemona,—   5

DESDEMONA.   My lord?

OTHELLO.   Get you to bed on th' instant; I will be returned forthwith. Dispatch your attendant there. Look 't be
done.

DESDEMONA.   I will, my lord.   10
            Exeunt OTHELLO, LODOVICO, *and* ATTENDANTS.

EMILIA.   How goes it now? He looks gentler than he did.

DESDEMONA.   He says he will return incontinent;
And hath commanded me to go to bed,
And bàde me to dismiss you.

EMILIA.   Dismiss me?

DESDEMONA.   It was his bidding; therefore, good Emilia,   15
Give me my nightly wearing, and adieu.
We must not now displease him.

EMILIA.   I would you had never seen him!

DESDEMONA.   So would not I. My love doth so
approve him,
That even his stubbornness, his checks, his frowns,—   20
Prithee, unpin me,—have grace and favor in them.

EMILIA.   I have laid those sheets you bade me on the bed.

DESDEMONA.   All's one. Good faith, how foolish are
our minds!
If I do die before thee, prithee, shroud me
In one of those same sheets.

EMILIA.   Come, come, you talk.   25

DESDEMONA.   My mother had a maid call'd Barbara;

[ACT IV · 3] 8 dispatch *dismiss* / 12 incontinent *immediately* / 19
approve *commend* / 23 All's one *no matter*

She was in love, and he she lov'd prov'd mad
And did forsake her. She had a song of "willow";
An old thing 'twas, but it express'd her fortune,
And she died singing it. That song to-night   30
Will not go from my mind; I have much to do
But to go hang my head all at one side
And sing it like poor Barbara. Prithee, dispatch.
    EMILIA.   Shall I go fetch your night-gown?
    DESDEMONA.   No, unpin me here.
This Lodovico is a proper man.   35
    EMILIA.   A very handsome man.
    DESDEMONA.   He speaks well.
    EMILIA.   I know a lady in Venice would have walked bare-
foot to Palestine for a touch of his nether lip.
    DESDEMONA.   [*Singing.*]

        The poor soul sat sighing by a sycamore tree,   40
            Sing all a green willow;
        Her hand on her bosom, her head on her knee,
            Sing willow, willow, willow.
        The fresh streams ran by her, and murmur'd her
            moans;
        Sing willow, willow, willow;   45
        Her salt tears fell from her, and soften'd the
            stones;
        Sing willow, willow, willow;

Lay by these;—
[*Singing.*] *"Willow, willow;"*—
Prithee, hie thee; he'll come anon;—   50
[*Singing.*]

        Sing all a green willow must be my garland.
        Let nobody blame him, his scorn I approve,—

Nay, that's not next.—Hark! who is't that knocks?
    EMILIA.   It's the wind.
    DESDEMONA.   [*Singing.*]

---

27 mad *wayward* / 28 "willow" *emblem of forlorn lovers* / 32 But to
go hang *to keep from hanging* / 34 night-gown *dressing gown* / 40
sycamore tree *emblem of vain hope*

     I call'd my love false love; but what said he then?   55
       Sing willow, willow, willow.
     If I court moe women, you'll couch with moe men.—

So, get thee gone; good-night. Mine eyes do itch;
Doth that bode weeping?
    EMILIA.   'Tis neither here nor there.
    DESDEMONA.   I have heard it said so. O, these men,
    these men!   60
Dost thou in conscience think,—tell me, Emilia,—
That there be women do abuse their husbands
In such gross kind?
    EMILIA.   There be some such, no question.
    DESDEMONA.   Wouldst thou do such a deed for
    all the world?
    EMILIA.   Why, would not you?
    DESDEMONA.   No, by this heavenly light!   65
    EMILIA.   Nor I neither by this heavenly light; I might do 't
as well i' th' dark.
    DESDEMONA.   Wouldst thou do such a deed for all the
world?
    EMILIA.   The world's a huge thing; it is a great price for   70
a small vice.
    DESDEMONA.   In troth, I think thou wouldst not.
    EMILIA.   In troth, I think I should; and undo't when I had
done. Marry, I would not do such a thing for a joint-ring, nor
for measures of lawn, nor for gowns, petticoats, nor caps,   75
nor any petty exhibition; but, for all the whole world,—'ud's
pity, who would not make her husband a cuckold to make him
a monarch? I should venture purgatory for 't.
    DESDEMONA.   Beshrew me, if I would do such a wrong
for the whole world.   80
    EMILIA.   Why, the wrong is but a wrong i' th' world; and
having the world for your labor, 'tis a wrong in your own
world, and you might quickly make it right.
    DESDEMONA.   I do not think there is any such woman.
    EMILIA.   Yes, a dozen; and as many to th' vantage as   85

---

57 moe *more* / 62 abuse *deceive* / 63 kind *way* / 73 undo't *deny it*
74 joint-ring *a love token* / 75 lawn *linen* / 76 ud's pity *God's pity* /
85 to th' vantage *in addition*

would store the world they play'd for.
But I do think it is their husbands' faults
If wives do fall. Say that they slack their duties
And pour our treasures into foreign laps,
Or else break out in peevish jealousies,   90
Throwing restraint upon us; or say they strike us,
Or scant our former having in despite;
Why, we have galls, and though we have some grace,
Yet have we some revenge. Let husbands know
Their wives have sense like them; they see and smell   95
And have their palates both for sweet and sour
As husbands have. What is it that they do
When they change us for others? Is it sport?
I think it is. And doth affection breed it?
I think it doth. Is't frailty that thus errs?   100
It is so too. And have not we affections,
Desires for sport, and frailty, as men have?
Then let them use us well; else let them know,
The ills we do, their ills instruct us so.

    DESDEMONA.   Good-night, good-night. Heaven me
        such uses send,   105
Not to pick bad from bad, but by bad mend.   *Exeunt.*

[ACT V • 1] *Cyprus. A street.*

Enter IAGO *and* RODERIGO.

    IAGO.   Here, stand behind this bulk; straight will he come.
Wear thy good rapier bare, and put it home.
Quick, quick; fear nothing; I'll be at thy elbow.
It makes us, or it mars us; think on that,
And fix most firm thy resolution.   5
    RODERIGO.   Be near at hand; I may miscarry in 't.
    IAGO.   Here, at thy hand; be bold, and take thy stand.

                        Retires.

    RODERIGO.   I have no great devotion to the deed,
And yet he hath given me satisfying reasons—

---

92 having *allowance* / 93 galls *capacity for resentment* / 94 revenge
vindictiveness / 98 change *exchange* / 99 affection *desire for pleasure*
/ 105 uses *practices* / 106 pick *learn*
    [ACT V • 1] 1 bulk *projecting structure* / 6 miscarry *fail*

'Tis but a man gone. Forth, my sword; he dies.   10
  IAGO.   I have rubb'd this young quat almost to the sense,
And he grows angry. Now, whether he kill Cassio,
Or Cassio him, or each do kill the other,
Every way makes my gain. Live Roderigo,
He calls me to a restitution large   15
Of gold and jewels that I bobb'd from him,
As gifts to Desdemona;
It must not be. If Cassio do remain,
He hath a daily beauty in his life
That makes me ugly; and, besides, the Moor   20
May unfold me to him; there stand I in much peril.
No, he must die. Be't so. I hear him coming.

                        Enter CASSIO.

  RODERIGO.   I know his gait, 'tis he.—Villain, thou diest!
                        Makes a pass at CASSIO.
  CASSIO.   That thrust had been mine enemy indeed,
But that my coat is better than thou know'st.   25
I will make proof of thine.
                        Draws, and wounds RODERIGO.
  RODERIGO.   O, I am slain.
        IAGO *from behind wounds* CASSIO *in the leg, and exit.*
  CASSIO.   I am maim'd for ever. Help, ho! murder! murder!
                                            Falls.

                        Enter OTHELLO.

  OTHELLO.   The voice of Cassio! Iago keeps his word.
  RODERIGO.   O, villain that I am!
  OTHELLO.   It is even so.
  CASSIO.   O, help, ho! light! a surgeon!   30
  OTHELLO.   'Tis he!—O brave Iago, honest and just,
That hast such noble sense of thy friends' wrong!
Thou teachest me. Minion, your dear lies dead,
And your unblest fate hies; strumpet, I come.
Forth of my heart those charms, thine eyes, are blotted;   35

---

11 quat *pimple* / 11 sense *quick* / 15 large *full* / 16 bobb'd *cheated*
/ 21 unfold *expose* / 25 coat *shirt of mail* / 33 Minion *darling* / 34
hies *hastens* / 35 of *from*

Thy bed, lust-stain'd, shall with lust's blood be spotted.

                                            Exit.

Enter LODOVICO *and* GRATIANO.

CASSIO.   What, ho! no watch? no passage?
    Murder! murder!
GRATIANO.   'Tis some mischance; the voice is direful.
CASSIO.   O, help!
LODOVICO.   Hark!   40
RODERIGO.   O wretched villain!
LODOVICO.   Two or three groan. It is a heavy night,
These may be counterfeits; let's think't unsafe
To come in to the cry without more help.
RODERIGO.   Nobody come? Then shall I bleed to death.   45

Re-enter IAGO, *with a light.*

LODOVICO.   Hark!
GRATIANO.   Here's one comes in his shirt, with light
    and weapons.
IAGO.   Who's there? Whose noise is this that cries
    on murder?
LODOVICO.   We do not know.
IAGO.   Do not you hear a cry?
CASSIO.   Here, here! for Heaven's sake, help me!   50
IAGO.   What's the matter?
GRATIANO.   This is Othello's ancient, as I take it.
LODOVICO.   The same indeed; a very valiant fellow.
IAGO.   What are you here that cry so grievously?
CASSIO.   Iago? O, I am spoil'd, undone by villains!   55
Give me some help.
IAGO.   O me, lieutenant! what villains have done this?
CASSIO.   I think that one of them is hereabout,
And cannot make away.
IAGO.   O treacherous villains!
What are you there?—Come in, and give some help.   60
                      [*To* LODOVICO *and* GRATIANO.]
RODERIGO.   O, help me there!
CASSIO.   That's one of them.

---

37 passage *passersby* / 55 spoil'd *crippled* / 60 Come in *approach*

IAGO.   O murderous slave! O villain!
                                                    Stabs RODERIGO.

RODERIGO.   O damn'd Iago! O inhuman dog!

IAGO.   Kill men i' th' dark!—Where be these bloody
    thieves?—

How silent is this town!—Ho! murder! murder!—   65

What may you be? Are you of good or evil?

LODOVICO.   As you shall prove us, praise us.

IAGO.   Signior Lodovico?

LODOVICO.   He, sir.

IAGO.   I cry you mercy. Here's Cassio hurt by villains.   70

GRATIANO.   Cassio!

IAGO.   How is 't, brother!

CASSIO.   My leg is cut in two.

IAGO.   Marry, heaven forbid!

Light, gentlemen! I'll bind it with my shirt.

Enter BIANCA.

BIANCA.   What is the matter, ho? Who is't that cried?   75

IAGO.   Who is't that cried!

BIANCA.   O my dear Cassio! my sweet Cassio!

O Cassio, Cassio, Cassio!

IAGO.   O notable strumpet! Cassio, may you suspect

Who they should be that have thus mangled you?   80

CASSIO.   No.

GRATIANO.   I am sorry to find you thus; I have been
    to seek you.

IAGO.   Lend me a garter. So. O, for a chair,

To bear him easily hence!

BIANCA.   Alas, he faints! O Cassio, Cassio, Cassio!   85

IAGO.   Gentlemen all, I do suspect this trash

To be a party in this injury.

Patience a while, good Cassio. Come, come;

Lend me a light. Know we this face or no?

Alas, my friend and my dear countryman   90

Roderigo! No:—yes, sure:—O heaven! Roderigo.

GRATIANO.   What, of Venice?

IAGO.   Even he, sir; did you know him?

GRATIANO.   Know him? ay.

---

83 chair *litter*

IAGO.   Signior Gratiano? I cry you gentle pardon;
These bloody accidents must excuse my manners,   95
That so neglected you.
    GRATIANO.   I am glad to see you.
    IAGO.   How do you, Cassio? O, a chair, a chair!
    GRATIANO.   Roderigo!
    IAGO.   He, he, 'tis he. [*A chair brought in.*] O, that's well
        said; the chair.
Some good man bear him carefully from hence;   100
I'll fetch the General's surgeon. [*To* BIANCA.] For
        you mistress,
Save you your labor. He that lies slain here, Cassio,
Was my dear friend. What malice was between you?
    CASSIO.   None in the world; nor do I know the man.
    IAGO.   [*To* BIANCA.] What, look you pale? O, bear
        him out o' th' air.   105
              CASSIO *and* RODERIGO *are borne off.*
Stay you, good gentlemen. Look you pale, mistress?
Do you perceive the gastness of her eye?
Nay, if you stare, we shall hear more anon.
Behold her well; I pray you, look upon her.
Do you see, gentlemen? Nay, guiltiness will speak,   110
Though tongues were out of use.

              Enter EMILIA.

    EMILIA.   Alas, what's the matter? What's the
        matter, husband?
    IAGO.   Cassio hath here been set on in the dark
By Roderigo and fellows that are scap'd.
He's almost slain, and Roderigo dead.   115
    EMILIA.   Alas, good gentlemen! alas, good Cassio!
    IAGO.   This is the fruits of whoring. Prithee, Emilia,
Go know of Cassio where he supp'd to-night.
[*To* BIANCA.] What, do you shake at that?
    BIANCA.   He supp'd at my house; but I therefore shake not.   120
    IAGO.   O, did he so? I charge you, go with me.
    EMILIA.   Oh, fie upon thee, strumpet!
    BIANCA.   I am no strumpet, but of life as honest

---

107 gastness *terrified look* / 108 anon *i.e., when she confesses*

As you that thus abuse me.

EMILIA.   As I? Fie upon thee!

IAGO.   Kind gentlemen, let's go see poor Cassio dress'd.   125
Come, mistress, you must tell's another tale.
Emilia, run you to the citadel,
And tell my lord and lady what hath happ'd.
Will you go on afore? [*Aside.*] This is the night
That either makes me or fordoes me quite.   *Exeunt.* 130

      [A C T   V • 2] *A bedchamber in the castle: Desdemona*
                        in bed asleep.

                Enter OTHELLO *with a light.*

OTHELLO.   It is the cause, it is the cause, my soul,—
Let me not name it to you, you chaste stars!—
It is the cause. Yet I'll not shed her blood,
Nor scar that whiter skin of hers than snow,
And smooth as monumental alabaster.   5
Yet she must die, else she'll betray more men.
Put out the light, and then put out the light.
If I quench thee, thou flaming minister,
I can again thy former light restore,
Should I repent me; but once put out thy light,   10
Thou cunning'st pattern of excelling nature,
I know not where is that Promethean heat
That can thy light relume. When I have pluck'd the rose
I cannot give it vital growth again,
It needs must wither. I'll smell it on the tree.   15
                           Kisses her.

Oh, balmy breath, that dost almost persuade
Justice to break her sword! One more, one more.
Be thus when thou art dead, and I will kill thee
And love thee after. One more, and that's the last;
So sweet was ne'er so fatal. I must weep,   20
But they are cruel tears: this sorrow's heavenly;

---

125 dress'd *i.e., his wounds treated* / 130 foredoes *ruins*
  [ACT V • 2] 1 cause *i.e., Desdemona's guilt* / 8 minister *servant* /
12 Promethean heat *heavenly fire* (*In classical legend, Prometheus
stole fire from heaven to give life to a clay image*) / 13 relume *relight*
/ 21 heavenly *like God's, in both loving and chastening the sinner*

It strikes where it doth love. She wakes.

DESDEMONA.   Who's there? Othello?

OTHELLO.   Ay, Desdemona.

DESDEMONA.   Will you come to bed, my lord?

OTHELLO.   Have you pray'd to-night, Desdemon?

DESDEMONA.   Ay, my lord.   25

OTHELLO.   If you bethink yourself of any crime
Unreconcil'd as yet to heaven and grace,
Solicit for it straight.

DESDEMONA.   Alack, my lord, what may you
    mean by that?

OTHELLO.   Well, do it, and be brief; I will walk by.   30
I would not kill thy unprepared spirit;
No; heaven forfend! I would not kill thy soul.

DESDEMONA.   Talk you of killing?

OTHELLO.   Ay, I do.

DESDEMONA.   Then heaven
Have mercy on me!

OTHELLO.   Amen, with all my heart!

DESDEMONA.   If you say so, I hope you will not kill me.   35

OTHELLO.   Hum!

DESDEMONA.   And yet I fear you; for you're fatal then
When your eyes roll so. Why I should fear I know not,
Since guiltiness I know not; but yet I feel I fear.

OTHELLO.   Think on thy sins.

DESDEMONA.   They are loves I bear to you.   40

OTHELLO   Ay, and for that thou diest.

DESDEMONA.   That death's unnatural that kills for loving.
Alas, why gnaw you so your nether lip?
Some bloody passion shakes your very frame.
These are portents; but yet I hope, I hope,   45
They do not point on me.

OTHELLO.   Peace, and be still!

DESDEMONA.   I will so. What's the matter?

OTHELLO.   That handkerchief which I so lov'd and
    gave thee
Thou gav'st to Cassio.

DESDEMONA.   No, by my life and soul!

---

30 walk by *step aside* / 32 forfend *forbid* / 37 fatal *deadly* / 45 portents *ominous signs*

Send for the man, and ask him.

OTHELLO.   Sweet soul, take heed,   50
Take heed of perjury; thou art on thy deathbed.

DESDEMONA.   Ay, but not yet to die.

OTHELLO.   Yes, presently,
Therefore confess thee freely of thy sin;
For to deny each article with oath
Cannot remove nor choke the strong conception   55
That I do groan withal. Thou art to die.

DESDEMONA.   Then Lord have mercy on me!

OTHELLO.   I say, amen.

DESDEMONA.   And have you mercy too! I never did
Offend you in my life; never lov'd Cassio
But with such general warranty of heaven   60
As I might love; I never gave him token.

OTHELLO.   By heaven, I saw my handkerchief in's hand.
O perjur'd woman! thou dost stone my heart,
And mak'st me call what I intend to do
A murder, which I thought a sacrifice.   65
I saw the handkerchief.

DESDEMONA.   He found it then;
I never gave it him. Send for him hither;
Let him confess a truth.

OTHELLO.   He hath confess'd.

DESDEMONA.   What, my lord?

OTHELLO.   That he hath us'd thee.

DESDEMONA.   How? unlawfully?

OTHELLO.   Ay.   70

DESDEMONA.   He will not say so.

OTHELLO.   No, his mouth is stopp'd;
Honest Iago hath ta'en order for 't.

DESDEMONA.   O! my fear interprets. What, is he dead?

OTHELLO.   Had all his hairs been lives, my great revenge
Had stomach for them all.   75

DESDEMONA.   Alas! he is betray'd and I undone.

OTHELLO.   Out, strumpet! weep'st thou for him
    to my face?

---

52 presently *at once* / 55 conception *belief* / 60 warranty *permission*
/ 63 stone *harden into stone* / 65 sacrifice *an act of justice* / 75
stomach *appetite*

DESDEMONA.   O, banish me, my lord, but kill me not!

OTHELLO.   Down, strumpet!

DESDEMONA.   Kill me to-morrow; let me live to-night!   80

OTHELLO.   Nay, if you strive,—

DESDEMONA.   But half an hour!

OTHELLO.   Being done, there is no pause.

DESDEMONA.   But while I say one prayer!

OTHELLO.   It is too late.

                    He smothers her.

EMILIA. [*At the door.*] My lord, my lord! What, ho! my lord, my lord!

OTHELLO.   What noise is this? Not dead? not yet quite dead?   85

I that am cruel am yet merciful:

I would not have thee linger in thy pain.

So, so.

EMILIA.   [*Within.*] What, ho! my lord, my lord!

OTHELLO.   Who's there?

EMILIA.   [*Within.*] O, good my lord, I would speak a word with you!

OTHELLO.   Yes:—'tis Emilia.—By and by.—She's dead.   90

'Tis like she comes to speak of Cassio's death.

The noise was high. Ha! no more moving?

Still as the grave. Shall she come in? Were 't good?—

I think she stirs again:—no. What's best to do?

If she come in, she'll sure speak to my wife.   95

My wife! my wife! what wife? I have no wife.

O, insupportable! O heavy hour!

Methinks it should be now a huge eclipse

Of sun and moon, and that th' affrighted globe

Did yawn at alteration.

EMILIA.   [*Within.*] I do beseech you   100

That I may speak with you, O, good my lord!

OTHELLO.   I had forgot thee. O, come in, Emilia.

Soft; by and by.—Let me the curtains draw.—

Where art thou?   *Opens the door.*

Enter EMILIA.

---

85 What noise *i.e., of a movement from Desdemona* / 99 alteration *some change in nature* / 103 curtains *bed curtains*

What's the matter with thee now?

EMILIA.   O, my good lord, yonder's foul murders done!   105

OTHELLO.   What, now?

EMILIA.   But now, my lord.

OTHELLO.   It is the very error of the moon;
She comes more nearer earth than she was wont,
And makes men mad.   110

EMILIA.   Cassio, my lord, hath kill'd a young Venetian
Call'd Roderigo.

OTHELLO.   Roderigo kill'd!
And Cassio kill'd!

EMILIA.   No, Cassio is not kill'd.

OTHELLO.   Not Cassio kill'd! Then murder's out of tune,
And sweet revenge grows harsh.   115

DESDEMONA.   O, falsely, falsely murder'd!

EMILIA.   O Lord, what cry is that?

OTHELLO.   That! what?

EMILIA.   Out, and alas! that was my lady's voice.
Help! help, ho! help! O lady, speak again!
Sweet Desdemona! O sweet mistress, speak!   120

DESDEMONA.   A guiltless death I die.

EMILIA.   O, who hath done this deed?

DESDEMONA.   Nobody; I myself. Farewell!
Commend me to my kind lord. O, farewell!   *Dies.*

OTHELLO.   Why, how should she be murder'd?

EMILIA.   Alas, who knows?   125

OTHELLO.   You hear her say herself, it was not I.

EMILIA.   She said so; I must needs report the truth.

OTHELLO.   She's, like a liar, gone to burning hell.
'Twas I that kill'd her.

EMILIA.   O, the more angel she,
And you the blacker devil!   130

OTHELLO.   She turn'd to folly, and she was a whore.

EMILIA.   Thou dost belie her, and thou art a devil.

OTHELLO.   She was false as water.

EMILIA.   Thou art rash as fire, to say
That she was false. O, she was heavenly true!

OTHELLO.   Cassio did tup her; ask thy husband else.   135

---

108 error *wandering from her course* / 131 folly *unchastity*

O, I were damn'd beneath all depth in hell
But that I did proceed upon just grounds
To this extremity. Thy husband knew it all.

 EMILIA. My husband?
 OTHELLO. Thy husband.   140
 EMILIA. That she was false to wedlock?
 OTHELLO. Ay, with Cassio. Nay, had she been true,
If Heaven would make me such another world
Of one entire and perfect chrysolite,
I'd not have sold her for it.
 EMILIA.   My husband?   145
 OTHELLO. Ay, 'twas he that told me on her first.
An honest man he is, and hates the slime
That sticks on filthy deeds.
 EMILIA.   My husband?
 OTHELLO. What needs this iterance, woman? I say thy
   husband.
 EMILIA. O mistress, villainy hath made mocks with love! 150
My husband say that she was false?
 OTHELLO.   He, woman;
I say thy husband; dost understand the word?
My friend, thy husband, honest, honest Iago.
 EMILIA. If he say so, may his pernicious soul
Rot half a grain a day! He lies to th' heart: 155
She was too fond of her most filthy bargain.
 OTHELLO. Ha!
 EMILIA. Do thy worst!
This deed of thine is no more worthy heaven
Than thou wast worthy her.
 OTHELLO.   Peace, you were best. 160
 EMILIA. Thou hast not half that power to do me harm
As I have to be hurt. O gull! O dolt!
As ignorant as dirt! Thou hast done a deed—
I care not for thy sword; I'll make thee known,
Though I lost twenty lives.—Help! Help, ho! help! 165
The Moor hath kill'd my mistress! Murder! murder!

   Enter MONTANO, GRATIANO, IAGO, *and others.*

---

144 chrysolite *a green stone* / 149 iterance *repetition* / 162 gull *dupe*

MONTANO.   What is the matter? How now, General!

EMILIA.   O, are you come, Iago? You have done well,
That men must lay their murders on your neck.

GRATIANO.   What is the matter?   170

EMILIA.   Disprove this villain, if thou be'st a man.
He says thou told'st him that his wife was false;
I know thou didst not, thou'rt not such a villain.
Speak, for my heart is full.

IAGO.   I told him what I thought, and told no more   175
Than what he found himself was apt and true.

EMILIA.   But did you ever tell him she was false?

IAGO.   I did.

EMILIA.   You told a lie, an odious, damned lie;
Upon my soul, a lie, a wicked lie.   180
She false with Cassio!—did you say with Cassio?

IAGO.   With Cassio, mistress. Go to, charm your tongue.

EMILIA.   I will not charm my tongue; I am bound
    to speak.
My mistress here lies murdered in her bed,—

ALL.   O heavens forfend!   185

EMILIA.   And your reports have set the murderer on.

OTHELLO.   Nay, stare not, masters; it is true, indeed.

GRATIANO.   'Tis a strange truth.

MONTANO.   O monstrous act!

EMILIA.   Villainy, villainy, villainy!
I think upon 't, I think. I smell't,—O villainy!   190
I thought so then,—I'll kill myself for grief—
O villainy, villainy!

IAGO.   What, are you mad? I charge you get you home.

EMILIA.   Good gentlemen, let me have leave to speak;
'Tis proper I obey him, but not now.   195
Perchance, Iago, I will ne'er go home.

OTHELLO.   O! O! O!   *He falls on the bed.*

EMILIA.   Nay, lay thee down and roar;
For thou hast kill'd the sweetest innocent
That e'er did lift up eye.

OTHELLO.   [*Rising.*] O, she was foul!
I scarce did know you, uncle; there lies your niece,   200

---

182 charm *silence*

Whose breath, indeed, these hands have newly stopp'd.
I know this act shows horrible and grim.
   GRATIANO.   Poor Desdemon! I am glad thy father's dead.
Thy match was mortal to him, and pure grief
Shore his old thread in twain. Did he live now,   205
This sight would make him do a desperate turn,
Yea, curse his better angel from his side,
And fall to reprobance.
   OTHELLO.   'Tis pitiful; but yet Iago knows
That she with Cassio hath the act of shame   210
A thousand times committed. Cassio confess'd it;
And she did gratify his amorous works
With that recognizance and pledge of love
Which I first gave her. I saw it in his hand;
It was a handkerchief, an antique token   215
My father gave my mother.
   EMILIA.   O God! O heavenly God!
   IAGO.   'Zounds, hold your peace.
   EMILIA.   'Twill out, 'twill out! I, peace!
No, I will speak as liberal as the north.
Let Heaven and men and devils, let them all,   220
All, all, cry shame against me, yet I'll speak.
   IAGO.   Be wise, and get you home.
   EMILIA.   I will not.
                     IAGO *offers to stab* EMILIA.
   GRATIANO.   Fie!
Your sword upon a woman?
   EMILIA.   O thou dull Moor! that handkerchief thou
      speak'st of
I found by fortune and did give my husband;   225
For often, with a solemn earnestness,
More than indeed belong'd to such a trifle,
He begg'd of me to steal it.
   IAGO.   Villainous whore!
   EMILIA.   She give it Cassio! No, alas! I found it,
And I did give 't my husband.
   IAGO.   Filth, thou liest!   230

---

205 Shore . . . twain *cut his thread of life in two* / 208 reprobance
utter damnation / 212 gratify *reward* / 219 liberal as the north *as
freely as the harsh north winds*

EMILIA.   By heaven, I do not, I do not, gentlemen.
O murderous coxcomb! what should such a fool
Do with so good a wife?   *The* MOOR *runs at* IAGO, *but*
    is disarmed by MONTANO *and others.* IAGO *kills* EMILIA.
OTHELLO.   Are there no stones in heaven
But what serves for the thunder?—Precious villain!
GRATIANO.   The woman falls; sure, he hath kill'd his wife.   235
EMILIA.   Ay, ay! O, lay me by my mistress' side.

                                              Exit IAGO.

GRATIANO.   He's gone, but his wife's kill'd.
MONTANO.   'Tis a notorious villain. Take you this weapon
Which I have here recover'd from the Moor.
Come, guard the door without; let him not pass,   240
But kill him rather. I'll after that same villain,
For 'tis a damned slave.

                      Exeunt MONTANO *and* GRATIANO.

OTHELLO.   I am not valiant neither,
But every puny whipster gets my sword.
But why should honor outlive honesty?
Let it go all.
EMILIA.   What did thy song bode, lady?   245
Hark, canst thou hear me? I will play the swan
And die in music. [*Singing.*] "Willow, willow, willow!"—
Moor, she was chaste; she lov'd thee, cruel Moor;
So come my soul to bliss, as I speak true;
So speaking as I think, alas, I die.   *Dies.* 250
OTHELLO.   I have another weapon in this chamber;
It was a sword of Spain, the ice-brook's temper,—
O, here it is. Uncle, I must come forth.
GRATIANO. [*Within.*]   If thou attempt it, it will cost
        thee dear.
Thou hast no weapon, and perforce must suffer.   255
OTHELLO.   Look in upon me then and speak with me,
Or, naked as I am, I will assault thee.

                      Re-enter GRATIANO.

---

232 coxcomb *fool* / 233 stones *bolts* / 239 recover'd *secured* / 243
whipster *whippersnapper* / 243 honor *reputation* / 243 honesty *honorable character* / 246 swan *cf. "swan song" sung by the dying bird* /
252 ice-brook's temper *tempered in ice-cold water, as with some of the
best Spanish swords* / 257 naked *unarmed*

GRATIANO.   What is the matter?

OTHELLO.   Behold, I have a weapon;
A better never did itself sustain
Upon a soldier's thigh. I have seen the day   260
That, with this little arm and this good sword,
I have made my way through more impediments
Than twenty times your stop. But, O vain boast!
Who can control his fate? 'tis not so now.
Be not afraid though you do see me weapon'd;   265
Here is my journey's end, here is my butt
And very sea-mark of my utmost sail.
Do you go back dismay'd? 'Tis a lost fear;
Man but a rush against Othello's breast
And he retires. Where should Othello go?   270
Now, how dost thou look now? O ill-starr'd wench!
Pale as thy smock! when we shall meet at compt,
This look of thine will hurl my soul from heaven,
And fiends will snatch at it. Cold, cold, my girl!
Even like thy chastity. O cursed, cursed slave!   275
Whip me, ye devils,
From the possession of this heavenly sight!
Blow me about in winds! roast me in sulphur!
Wash me in steep-down gulfs of liquid fire!
O Desdemona, Desdemona! dead!   280
Oh! Oh! Oh!

     Enter LODOVICO, MONTANO, CASSIO *carried in a chair, and*
          OFFICERS, *with* IAGO *prisoner.*

LODOVICO.   Where is this rash and most unfortunate man?

OTHELLO.   That's he that was Othello; here I am.

LODOVICO   Where is that viper? Bring the villain forth.

OTHELLO.   I look down towards his feet; but that's a fable.   285
If that thou be'st a devil, I cannot kill thee.

                        Wounds IAGO.

LODOVICO.   Wrench his sword from him.

IAGO.   I bleed, sir; but not kill'd.

---

266 butt *the end of my arrow's flight* / 267 sea-mark *landmark* / 267
utmost sail *end of my final voyage* / 269 Man but a rush *take up a
reed as a spear* / 272 compt *judgement* (*day*) / 279 steep-down gulfs
whirlpools / 285 feet *the devil has cloven hooves*

OTHELLO.   I am not sorry neither. I'd have thee live;
For, in my sense, 'tis happiness to die.

LODOVICO.   O thou Othello, that wert once so good,   290
Fallen in the practice of a cursed slave,
What shall be said to thee?

OTHELLO.   Why, anything.
An honorable murderer, if you will;
For nought did I in hate, but all in honor.

LODOVICO.   This wretch hath part confess'd his villainy.   295
Did you and he consent in Cassio's death?

OTHELLO.   Ay.

CASSIO.   Dear General, I never gave you cause.

OTHELLO.   I do believe it, and I ask your pardon.
Will you, I pray, demand that demi-devil   300
Why he hath thus ensnar'd my soul and body?

IAGO.   Demand me nothing; what you know, you know.
From this time forth I never will speak word.

LODOVICO.   What, not to pray?

GRATIANO.   Torments will ope your lips.

OTHELLO.   Well, thou dost best.   305

LODOVICO.   Sir, you shall understand what hath befall'n,
Which, as I think, you know not. Here is a letter
Found in the pocket of the slain Roderigo,
And here another. The one of them imports
The death of Cassio to be undertook   310
By Roderigo.

OTHELLO.   O villain!

CASSIO.   Most heathenish and most gross!

LODOVICO.   Now here's another discontented paper,
Found in his pocket too; and this, it seems,
Roderigo meant t' have sent this damned villain;   315
But that belike Iago in the nick
Came in and satisfi'd him.

OTHELLO.   O thou pernicious caitiff!—
How came you, Cassio, by that handkerchief
That was my wife's?

CASSIO.   I found it in my chamber;

---

289 sense *opinion* / 291 practice *stratagem* / 296 consent in *agree upon* / 309 imports *concerns* / 316 belike *probably* / 317 Came in *interposed*

And he himself confess'd but even now 320
That there he dropp'd it for a special purpose
Which wrought to his desire.
    OTHELLO.   O fool! fool! fool!
    CASSIO.   There is besides in Roderigo's letter
How he upbraids Iago, that he made him
Brave me upon the watch, whereon it came 325
That I was cast; and even but now he spake,
After long seeming dead, Iago hurt him,
Iago set him on.
    LODOVICO.   You must forsake this room, and go with us.
Your power and your command is taken off, 330
And Cassio rules in Cyprus. For this slave,
If there be any cunning cruelty
That can torment him much and hold him long,
It shall be his. You shall close prisoner rest,
Till that the nature of your fault be known 335
To the Venetian state. Come, bring away.
    OTHELLO.   Soft you; a word or two before you go.
I have done the state some service, and they know't—
No more of that. I pray you, in your letters,
When you shall these unlucky deeds relate, 340
Speak of me as I am; nothing extenuate,
Nor set down aught in malice. Then must you speak
Of one that lov'd not wisely but too well;
Of one not easily jealous, but being wrought
Perplex'd in the extreme; of one whose hand, 345
Like the base Indian, threw a pearl away
Richer than all his tribe; of one whose subdued eyes,
Albeit unused to the melting mood,
Drops tears as fast as the Arabian trees
Their med'cinable gum. Set you down this; 350
And say besides, that in Aleppo once,
Where a malignant and a turban'd Turk
Beat a Venetian and traduc'd the state,
I took by th' throat the circumcised dog,

---

322 wrought to *worked out in accordance with* / 344 easily *naturally* /
344 wrought *worked upon* / 346 Indian *Indians proverbially had no
knowledge of the value of precious stones or gold* / 350 med'cinable
medicinal

And smote him, thus.   *Stabs himself.*   355
 LODOVICO. O bloody period!
 GRATIANO.   All that's spoke is marr'd.
 OTHELLO. I kiss'd thee ere I kill'd thee. No way but this,
Killing myself, to die upon a kiss.
        Falls on the bed, and dies.
 CASSIO. This did I fear, but thought he had no weapon;
For he was great of heart.
 LODOVICO. [*To* IAGO.] O Spartan dog,   360
More fell than anguish, hunger, or the sea!
Look on the tragic loading of this bed;
This is thy work. The object poisons sight;
Let it be hid. Gratiano, keep the house,
And seize upon the fortunes of the Moor,   365
For they succeed on you. To you, lord governor,
Remains the censure of this hellish villain;
The time, the place, the torture. O, enforce it!
Myself will straight aboard; and to the state
This heavy act with heavy heart relate.   *Exeunt.*   370

---

356 period *conclusion* / 360 Spartan *ferocious, but also, stony calm* /
361 fell *cruel*

Rinehart Editions